IT HAD TO BE REVOLUTION

It Had to Be Revolution

Memoirs of an American Radical

∾ CHARLES SHIPMAN

WITH A FOREWORD BY

HARVEY KLEHR

Cornell University Press

Ithaca and London

A volume in the series Studies in Soviet History and Society, edited by
Joseph S. Berliner, Seweryn Bialer, and Sheila Fitzpatrick.

First published 1993 by Cornell University Press.

International Standard Book Number 0-8014-2180-2
Library of Congress Catalog Card Number 91-57896
Printed in the United States of America
Librarians: Library of Congress cataloging information
appears on the last page of the book.

⊗ The paper in this book meets the minimum requirements
of the American National Standard for Information Sciences—
Permanence of Paper for Printed Library Materials, ANSI Z39.48-1984.

To Pick, who is always with me

CONTENTS

vii

Contents

FOREWORD

by Harvey Klehr

The collapse of communism in the former Soviet Union and Eastern Europe closes one of the great epochs in modern history. The
intellectual and political warfare between democracy and communism has ended with the triumph of the former and the utter rout of
the latter. While a few communist regimes cling desperately to
power and a handful of communist insurrections take advantage of
particular situations, few observers doubt that communism has lost
its vision, allure, and confidence. Marxism-Leninism touted itself
as a scientific answer to the problems of capitalism. Whatever dilemmas capitalism faces, even its critics can see few answers coming from the sclerotic categories that guided Marxism-Leninism for
the past seventy years.

Ever since 1917 the USSR has been the intellectual and moral
center for radicals and revolutionaries from around the globe. The
world socialist movement was split apart by the Russian Revolution. That part which rejected the Leninist model gradually came to
terms with capitalism and democracy and evolved into today's
moderate socialist and social-democratic parties. Moscow became
the Mecca for those committed to revolution. Even if some revolutionaries were eventually repelled by Stalinism or seduced by other,
competing forms of communism, a substantial part of their ideological baggage was made up of assertions and theses about where the
Soviet experiment had gone wrong. The New Left that emerged in
the 1960s justified itself as radical but not communist, a distinction

that collapsed as Marxism-Leninism increasingly infected the movement in the late 1960s.

By the end of its seventy-year run, it was hard to remember the caliber of the early recruits to the communist cause. Marxism-Leninism, having failed as a predictor of the future or a guide for the present, survived only as a ponderous justification for the continued hold on power of a parasitic bureaucracy. Its adepts rarely pretended to believe what they were saying. Even Western intellectuals sympathetic to Soviet positions in international affairs avoided talking about a world revolution. In Western Europe and the United States communist parties were everywhere losing whatever influence and significance they once had. Their members and sympathizers were marginalized and rarely people of talent.

The heroic age of communism was in its early years. The most successful period for most communist parties came in the 1930s, particularly in the last half of the decade when, responding to the threat of Adolf Hitler, the Soviet Union inaugurated the Popular Front. But this was clearly a tactical maneuver designed to combat Hitler and required Communists to shelve some of their most cherished principles and to cooperate with capitalists and bourgeois political parties.

It was the first, heady years after the Russian Revolution when the communist dream shined most brightly, before the disappointments and the tragedies of the Russian Revolution were too obvious. In those early years, before millions of people had to be liquidated to create the new society or on the pretext that they were enemies of the revolution, it was still possible to imagine that a new society and a new man were being created. In that first decade it was still plausible to hope that idealism in the service of disciplined intellect could eliminate evil. A band of dedicated, talented, and altogether remarkable people signed up in the ranks of revolution. Adventurous, reckless, arrogant, often brilliant, they stampeded around the globe, intoxicated by the belief that, armed with this wondrous new doctrine of revolution, faith in the working class, and enough determination, they could overthrow decrepit governments and institute the reign of equality.

Most of them died very young. By its very nature, their job was a dangerous one. They were killed by police or troops or vigilantes in the countries whose governments they were trying to overthrow. Others died fighting in Spain or during World War II. Far more often, they were executed in the cellars of the Lubyanka, by the government whose interests they had tried to serve. Only a lucky few survived in the Soviet Union; to have done so required them to forget or lie shamelessly about their early exploits and, most certainly, to enlist in Stalin's ranks.

Relatively few American Communists were sent on assignments outside the United States in the first years after the Russian Revolution. While Comintern postings became more frequent in the next two decades, surprisingly few American Communists or ex-Communists have written about the experience. Most American Communists eventually became ex-Communists. But a much smaller percentage of the Party's cadres abandoned the cause, and an even smaller percentage of those selected for international work did so.

The man who ended his life as Charles Shipman was not selected for such work; he stumbled into it. And his involvement with the American Communist Party came after he had played an interesting role in two other communist parties. Moreover, his experience in the CPUSA was hardly typical. Never in the top ranks of the Party, he held several key assignments. Although he was a participant in the factional wars that divided the CPUSA in the 1920s, his expulsion was unrelated to the factionalism. Finally, his life as an ex-Communist differed significantly from most—he was never called before a congressional committee and his Party past, while it occasionally caused difficulties or problems, did not dominate or cloud his life.

While Shipman's story is not typical, it does provide a fascinating picture of one journey of commitment and disillusion. This autobiography brings back to life those heroic years before the revolution devoured its children. It wonderfully evokes that period when the Russian Revolution seemed to signal a liberation from the staid conventions of the past and promised a model for the liberation of mankind. All kinds of rebels and activists found themselves in its emotional grip. Few had any idea of what enlisting in the revolutionary army might portend. It was still a grand adventure. Charles Phillips was one of those rebels who found himself caught up in the whirlwind. Without much political experience or thought for the consequences, he became for a brief period of time a professional revolutionary, one of those who committed "the whole of their lives" to overthrowing the capitalist system.

It was an unlikely course for a young man from a middle-class, conservative family who was destined to live several very different lives under a variety of names. Like many of the young people attracted to Bolshevism in its early days, Charles Phillips was born Jewish. Unlike them, he knew virtually nothing about his heritage. His father had changed the family name, pretended to be of German descent, and made sure that his children had little to do with Jewish life, culture, or religion. And, as Shipman's comments on a trip to Israel late in his life attest, he felt no ties to either religious or ethnic values.

The elder Phillips was a successful clothing manufacturer. A confrontation with some of his father's striking employees at the family home first convinced Charles of the justice of workers' struggles. A poor student, he dropped out of school and displayed little talent for business. A meeting with Walter Lippmann changed his life. Impressed by his intelligence, Lippmann persuaded Charles's father to send him to college. At Columbia Journalism School, Morrie Ryskind, later a conservative Hollywood screenwriter, got Charles to join the Socialist Club.

Phillips became an active participant in the Bohemian left wing centered in Greenwich Village. Unlike many of his contemporaries, he pressed activism well beyond revolutionary rhetoric. He traveled to Europe on Henry Ford's Peace Ship and was prominently involved in antiwar activity after returning to New York. Arrested for conspiracy to obstruct conscription, he was convicted and given a minimal sentence after his own father testified against him, leading to a break in relations with his family.

Conscription drove Phillips into exile. He refused to report for induction into the army and was seized and deposited in an army camp. Refusing to cooperate, he was eventually given a dishonorable discharge. About to face reinduction, he decided to flee to Mexico. After a long and difficult journey, including an illegal flight across the border, he arrived in Mexico City and began his second and most adventurous life, that of international communist agent.

In Mexico City Phillips made contact with a handful of people active in the labor movement. Along with Mike Gold, the future communist literary critic, he wrote for a Mexican newspaper. He played a major role in converting M. N. Roy, the young Indian nationalist, into a socialist. Using the name Frank Seaman, Phillips was one of the founders of the Mexican Communist Party, which elected him and Roy delegates to the Second Comintern Congress scheduled for 1920 in Moscow. Nothing could better illustrate the internationalism and the weaknesses of the early communist movement than the choice of an Indian Brahmin and an assimilated American Jew as the representatives of the newly formed Mexican Communist Party.

In Mexico, Phillips and Roy came under the influence of one of the Comintern's legendary agents, Michael Borodin. Borodin quickly enlisted Phillips into Comintern activities, sending him on a mission to search for a missing suitcase with blueprints and diamonds intended to finance revolutionary activities. More important, Borodin tutored Phillips in Marxism-Leninism, impressing on him the duties of a revolutionary.

En route to Moscow late in 1919, Phillips (now using the pseudonym Jesús Ramírez) and Borodin stopped in Spain, where they convinced a small group of dissident socialists to affiliate to the Third International, forming the basis of the Spanish Communist Party. To reach the Soviet Union, Ramírez had to evade Estonian border police. Like many young foreign Communists, he was deeply moved by the sense of mission and purpose he found among a people bearing up under severe economic shortages. Phillips met with Lenin and was even more convinced that the corrupt old world was doomed.

It is striking how informal and haphazard the early Comintern agents were about their activities. Ramírez had to scrounge train fares, depend on luck to find key people, and accept confusing or no directions about personnel, policies, or tactics. As the organization became more bureaucratized, the grand sense of adventure that this autobiography captures so well gave way to stricter controls and factional maneuvering.

The Comintern decided to send Ramírez back to Mexico with Sen Katayama, a legendary Japanese revolutionary who had spent years in the United States, and Louis Fraina, John Reed's rival for the leadership of the American communist movement. Their task was to set up a Latin American Bureau of the Profintern, or Red International of Trade Unions. Ramírez, however, was the only one of these erstwhile revolutionaries who spoke Spanish. Fraina, disillusioned, vanished one day with thousands of dollars of Comintern money. He reappeared, years later, in the United States as Lewis Corey and carved out a distinguished career as an economist and founder of the anticommunist Americans for Democratic Action.

Back in Mexico, Ramírez's activities in the Mexican labor movement led to his deportation to Guatemala, where he assumed the new identity of Manuel Gómez and soon slipped back into Mexico. Living underground and evading the police proved impossible. Gómez and his Russian wife (they had married in Moscow even though he was still legally married to an American woman) moved to Chicago, where he joined the American Communist Party and began still another phase of his revolutionary career.

As Manuel Gómez, he quickly worked his way up the Party ladder, beginning as an ordinary recruit, taking on local responsibilities, and rising to direct anti-imperialist work for the World Congress against Imperialism and the 6th Comintern Congress.

The inner life of the American party in the 1920s was fractious. From his Chicago base, Gómez was a natural ally of the midwesterners who looked to William Foster for leadership and scorned the allegedly intellectual and middle-class adherents of Jay Lovestone. Although Gómez was an active participant in these battles, he managed to hold on to his Party positions even when his faction lost its hold on the Party.

While his picture of Party life is fascinating, it also has gaps. His comrades knew him as Manuel Gómez and assumed he was Mexican. Did he ever talk about his Comintern past? Some comrades, notably Mike Gold, had known him in Mexico as Phillips and Seaman. Was the Party leadership aware of this background? Did the Lovestone faction assume that he still was a Comintern agent, sent to America on some special assignment? When he went to Europe and Russia in the late 1920s, did anyone make the connection between Gómez and Ramírez? The autobiography is silent about these issues, and the numerous identities—Phillips, Seaman,

Ramírez, and Gómez—may have convinced anyone who had an inkling that they were one and the same that this was a very important comrade.

By the end of the 1920s Gómez was beginning to have doubts about the cause to which he had devoted his life. After breaking up a Trotskyist meeting, he felt ashamed of this behavior. The adulation of Stalin was distasteful; but, like many Communists, he found it difficult to make a clean break with the Party. In 1929 he adopted a new name, Charles Shipman, in order to take a job on a Wall Street newspaper, beginning a double life that was to last almost a decade. Gómez within the Party, Shipman on Wall Street, he juggled two contradictory identities and styles. Still a good Marxist-Leninist, convinced that capitalism was on its way to destruction, he advised investors in one of his columns to sell their stock. When the market crashed shortly afterward, he gained a reputation as an astute analyst, and when his paper was absorbed by the *Wall Street Journal*, Charles Shipman was a daily columnist.

Even when he was formally expelled from the CPUSA in 1932 for "petty-bourgeois" tendencies, Gómez continued to think of himself as part of the movement and retained many of his friends. He began to devote himself to cultural work on behalf of the Party. His new companion, Sylvia Feningston, was one of the original members of the Group Theatre. When she and a number of left-wing intellectuals formed the Theater Union, they asked Gómez to sit on the board because of his communist connections. In this capacity, he was responsible for bringing Bertolt Brecht on his first trip to America. Not until 1937 did Shipman break with the CPUSA. Disturbed by the purges in the USSR, he tried to recruit some friends in the Party to oppose Stalin. Fervently denounced by the *Daily Worker* and repudiated by old friends, he abandoned his revolutionary illusions and his Manuel Gómez identity for good.

The final portion of Shipman's life was far more prosaic. Although he fled from New Jersey to Kansas City in 1941, convinced that the FBI was on to him, it proved a false alarm. His communist past rarely intruded into his successful business career. He did balk at applying for a passport during the McCarthy era, concerned that an investigation might turn up Charles Phillips. When Robert Young, his boss and a noted railroad tycoon, learned about his revolutionary past, he eased Shipman out of the Allegheny Corporation but helped find him another challenging job. Shipman never testified before congressional committees, and the one or two times the FBI did visit him, he was unable to identify anyone they asked him about. It was as if the tumultuous first forty years of his life had simply vanished.

Autobiography is not, of course, history. An individual who is telling his own life is often prone to error or wishful thinking or distortion. Historians of the American communist movement will not agree with all of Shipman's observations about the Party or the individuals with whom he came in contact. And, there is the possibility that he is not telling us everything he could. It is possible that the opening of the files of the Communist International will add more details about his life or activities, particularly in Mexico and Spain. For the present, however, this lively memoir will enrich our understanding of the world of international communism and the people who participated in it.

PREFACE

Holmdel, New Jersey, March 1941; the trees still bare. On the other side of the world Britain was reeling under the German blitz. In Washington President Roosevelt had just signed Lend-Lease. The atmosphere was tense. Widespread speculation about the United States entering the war. But the little village of Holmdel was quiet and peaceful.

A Sunday evening, around eight. We had put Carlota to bed ourselves. Emma had Sundays off. She wanted to spend this one with her daughter; we would be picking her up at the ten o'clock train from New York. Sylvia, alone in the front room, heard a faint knock at the door. It was unusual. In fact it had never happened before. A little after answering Sylvia called me in. The visitor was a polite though expressionless young fellow, twenty-five or twenty-six, a neat dresser. In city clothes. He asked if Sylvia wouldn't mind stepping into another room. I noticed his southern drawl.

When Sylvia had left us he produced a credential. The FBI.

"Mr. Shipman," he began. . . . Now an ingratiating smile. "You are Mr. Shipman?"

"Yes."

"Mr. Shipman, we would like for you to assist us. As an American, sir. The Bureau has reports of suspicious characters out this way. Would you possibly know some suspicious-looking individual, sir?"

"In Holmdel?"

"Anywhere around."

"We're pretty new here. We don't even know our neighbors."

"I see. Well would you be willing to assist us, Mr. Shipman? Regardless."

"Of course. But I don't see how ... "

"Would there be Commies in this particular neck of the woods?"

"Commies?"

"Com-nists."

I shrugged.

"Any feller who maybe used to be a Com-nist?"

"I told you we don't know a soul. I suggest you ask someone else. There's a house half a mile up the main road."

"Thank you sir. I'll sure do that. For the record, Mr. Shipman, what is your occupation?"

"Financial analyst."

"Employed where, sir?"

"Standard & Poor's Corporation, in New York."

"And the address, sir?"

I gave it to him.

He said, "I sure am sorry you can't put us on to those Commies. Ever been a Com-nist yourself, Mr. Shipman?"

So ... ! I was apprehensive before. Now I was scared. But I answered unhesitatingly. "No. Why do you ask?"

"Well we understood you were. Or had been? Maybe once?"

"You must be mistaken."

"Is Shipman your real name?"

"Yes."

"Ever had another?"

"No."

"Never?"

"Never."

Then, after reflection: "I see. Guess we got a bum steer. The wrong Shipman. I sure hope you'll excuse it. I'll go talk to those folks on the main road. Well, we know how to reach you. Thank you for your cooperation, Mr. Shipman. Will you convey my respects to Mrs. Shipman, sir?"

He shook hands before departing.

"What was it?" asked Sylvia, coming back in.

"Not good," I told her. He was FBI. Not good at all. A little pre-liminary sparring, transparent as hell, and he asks am I a Commu-nist. Have I ever been a Communist? Is Shipman my real name? Now, God damn it, he's got the S&P address.

"You told him?"

"He asked for it. I'd have been a fool to fake it. Darling, I can't go to work tomorrow. We can't stay here either."

"I don't know what you mean." She was trembling.

We couldn't afford to chance it, I told her. I was just too vulner-able. Maybe he was only fishing. Maybe. But why send an FBI man to Holmdel? A poky place like this? Borodin taught me—when in doubt, move. Move fast and leave no traces.

We resolved to wake our daughter and decamp. We would go where Sylvia and I could find jobs and pass unnoticed. I liked Chi-cago but was known there. We chose Kansas City because it was the most unlikely large city we could think of. We would change our names, leave no ties, start fresh. I was forty-four years old, Sylvia thirty-eight, Carlota six.

Neither of us had much cash. The bank was closed—and our account there insignificant. I phoned my ardently respectable brother Harry. He agreed to meet me at the Hotel Pennsylvania in New York at midnight with $400. I did not tell him what for, and the little I did say scared him—anything clandestine would have scared him.

Sylvia and I split forces. I drove into the city with Carlota. Sylvia had to meet Emma at the Holmdel station at ten, head Emma off with some vague how-come, and accompany her on the next train back. She told Emma that an urgent business call had obliged me to leave for some distant city, that I'd be gone indefinitely, and that she and Carlota were going along, in fact Carlota and I were already in New York.

Obviously we would have to stay overnight at the Hotel Pennsyl-vania. I registered with Carlota in my arms—too sleepy to ask ques-tions. I got her to bed and returned to the lobby. Harry was there, accompanied by his faithful wife, and both of them were very ner-vous. I saw him look around cautiously before approaching me. Edith had already moved to the door as he handed me an envelope and murmured, "Please don't talk, Charlie; g'bye." They fled.

While this was happening Sylvia tottered into the lobby, weary and almost as nervous as Harry. Her dirty work was accomplished, and Emma, uncomprehending and bewildered, had been dispatched to her daughter in Harlem.

Carlota was sound asleep in the room. We telephoned Liston Oak, our most trusted friend. Liston and I had been Communists together, disenchanted together, expelled together, publicly denounced together ("tools of the capitalist system"). Liston did not have anything to hide, but I did. He was in bed when we phoned (after 1 A.M.).

"This is Charles Shipman. I'm calling from the Hotel Pennsylvania. Sylvia and I want to see you."

"I'll be there in forty-five minutes."

He made it in thirty-five. We talked in the small bathroom, in whispers, so as not to wake up Carlota. "Liston," I began, "we're going to disappear. We can't tell anybody where. Not even you." I told him about the FBI man. Yes, our conclusions might prove wrong, our steps hasty—perhaps a big and expensive mistake. A mistake in the opposite direction, however, would prove a damn sight more expensive.

Liston was superb. He undertook to close the house, settle the lease, dispose of the books and furniture, take charge of our dog, do something about the cat and five newborn kittens. He would reclaim his own ramshackle car at the Holmdel station. He would try to sell ours. He would take care of Emma, too, one way or another. Typical Liston. A unique and precious human being. After goodnight and *abrazos* he was back by ten to drive us to our railroad station. Not Penn Station, not Grand Central, but Elizabeth, New Jersey.

We made but one stop en route, a prearranged street-corner meeting between Sylvia and her sister Madeleine. It lasted just long enough for us to say, "We are disappearing, may never see you darlings again, won't be able to write; reassure mother and father; love, love, love." Then we kissed and hugged and waived *adios*—with no hint of the wherefore.

During that whispered bathroom colloquy we had arranged a way for Liston to reach us once we had disappeared. For two weeks, wherever we might be we would visit a library every day and scan the classified ads in the *New York Times* for a message signed

"Eliphalet." We had a simple code. One sort of phrase meant "Stay away." Another, "Come back." If no message appeared in fourteen days we could forget it. In the meantime Liston would manage to discuss the whole story confidentially with Roger Baldwin at the American Civil Liberties Union. Roger knew me well (had known me since 1915) and knew all about my legal trouble.

Sylvia was near panic now. I tried to give her a sense of adventure about our hegira, but adventure exerted no appeal. Carlota, agog since waking up in a room at the Hotel Pennsylvania, had become all curiosity. Once on the train we trotted out the story we had prepared for her: the company where daddy works is paying him extra to find out everything he can about the plans of some very shifty competitors—operating from another city. It will be what people call undercover work—like a mission in an enemy country. Getting the information daddy's company wants might take a long time, and none of us must let anyone know who we are or why we are there. We will have to change our names, become totally different people.

"Do you think you can do that?" I asked.

"I think it will be fun! I want to be JULIA GORDON." (After a radio series heroine.)

"Okay, sweetie. You just named the whole family. Now you and mommy and I are all GORDONS."

I began to think it was fun myself.

She never made a slip. (I did—once.)

Although we traveled in the isolation of a compartment until the change of trains at St. Louis, it had to be seats in the chair car the rest of the way. Who could tell how long our few hundred dollars would last?

Kansas City was dark when we got there. Leaving Carlota ("Julia") at the hotel the next morning, Sylvia and I went apartment hunting. A kindly sexagenarian maid promised to keep an eye on cute little Julia while Mr. and Mrs. Gordon were away. We looked in cheap neighborhoods. Anything would do until we both had jobs, so we were satisfied with the first place we looked at. The landlady required references—something we hadn't anticipated. Cursorily flipping the pages of my address book, I let her have the name and address of my first wife—my one slip. As soon as we walked away we realized we couldn't go back there. We ended up with a place far less desirable, which we took on a week-to-week basis. It was an "efficiency," a room with a Murphy bed and an electric plate. When the bed was down instead of folded into the wall, there was not much space to move around. But at least the owners had not required references.

There was a public school within walking distance, and Carlota (Julia), a few months short of seven, was accepted—welcomed—in mid-term. The school wanted a Julia Gordon birth certificate for the new second grader—but it could wait, since we were from out of town. Sylvia sought a job through an employment agency. Impressed, no doubt, by her engaging charm, modulated voice, and native dignity, they hired her to work right there—as an interviewer. A few days later I was on my way to becoming a reporter for the *Kansas City Star*. The city editor liked me but needed the managing ed's okay (I did, after all, have considerable newspaper experience).

Every day at noon Sylvia and I met at Kansas City's main library and studied the classified ads in the *New York Times*. Little more than a week had passed when a jumble of words subscribed *Eliphalet* appeared. Decoded it meant, *Everything okay; come back.*

Was everything okay? What had Liston found out? Could he have been misled? Should we or shouldn't we? Not—we decided—on the unsupported assurance of Liston's cryptic message. We felt reasonably safe where we were—as Gordons. And we were adjusting. Julia was well settled in school, the financial problem was on the way to solution, we had found a community center nearby, people were friendly. With the newspaper job in prospect, Kansas City promised an advantageous enough new start for us. We concluded that I should go to New York alone and investigate. I took a bus.

IT HAD TO BE REVOLUTION

1 The Right or Wrong School for a Bad Boy

I was born August 10, 1895, in New York City to Harry and Eva Phillips. We lived on the top floor of a four-story brownstone on 116th Street, east of First Avenue (two blocks from the East River). My grandparents (the Jacobs) and assorted uncles and aunts occupied the rest of the house. Grandpa owned it. I have vivid recollections of my earliest years but nothing of consequence apart from my being a Bad Boy. Everybody said Charlie was a bad boy. Including Charlie himself (me). I stole onions from Grandma's kitchen and put them on the rails of the 116th Street horse-car line. On my way home from the First Avenue grocery I smashed a bagful of eggs against another boy's head. Just before guests arrived for a celebration dinner (my parents' tenth wedding anniversary), I took the place settings off the table and carefully rearranged them on the floor.

These common pranks are all I or anyone else has remembered to document the certainty of my fledgling waywardness. But there must have been worse, because I was always in trouble and being punished. My big-muscled father used his razor strap on me. I would squirm away but he would keep after me, whipping me all over the dining room floor, getting at me even way under the table. My mother, looking on, would soon tell him to stop. Afterward she would cry with me, pet me, and importune me to be a good boy. She never doubted the whipping was deserved, and neither did I. But I could not help doing the wrong things.

A crisis developed when I was five years old. We were summering at Anverne or Edgemere. Walking between the tracks of the Long

Island Railroad with two other little boys, I had a sudden impulse to touch the electrified third rail. I'd been warned it would kill me but I guess I refused to believe it could be that terrible. Unaccountably I escaped with a shock that sent me sprawling. But the exploit brought Pop and Mom to despair: Charlie constituted a case too serious to be handled at home; he had to be placed in a disciplinary institution, a military school. As soon as it could be arranged my father took me on the train to Mt. Pleasant Military Academy at Ossining, New York, and left me there.

So before I was old enough to know what kind of family world I had been born into I was out of it. I loved my protecting mom and thought I loved (while resenting) my retributory pop, without being more than dimly aware of who or what they were, except as they affected me. My sister, Anna, had her own friends; she was too old for me. My brother, Harry junior, was too young: only two years old when I was five. And in five years of life how much could I have been expected to learn about the numerous Jacobs downstairs?

I remained a Mt. Pleasant student until nearly fourteen. Mom rarely came to see me, Pop never. I got home only during Christmas vacations and, briefly, in summertime. Spent the best part of the summers in one or another expensive boys' camp: Weingart's in the Catskills; Natural Science Camp in the Finger Lakes region; Camp Kennebec in Maine. Why did my parents want to see so little of me? They must have felt it was for my own good. I know I was Mom's favorite child (she often told me so.) And Pop, when not exasperated with me, used to say: "All Charlie needs is to get hold of himself, because he's got more brains than anybody."

Mt. Pleasant Military Academy proved to be only superficially military. We wore uniforms, responded to reveille and taps, marched to the dining hall and to church in town, and rehearsed the manual of arms for an hour once a week. Overall, though, the atmosphere was that of a fashionable prep school. With a devoted teaching staff, tree-lined campus, handsome library, and ample playing fields, it might have been a small-scale Andover or Exeter— with overtones of Eton and Harrow. Early in my stay the school dropped "military" from its name in favor of plain Mt. Pleasant Academy.

Little Charlie, "the bad boy"

I don't think the church-going was obligatory, for the school was nonsectarian. Most students went to the Episcopal church but some to the Presbyterian and a few to the Catholic. I marched with the Episcopalians. It may have been by an understanding between Mr. Brusie (the distinguished headmaster) and my father. Pop, I learned years later, had no religion at all. I think I knew, without a notion of where from, that we were Jews. In spite of my un-Jewish appellation of Charles Francis Phillips, Mr. Brusie must have known it too. Because the first roommate assigned to me was a dark-skinned Cuban named Anastasio Maldonado—"Anny" and I being the only "racial aliens" in the school. However, aside from this first-year roommate pairing (which seemed coincidental to me at the time), I recall nothing suggestive of discrimination in all my Mt. Pleasant years. I participated fully in all school activities and seem to have been accepted without qualification by students and faculty equally.

The student body of a hundred or more ranged from youngsters in the most elementary grades ("forms") to upperclassmen in their final semester of preparation for college. To a certain extent the fifteen or twenty youngest had a regime apart. They lodged in a wing added on to the fine old building that housed the headmaster and his family. My fondest recollections of Mt. Pleasant are of Sunday evenings before bedtime when we kids were admitted to the parlor of that house, gathering in a circle on the Oriental rug and listening to Miss Etta reading to us from her easy chair by the big kerosene table-lamp. *Treasure Island, Robinson Crusoe, Oliver Twist, Tanglewood Tales, The Prince and the Pauper, The Man without a Country* . . . I believe my lifelong love of literature stems from those enchanted evenings.

Though I liked most of my studies—except math—I was apt to become restless in class as recreation time neared, my mind gravitating to the playing fields. I loved baseball (though it gave me a busted nose). And tennis. I "flunked" hockey—never even being able to stand up on skates. But I excelled at football—eventually made the school team—and reveled in it. Especially the feel of butting through an opponent's defensive line.

Wednesdays and Saturdays were half-holidays when students were free to leave the academy grounds, roam the streets of Ossining, and spend their allowances on ice cream sodas, candy, and such. (My starting allowance was fifteen cents a week. Other boys got twenty-five.)

We had monthly dancing lessons, together with girls invited from Miss Tewksbury's school at Briarcliff. We wore dress uniforms and white cotton gloves. The girls excited and terrified me. Self-conscious, clumsy, and tone-deaf, I balked at approaching them in my squeaky patent leather pumps. My nose (troublesome at best since the baseball accident) refused to breathe. I stumbled badly. I was glad when the music stopped—and so undoubtedly were my partners. In spite of the lessons I did not learn to dance, and never have.

As I grew to puberty my most notable sex experiences were group masturbation with boys in the same dormitory. Once, I remember, we all compared penises. I was surprised to find mine was the only one without a foreskin. None of the other boys could account for this and neither could I. I thought about it later on and only then reasoned that it must have something to do with being Jewish.

From start to finish—as a kid in the first or second form and on through my later Mt. Pleasant years—the academy's monthly scholastic Honor Roll posted on the assembly room blackboard showed my name at the top of the list. But I got no honors for "deportment." At Mt. Pleasant too I was the bad boy who broke all the rules: climbing over the playing-field fence to sneak into town, getting caught smoking in the washrooms, getting caught pulling up the skirts of twelve-year-old Elizabeth Brusie (the headmaster's daughter). Other boys did such things, but I seem to have been the most persistent—and most often caught. I think now that sometimes I actually wanted to be caught (vanity? a need to prove myself as good/bad as anybody? probably so).

If you received bad marks for deportment (demerits) you had to work them off "on the Guard Squad"—walking round and round a circular path behind the gym during free time (Wednesday and Saturday afternoons, holidays, etc.). When my mother came to see me one Saturday afternoon I had to be summoned from the Guard Squad. It was my customary free-time habitat. Still, my dominant recollections of the eight Mt. Pleasant years are happy ones.

When my parents withdrew me from the school (doubtless feeling they had spent enough on me), I was going home as if for the first time. Home to a businessmen's world, with circumstances, usages, habits, proclivities, aspirations, and ideals remote from those nurtured in the halls of Mt. Pleasant. Pop had come to this country from a Jewish *shtetl* in Russia at the age of eleven with his older brother, Louis. Almost immediately he got a job on a tailor's bench,

5

and by devotion to the craft, hard work, and thoroughness wound up a supplier of men's suits (under contract) to the well-known retail firm of Rogers Peet & Co., with some two hundred men and women in his employ. (That he had originated in Russia I learned only many years later and by accident. Pop had always claimed Germany. I learned also that we were "Phillips" by derivation from "Fischel.")

Mom was American born but her (Jacob) family background was Old Country—and utterly dominated by Grandpa. This undersized, wiry, hawk-nosed old Hyman Jacob personified the poor Russian-Jewish immigrant who made good. Religiously Orthodox, he never did a scintilla of work on Saturdays (someone else even had to light the gas), but he made up for it on weekdays. Hyman Jacob was like Pop. But different. A pious, strictly Orthodox Jew. Also far more enterprising than my plodding father. More aggressive, tougher, sharper. And a lot richer. He made a bundle selling canvas leggings to the army in the Spanish-American War, then built himself a big footwear manufacturing business with two of his four sons, Uncle Moe and Uncle Ike—H. Jacob & Sons.

All the Jacobs were go-getters and showed little interest in intellectual matters. As boys, Uncle Moe and Uncle Ike sold newspapers by day and candy in vaudeville theaters at night. Uncle Manny started work early in life and in due course established E. Jacob & Co. (with Uncle Ben as the "Co." and star salesman). They started out importing ladies' veilings (then the fashion) and later diversified into other fabrics. The fierce old man, the four sons, three surviving daughters (including Mom), and a number of satellite in-laws made up a formidable clan. There were "Moe's Lillie" (Michaels), "Manny's Lillie" (Bleyer), "Ike's Millie" (Strauss), "Jenny's Alfred" (another Bleyer), "Eva's Harry" (my father), and so on. They were much in one another's company, especially on Friday nights—a social must for them and their children, and later their children's children. Despite Mom's persistent nagging, I dodged every Friday night social I could.

2 Trying—Not Very Hard—to Adjust

Among the Jacob family and the satellite in-laws, Grandpa was alone in his Orthodox religiosity. Such religious affiliations as the others maintained were Reformed. But one and all were united in reverence for America as the Land of Promise, and by faith in the American credo as they understood it. Honest in their beliefs—and in their private and business practices—they were profoundly conscious of their stake in the existing order. If you stayed poor in this country it was your own fault. They voted Republican as a matter of course, and held organized labor anathema.

So it went in my home. Either you made it or you were nobody.

By this time we were no longer living in Grandpa's house. Neither, for that matter, was Grandpa. Everyone we knew had moved to the then "better neighborhood" of the Upper West Side. In my fourteenth year, presumably equipped with a good primary education, I was enrolled in the eighth grade at public school (P.S. 10)—for a few months—to get a diploma. I barely made it, emerging with a C− average. It seemed my Mt. Pleasant courses had been no preparation at all!

Confused, frustrated, not knowing where I was headed, I began to do all sorts of reckless things. Once, before a crowd of horrified onlookers, I climbed the grooved façade of a neighboring eight-story apartment house to the roof. And one day my mother came home to find another crazy kid and me in the kitchen fighting a mock duel with carving knives. Just at that moment a misdirected knife cut deep into my right wrist, and blood spurted all over me and the kitchen floor. (I still carry the scar.)

The carving knife experience evidently sobered me, for it was the last such antic I can remember. But I was still unable to adjust. My mother's overdemonstrative affection embarrassed me, while my father, with his custom-made suits and cigar, struck me as the quintessence of self-satisfaction. (Actually he was unsure of himself.) If Pop looked up from his *New York Herald* with an observation, I instinctively said something contrary. We argued about everything. He was home much of the time just then because his

7

employees (Jewish and Italian sewing machine operators, cutters, pressers, etc.) had gone on strike. Alleging sweatshop conditions in his two lofts on East Houston Street. A delegation of three ratty-looking men and an adolescent girl broke in on us one evening while we were eating dinner. Lena, our cross-eyed Hungarian housemaid, announced, "Some people here . . . ," and suddenly they were in the dining room. Pop, outraged (and dismayed), refused to talk to them. All he would say was "Get out of my house!" I pitched in with "Pop, why won't you listen to these . . . " He leaned across the table and slapped me. I started to hit him back but Mom hung on to my hand. As I remember it, the intruders then said he would be sorry and departed. My father shrieked to Lena to fasten the door after them—with the chain. "Monsters, ingrates," he muttered. "But Pop . . . ," I protested. My mother stopped me. "Don't say anything, Charlie! Pop's right." I got up from the table and stamped into my room.

"Monsters" and "ingrates"?! The terms, in combination, were not new to me. Along with "villains," "cutthroats," and "goniffs," they had been the words applied in our home (and Grandpa's) to striking workers anywhere. And I had not objected, assuming, indeed, that those so stigmatized must be a species of demons. But these people seemed so inoffensive that the virulence of my parents maddened me. Particularly against Mom, whose "do unto others" homilies I thought of with nausea. Sweet mottoes were Mom's speciality. She had more of them than a greeting-card manufacturer—her best loved being "If you can't say anything good about a person don't say anything." (To be fair to her, she herself was true to that bromidic maxim. I never heard her speak ill of a single individual.) Mom was shallow, ignorant, biased, and egocentric but generally well-meaning and utterly without malice. She followed me into my room, and after much lamentation, we embraced. But from then on my sympathies were on the side of striking workers.

I marveled that during the entire scene in the dining room Anna and Harry had sat at the table expressionless. As if insulated. They were used to flare-ups between Pop and me. They themselves never had any serious differences with Pop. There was empathy between them and him. And mutual attachment. Anna, his favorite, was a sweet kid: placid, incurious, and as agreeable as sunshine. Harry, his particular pride, promised, even then, to satisfy every ambition Pop could have had for him. Comparatively uncomplicated, uncontemplative, free of maverick impulses, he fitted comfortably into his environment. Brothers could hardly have been more dissimilar than Harry and I. We were never close. But we liked—and respected—each other through careers that took us into situations incompatible *ad extremum*.

Except for what happened in front of the strike committee, my settos with Pop were comparatively restrained. Pop's everyday attitude toward me was not so harsh as I may have suggested. His normal tendencies were indulgent—and forbearing. Mom, his inferior in wit but nobody's inferior in will, dominated him whenever she chose to.

Before my father was much past fifty he retired from business. Rogers Peet had decided to do their own manufacturing, and he lacked both the know-how and the gumption to start something new. Although not so rich as those aggressive Jacobs, he was by ordinary reckoning a comparatively wealthy man and could now take life easy. His capital, invested, actually grew.

Meanwhile, it was expected that, after four years of high school, I would go to work for E. Jacob & Co., "starting at the bottom to learn the business" and within a reasonable period entering upon the golden route of salesman to the trade. I considered De Witt Clinton High School but chose the High School of Commerce—not, as Pop approvingly assumed, for an introduction to business, but because it had a good football team. I hated it. In the middle of the second year I dropped out, feeling I might as well plunge directly into business. E. Jacob & Co. assigned me to "call on the trade" with Uncle Ben. My job being to carry his sample case. It did not work out. I insulted a customer, Uncle Ben and I quarreled, and Uncle Manny fired me (with regrets to my parents). Pop was philosophical about it, but said, "Charlie, if you can't get through high school and you can't manage to get along at E. Jacob & Co. maybe you're not so smart as I thought." Mom said that maybe it was a mistake to go with E. Jacob & Co.; they were not the only people in the business and Charlie probably would do better with strangers. I thought she might have been right; certainly the Jacob style was uncongenial to me.

Since I now had at least a nodding acquaintance with the field, I approached a small wholesale piece-goods firm—and was hired as a salesman! By sheer good luck I was handed an order on the first day. After that nothing. I did not insult anyone but I did not arouse much interest either. I had no spirit for it. Thanks to that first day's order I lasted nearly a month before being fired. A jobber of lace and embroidery engaged me to sell on commission to small stores. I barely went through the motions. My employer soon refused to keep me (even on a commission basis; I was collecting against a "drawing account" and not earning). Commission jobs are easy to find—though not always with drawing accounts—and I acquired several. But to no purpose. I formed the habit of going out with my samples in the morning, calling on one customer (to quiet my conscience), and spending the rest of the day in the reading room of the Forty-second Street Public Library. (In the library I discovered E. L. Voynich's *The Gadfly*—with an enthusiasm that is rekindled with every rereading.) This went on as long as the job lasted.

Six or eight months of such pretense were more than plenty. The new publishing firm of Boni & Liveright wanted a stock boy. I applied—on my knees—successfully. Residing at home expense-free, I managed, out of my scanty salary, to pay for two Columbia University extension classes, one night each week: European history (with James Harvey Robinson) and English literature (with a junior but inspired professor whose name I no longer remember). They were water in the desert. The history class enrollees included a young Will and Ariel Durant (both of them scrawny, wild-haired, shabby, and, I would judge, very poor). The lit class gave me Burns, Wordsworth, Coleridge, Byron, Shelley, and Keats. And Blake: *Songs of Innocence, Songs of Experience, The Marriage of Heaven and Hell.* Also Godwin, Maria Edgeworth (*Castle Rackrent*), Hazlitt, De Quincey, and the beguiling Charles Lamb of *Essays of Elia.*

There was in our neighborhood a fellow of my age (then about seventeen) who shared many of my questionings, anxieties, susceptibilities, and yearnings. Edwin Justus Mayer. We were close friends and confidants. He was the one who learned of the Boni & Liveright opening. Though he'd been tempted himself, necessity chained him to his better-paying job at the BVD company. His father had plunged from great wealth to bankruptcy—and suicide—during the panic of

1907. Eddie, providing considerable support to a prodigal mother, lived with her and her bemusement with past grandeur in a modest apartment across the street from us. He had a weak stomach (it eventually killed him) but a lively and roving mind. We discussed the "humanities" together day after day. Walt Whitman in poetry. In prose most particularly Wells, Shaw, Ibsen, Samuel Butler, Frank Norris, Dreiser. When Teddy Roosevelt ran for president on the Progressive ticket in 1912 we both wore Theodore Roosevelt/Hiram Johnson buttons and distributed Bull Moose leaflets. (My father, a thoroughgoing Taft conservative, would not even argue with me.) Eddie and I also listened to street-corner speakers like August Claessens and Jacob Panken. Socialists. Their shrill harangues abashed but excited us.

Eddie's ambitions had a point of focus that mine lacked. He knew he wanted (lusted) to become a writer. And he became one. Precociously. In his early twenties he wrote a presumptuous yet percipient autobiography entitled *A Preface to Life* (in which I figure briefly). Its publication won better than average first-book attention. Eddie had taste and talent and achieved both public and critical recognition with two delicious Broadway comedies that had an Oscar Wilde—like polish: *The Firebrand* and *Children of Darkness*. Later he dropped into junk writing and affluent anonymity in Hollywood. Eddie had gotten an occasional story printed while he was still at BVD. At the same time I was writing, brashly, about the sorry human condition. I actually sold a 300-word article to *Pearson's Magazine*, and a bit of satirical light verse to *Puck*.

Literature and politics claimed only a portion of my spare time. I saw Lillian Walker, Max Linder, Mabel Normand, John Bunny et al. in movies; dark beer at five cents a glass (with "free lunch!") at the Lion saloon, 110th Street and Broadway; played poker and tennis. Sometimes a bunch of us went down to the Times Square area— maybe for a Broadway show. I got a mad crush on a musical comedy starlet named Gertrude Bryan, saw her show (*Little Boy Blue*) over and over, and once even followed her furtively to the Woodstock Hotel, where I telephoned her room in order to hear her say "hello." Then hung up. Uncle Ben gave me the address of a two-dollar whorehouse. I had been taught fornication by one of our "servant girls" and had gone to bed with "pick-ups," but this whorehouse experience was a first. Girls in kimonos and silk underwear lounged on benches in a large bare reception room, waiting to be selected. I picked a tall blonde with gold slippers and she took me upstairs. It was all over in a few minutes. A nothing!

3 Columbia, the Socialist Club, and a Wonderful Magazine

Pop, though alarmed by my tendencies, was proud to see something of mine printed. At Mom's suggestion he sent the *Pearson's* piece to Walter Lippmann. Neither of them knew Walter Lippmann, and the fact that he had recently been secretary to the socialist mayor of Schenectady hardly recommended him to them. But he was a scion of the immensely rich third-generation German-Jewish elite, and in spite of that a relative of a relative (by marriage) of one of the Jacob offspring. Besides, he had a measure of prestige in the cultural world, which somehow seems to have penetrated, directly or indirectly, my parents' consciousness. Only a few years out of Harvard, he was being declared "noteworthy" and "brilliant" by critics of his just-published book, *A Preface to Politics*.

Lippmann invited me to visit him one morning in his family's brownstone mansion off Fifth Avenue. Tall, blue-eyed, handsome, well fed and well groomed, he struck me at the start as athletic, scholarly, serious yet detached—perhaps a bit smug. Still, he had headed the Harvard socialist club and was now (in 1913) on the editorial board of an independent socialist monthly, *The New Review* (he quit that board two years later). He addressed me simply and encouragingly, without condescension. Our conversation lasted about two hours, beginning in his book-lined study, carried further during a walk to the Harvard Club, and continued there during lunch. He talked of Wordsworth and Blake and Ibsen, and of Teddy

Roosevelt's Bull Moose campaign, which he had supported. I remarked that Blake was my favorite poet, and felt flattered when he said he was his, too. He questioned me a little, chiefly on my educational background. When I told him of listening to socialist street-corner speakers, he merely nodded. Though he made no mention of his own socialist work, what I knew of the record fired my imagination. In a few years I would be cursing him, but he was an example to me now, the expression of a politico-literary ideal. Before I left he confided that he and some others were about to launch a new weekly to be called *The New Republic*. "After Plato's *Republic!*" I exclaimed appreciatively. He smiled and said, no, it came from Herbert Croly.[1]

A week after the lunch at the Harvard Club, I learned that Walter Lippmann had telephoned my father and persuaded him that I ought to have a chance at college. Pop agreed to finance me, with two provisos: that it be in New York, where I would avoid unnecessary expense by living at home, and that I could pass the entrance exams within one year. I took extension classes day and night, and summer session. More lit. More history. Economics. Geology. French (from scratch). I studied as never before, or since, and by the skin of my teeth passed the needed entrance exams (including three years of French) on schedule. The exams I took were for the Pulitzer School of Journalism. It was my only possible choice, because the S. of J., though a full, four-year undergraduate unit of Columbia University, did not require math for admission. Happily it was a choice that appealed to me anyway.

Besides practical instruction in newspaper reporting, feature writing, and so on, the School of Journalism offered courses in literature, history, politics, economics, and philosophy. Only two or three of the professors were exclusively S. of J. Among the others were Columbia University greats like Charles A. Beard, James T.

---

1. Croly's *The Promise of American Life*, published in 1909, was recognized as a major influence in both the Progressive Nationalism of Theodore Roosevelt and the New Freedom of Woodrow Wilson. Not only had Croly supplied the *New Republic* name; the magazine was actually his project. He had planned it; he had inspired Willard Straight to underwrite it, and he had put together the editorial board of Walter Lippmann et al. Croly himself remained a *New Republic* editor until his death in 1930.

Shotwell, and Brander Matthews. Also a smart, provocative, fledgling economist named Leon Fraser who one day was to become president of the Bank for International Settlements. The gaunt, graying, but spirited Beard, whose *Economic Interpretation of the Constitution* and *Economic Origins of Jeffersonian Democracy* meant more to me than any textbooks, was pithy in the classroom and unfailingly genial out of it, whether in his office or walking (striding) with you across the campus. No less genial was the amazing Walter B. Pitkin, who taught psychology, Aristotelian philosophy, and journalism, all brilliantly, and at the same time pounded out scores of popular detective stories (under a variety of pseudonyms) along with his *History of Human Stupidity* and the best-selling *Life Begins at Forty*—all the while operating a profitable duck farm at his home on Long Island.

My freshman year started in September 1914—an ominous period in the world outside. World War I had begun in Europe. Diplomatic relations between the United States and Mexico had been in suspension since a bloody incident at Vera Cruz early in the year.[2] Our country itself was suffering wholesale unemployment, desperate labor struggles. Militiamen had fought a pitched battle in April with striking miners at the Rockefeller-dominated coal fields of Ludlow, Colorado, and women and children had been killed. The strike persisted into September, with federal troops in control.

Now nineteen, I was old for a freshmen. As the term began, the S. of J. sophomores gave us a welcoming party. One of our young hosts, a thick-nosed, thick-spectacled, broad-smiling guy, singled me out and introduced himself as Morrie Ryskind. (He was the "Morrie" whose witticisms in F.P.A.'s "Conning Tower" I was al-

2. On April 9, 1914, a party from U.S.S. *Dolphin*, going ashore for supplies, accidentally entered a restricted area and Mexican troops arrested them. Although they were released promptly, with apologies, Admiral Henry T. Mayo demanded that the port commander apologize formally in person, promise to punish the responsible officer, hoist the American flag, and give it a twenty-one-gun salute. The salute refused, American forces on April 21 bombarded Vera Cruz and occupied the city. General Victoriano Huerta, then enjoying his brief tenure of the Mexican presidency, broke off diplomatic relations with the U.S. The incident temporarily united Mexican opinion behind Huerta and brought Mexico and the U.S. close to war.

ready acquainted with, and much admired.[3] In time he was to write
the book and lyrics of one of Broadway's best musical comedies, *Of
Thee I Sing*.) I asked him about extracurricular organizations at Columbia. Was there some interesting group a new student might like
to join? "Sure thing," he said. "Whatever you want. Like the Socialist Club for example." I was amazed. Not that it existed, only that it
had been mentioned to me before any other. But of course it was just
what I wanted to hear. I joined the Columbia Socialist Club, the
Columbia University chapter of the ISS (Intercollegiate Socialist
Society), and was promptly elected secretary. I found Journalism
students predominating there. Three or four of the members were
Columbia College, not more, plus a handful of postgraduates and
three Barnard girls.

Morrie was a member himself, and most of the other S. of J.-ers in
the club were classmates of his. Socialists, near-socialists, syndicalists, feminists, and at least one anarchist (George E. Sokolsky) had
made the S. of J. sophomores, Class of 1917, "a hotbed of radicalism," at least among university gossips. They were determinedly
avant-garde as to politics, art, literature, free love, and life generally.
The freshmen, Class of 1918 (mine), proved "nearly as bad." The
two classes intermingled, and I soon had a set of good friends:
Morrie Ryskind, Howard Dietz ("Freckles"), Irwin Edman, Al and
Si Seadler, Max (M. Lincoln) Schuster, Larry (Lorenz) Hart, Phyllis
Perlman, Otis Peabody ("Opie") Swift, Morrie (Morris R.) Werner,
and Bill (William Slater) Brown. All but Larry Hart (too cynical)
were in the Socialist Club with me. Irwin Edman, a bibliomaniac,
shy and near-sighted (Irwin was an albino), stayed in Journalism
only halfway through the first semester of his sophomore (my freshman) year. After he shifted to Columbia College, I continued to see
him in the Socialist Club (till he dropped out of that) and in Boar's
Head, the university's literary society. All of us saw in him the celebrated philosopher to be.

George Sokolsky, our flamboyant anarchist, affected his own little
sophomore clique. From a family of Russian-Jewish Bakuninists in

3. Franklin Pierce Adams (F.P.A.) was a central figure in the group (which included Dorothy Parker) that lunched together weekly at the Algonquin. His column, signed F.P.A., ran first in the *New York Herald-Tribune*, then in the *Evening
Sun*, where it was headed "The Conning Tower."

the East Side slums, he had learned the lore of nihilism when the rest of us were only a few years out of kindergarten. He had a quick mind, a gift for starting conversation, and a scornfully truculent manner. "Sock" was unpleasant to look at, his complexion muddy and pimpled, his small eyes myopic, his tangled mass of kinky hair evidently neither combed nor washed. But he had a hold on his chosen companions. Hypnotically, it seemed, in the case of his inamorata, the willowy, delicately featured Esther Norton, patrician heiress and prettiest girl in the class. Esther groveled before him.

Radicalism in the S. of J. student body did not reflect the attitude of the school's administration. Octogenarian Talcott Williams, its director, was as conservative as the university's pompous right-wing-Republican president, Nicholas Murray Butler. And as prissy as Queen Victoria. Phyllis told me Talcott Williams, Ph.D., Litt.D., LL.D., once said to her: "Miss Perlman, never touch a doorknob if a man is present."

My closest friend at the S. of J. was William Slater Brown. He came from old New England stock; an ancestor established this country's first textile factory, the Slater Mill near Boston. But Bill, when sixteen, had supported the 1912 Lawrence textile strike as messenger for Arturo Giovannitti, the flaming IWW (Industrial Workers of the World) poet-strikeleader. Soft-spoken and self-deprecatory, Bill was a poet himself—with leanings toward French modernism (in which he was astonishingly well-read). He was also a connoisseur of French wines. I introduced Eddie Mayer to him and the three of us spent long evenings together in Bill's dormitory cubicle on campus. We drank cheap booze, gabbed, and dreamt up Socialist Club agendas until Bill's eyes began to dim and his mouth sagged, and Eddie and I could barely see the open copies of Clive Bell's *Art* and Remy de Gourmont's *Luxembourg Nights* on Bill's desk, or even the silhouette of a burly workingman climbing over a factory rooftop in the huge black and red IWW poster on the wall. An uncle of Bill's had an apartment off Washington Square in Greenwich Village. Bill suggested that we go down and "pay the old boy a visit," unannounced, just to get a look at the place. We went— along with Morrie, Freckles, Al, Si, Phyllis, and the three Socialist Club Barnard girls. The old boy wasn't home! But we had fun at Polly's Place, a second-floor tearoom on Eighth Street.

The Barnard girls were Eleanor Wilson Parker, Elizabeth Bigelow Hall, and Estelle Albert. The cute little Estelle Albert and the leggy blonde Betty Hall I knew only slightly—through their infrequent attendance at meetings. Eleanor Parker I knew better. A year younger than I, she could have posed for a Norman Rockwell–*Saturday Evening Post* version of exuberant American girlhood. She happened also to be a passionate idealist. And one of the hardest-working members of our Socialist Club.

I liked going to Greenwich Village; its bohemianism was such a relief from my home. Now and then I went back to Polly's Place sometimes greeted by the legendary Polly (Holladay) herself. It was there that I first saw Stuart Chase, a young instructor in economics who had published a sharp and lucid first book. Also Alfred Kreymborg, Maxwell Bodenheim, Harry Kemp, and other Village luminaries. There I met and talked with the talented but ill-fated Harold Stearns. He told me an unknown chap in his twenties named Eugene O'Neill possessed a sure-fire formula for playwriting. I went (less often) to other "tearooms": Romany Marie's (she was a fortune-telling gypsy), The Mad Hatter, The Dutch Oven. I prowled in the amiable Frank Shay's bookstore—and in the back room listened to Vachel Lindsay chanting "The Congo." And Alfred Kreymborg reading his imagist poems. (In the 1940s my Sylvia and I were to encounter the then decrepit, whiskey-soaked, and very mundane but still gentle Frank Shay on Cape Cod, with his wife, Edith Foley. And become their friends.) I admired the current imagist poetry, particularly Amy Lowell's and John Gould Fletcher's. But I preferred the poetry of vigorous social protest. New books like Carl Sandburg's *Chicago Poems*, James Oppenheim's *War and Laughter*, and Louis Untermeyer's *Challenge*. The poems in *Challenge* excited me. I read, reread, and memorized many. One, "Caliban in the Coal Mines," stays with me. ("God if you wish for our love / Fling us a handful of stars.")

Greenwich Village meant most to me as the home of a wonderful magazine, the *Masses*, which appeared monthly in illustrated outsize format. Its like never existed before and never could exist again. (The later Communist-spawned *New Masses* was a sectarian and spiritless counterfeit.) The *Masses* characterized itself like this:

It Had to Be Revolution

> A free magazine owned and published cooperatively by its edi-
> tors. . . . A revolutionary and not a reform magazine; a magazine
> with a sense of humor and no respect for the respectable; frank, ar-
> rogant; impertinent; searching for the true causes; a magazine di-
> rected against rigidity and dogma wherever it is found; printing
> what is too naked and true for a money-making press; a magazine
> whose final policy is to do what it pleases and consult nobody, not
> even its readers.

With Max Eastman as guiding genius and Floyd Dell as managing
editor, its buff-colored pages offered brilliant works by writers, artists, intellectuals, labor leaders, and philosophers representing every phase of antiestablishment ideology. Marxist and non-Marxist
socialists. Syndicalists. Anarchists. All more or less comrades together in that innocent period of the revolutionary movement. The
Masses office off Union Square was hospitable to sympathetic visitors, especially young ones. If Max Eastman and Floyd Dell were
tied up you could be sure of a cordial welcome from one of the other
editors usually around: Robert Carleton Brown, Howard Brubaker,
or H. J. Glintenkamp ("Glint").

During one of my visits John Reed dropped in, full of beans. I had
first met the hulking guy in 1913, when he and the flashing-eyed
IWW glamor girl, Elizabeth Gurley Flynn, attended a rich woman's
fund-raising soiree on behalf of the striking Paterson silk workers.
We'd met again when I journeyed to Paterson to join the picket line,
but I could not claim actually to know this likable, boyish paladin.
Eight years younger than he, I was a novice in comparison. Jack (I
hesitated before calling him that) had been in Walter Lippmann's
class at Harvard and they had been buddies in the Harvard Socialist
Club. He had since won recognition as a daring and talented war
correspondent, reporting brilliantly on the revolution in Mexico,
and becoming a partisan (and chum) of Pancho Villa in the process.
He'd also covered the Balkan War, writing vivid stories from the
Serbian front lines. In the meantime, his socialist thinking had
trended steadily more "revolutionary"—away from "parliamentarism" and toward "mass action"—and now, under IWW influence,

he was practically a syndicalist. At the time, I hardly knew what a syndicalist was. I was for Socialist Party "parliamentarism," and for the IWW too.

Floyd Dell shared a floor-through Village apartment—it seemed like one enormous room—with David Karb (advertising manager of the *Masses*) and Merrill Rogers (its business manager) and a pasty-faced, impishly profane young Dorothy Day (the future Catholic saint). He regularly had some thirty or forty people there for Sunday brunch. Once even me. I found myself rubbing shoulders with Max Eastman, Jack Reed, Clement Wood, Boardman Robinson, Robert Minor, Lydia Gibson, Ida Rauh, Mary Heaton Vorse, Susan Glaspell, Louis Untermeyer, and darling old Art Young, cartoonist nonpareil. Meeting Louis Untermeyer gave me a palp because his *Challenge* meant so much to me. I got an added palp when he asked me to dinner at his apartment uptown. There I met his (first) wife, Jean Starr—a poet herself, and a good one. Untermeyer looked more the bourgeois jewelry salesman (at which he earned his living) than the revolutionary poet, but I found the conversation satisfyingly literary-radical.

In those days some prominent rebels wore black flowing windsor ties to proclaim their bohemian individuality. Arturo Giovannitti did. And Ben Reitman. It had become a fashion, a badge. In effect a convention of unconventionality. (No laughing allowed.) I wore one for a while (at least a short while) until I realized that a person concerned with the remaking of society should not risk compromising the issue with something so frivolous as eccentricity in dress. I had a different but seemingly related objection to some things appearing in the *Masses*—pieces on psychoanalysis, birth control, and so on. Okay in themselves, they were out of place, I thought, in a class-struggle publication of limited space. Outline drawings of nude women, science fiction, love poems—all hints, I believed, of a disconcerting element of irresponsibility in some of the editors. (I was stupid about it. The things I objected to helped give the *Masses* its encompassing sense of life.) I loved the magazine regardless. It was, as someone (Theodore Draper?) says, "a meeting ground for revolutionary labor and the radical intelligentsia."

The *Masses* inspired me to promote a radical student magazine at Columbia. In little more than a week I had an editorial board consisting of Bill Brown, Morrie Ryskind, Irwin Edman, Phyllis Perlman, Esther Norton, Opie Swift, Al and Si Seadler, Max Schuster, Donald Stern, Wayne Wellman (president of the ISS Columbia chapter), and myself. Freckles, Eleanor Parker, and Marshall D. ("Bishop") Beuick constituted our business board. Betty Hall and Dorothy Metzger, staff members originally, resigned when Barnard's Dean Gildensleeve "dissuaded" them. (They were seniors and anxious about their diplomas.) The magazine, *Challenge* (after Louis Untermeyer's), was out in a couple of months' time. Twenty-four pages of irreverent prose, verse, and cartoons. We copied the *Masses* format, and H. J. Glintenkamp did a cover for our first issue. It showed Nicholas Murray Butler ("old Nick") at the Hamilton Hall door cutting off entering students' tongues. Demand for it—throughout the university—exceeded our youthfully enthusiastic expectations. The *New York Evening Sun* printed a story by its part-time campus newshound (Frank Scully) reading: "*Challenge* is out today and judging from the excitement on the campus the editors will be out tomorrow." A wisecracking sophomore at Columbia College, Herman J. Mankiewicz, put out a six-page anti-*Challenge* magazine, entitled *Dynamite*, half in random Japanese characters and the other half blank. He came over to the S. of J. and handed me a copy. We became sometime friends—banteringly. Quick-witted, convivial, and thoroughly cynical, Mank was an entertaining rogue—and a sponger. Morrie quipped: "I'll say this much for H. J. Mank, / if anybody blew he drank." (Brother of Hollywood's Joseph R. Mankiewicz, Herman J. ultimately became something of a Hollywood figure himself.)

It would be absurd to imply I thought of nothing those days but the need for a better world. There was many an evening ramble in Riverside Park with S. of J. intimates. Picking up girls. Listening to "We were sailing along on Moonlight Bay." Like Morrie and the rest I contributed paragraphs and light verse to F.P.A.'s "Conning Tower." (My signature was "Gulliver.") Larry Hart and I collaborated on a little play burlesquing Talcott Williams; we called it "The Oracle of Talcum Bill." We acted it in the school and it went over big, thanks to Larry's rhymes—foreshadowings of the brilliantly sardonic lyrics of the Rogers and Hart musicals.

Getting out *Challenge,* we soon realized how much copy a twenty-four-page magazine demanded. New as we were, we had to contribute much of the material ourselves. Inevitably the war in Europe dominated our pages. Both the Entente allies and the Central Powers had apologists in this country. We supported neither. Socialist and internationalist, we reiterated the timeworn adage that whichever side won, the people would lose. We advocated two things: end the fighting, and prevent our country from being drawn into it.

No subsequent issue of *Challenge* enjoyed the on-campus demand of the scandalous first. Since we of course had to be subsidized we were fortunate to have an angel. He had appeared at the outset, from an unlikely quarter, and nothing could scare him off: Professor James McKeen Cattell, venerable head of Columbia's Science Department. Professor Cattell had no ties with radical political movements, nor was he acquainted in advance with anyone on our staff. He said he liked our nonconformity, our "youthful gusto." And he hated war.

4   The Ford Peace Expedition

I was not a pacifist (and never have been). I was ready to concede that some wars could be justified with all the suffering. But not this one. The result, I believed, of unprincipled politico-economic power grabs on both sides (in Africa, parts of Asia, southeastern Europe, the Dardanelles). I still believe I was right. (Witness the war aims made explicit in the secret treaties revealed after the war.)

When the guns of August began to boom in 1914, President Wilson proclaimed U.S. neutrality and admonished Americans to be "impartial in thought as well as in action." Neither side respected American rights or interests. The British intercepted American ships and confiscated cargoes. The Germans announced that neutral vessels entering waters around the British Isles would do so at their own risk. British ships flew neutral flags in the area. The Germans retaliated with indiscriminate submarine warfare. Protests to both sides proved ineffectual. On May 7, 1915, a submarine sank the *Lusitania* off the Irish coast without warning. Over a thousand innocent passengers lost their lives, including 128 Americans. The ship had been carrying munitions as well as people (a sneaky business on the part of the British). But nothing could have made the German action less of an atrocity. Our government's response was prompt and tough. The president drafted a note which Secretary of State William Jennings Bryan considered so warlike that he resigned rather than sign.

Wilson now "adopted" Preparedness—previously identified with Theodore Roosevelt, Henry L. Stimson, the Anglo-American Union, the American Defense Society, and other pro-Entente stalwarts. Meantime (September 1915) an American banking syndicate announced a $500 million loan to France and Britain with Wilson's approval. (On August 15, 1914, the president had asseverated: "Loans by American bankers to any foreign nation which is at war are inconsistent with the true spirit of neutrality.")

Preparedness propaganda had influential private support. Those who disliked it (undoubtedly the majority of Americans) lacked an authoritative voice. Organized opposition to it came chiefly from such pacifist groups as the Quakers, civil libertarians, the IWW and the few other (relatively small) radical labor unions, and of course the Socialist Party. A Socialist Party referendum (11,041 to 782) called for expulsion of any party member holding public office if he voted for army or navy appropriations—or for war. The real test for American socialists was still to come. Before August 1914, the European socialist parties—the British Labour Party, the German and Austro-Hungarian Social Democrats, the French, Italian, Belgian, and Russian parties, and so on—had committed themselves to a similarly uncompromising antiwar policy. But when hostilities began the big socialist parties in the belligerent European countries all "loyally" supported their respective governments. The alternative was to face persecution. Up against no such emergency, the American socialists could oppose the war without defying their government, but only so long as the United States stayed out.

The peace movement as such tended to be vague in outlook. And negative. Occasionally, though, some action project emerged. The most spectacular of these was Henry Ford's late 1915 Peace Ship— with its slogan: "Out of the trenches by Christmas!" The slogan was ballyhoo. To be fair to him, Ford hardly expected such a miracle. His expedition had a plan that, to its leading participants, seemed sober and realistic: to lay the foundation for "a standing conference of neutral nations" (Holland, Switzerland, the Scandinavian countries, Spain, and the United States). This standing conference would offer, continuously, to mediate between the warring nations. "Every single day" it would renew its offer of immediate mediation, "until the warring nations were ready for tentative discussions."

The idea did not originate with Ford. He got it from a Hungarian leader of the international Women's Movement, Rosika Schwimmer. She sold him on it—Peace Ship and all—in no time. The high-powered lady had gotten to him, after repeated tries, only a month before the Peace Ship left Hoboken! He promptly announced it to the press, saying he was prepared to spend $10 million on the undertaking. (He actually spent $600,000.) Ford had an uncanny publicity sense. The project was front-page news day after day. Reporters flocked around him. He took fifty of them on the Peace Ship in company with the fifty-seven constituent members of the expedition and thirty-six college and university students (brought along to watch, and perhaps to cheer). All were guests of Henry Ford. Constituent members, probably chosen on Madame Schwimmer's advice, received telegrams of invitation signed with his name. Similar telegrams went to the student observers.

At the last minute, the day before the ship sailed, I was invited as the representative of Columbia, stepping in for another student, invited earlier, who was unable to go. I had known such a chance might come, had reasons for welcoming it and enough foresight to be ready with a passport. The ship was the Scandinavian-American liner *Oscar II*, engaged (all but the steerage) for the expedition. The pre-departure period was hectic. (This from a clipping: "New York's Hotel Biltmore, Peace Expedition headquarters for the eleven days

Student contingent with Henry Ford's 1915 Peace Expedition. Including
Charles Francis Phillips (rear row, 4th from right) and Betty Hall (seated,
5th from right).

before sailing, seethed with excitement. Besieged by hordes of reporters, messengers, pacifists, assorted reformers and intrepid
cranks, it was a miracle that the harrassed [sic] managing team—
Ford, Rosika Schwimmer and Louis Lochner of the Chicago Peace
Society—survived.")

The old, 12,000-ton *Oscar II* sailed for Europe on December 4,
1915, with a great big dove of peace stationed in the first-class
lounge. Henry Ford stood on deck, gaunt and careworn, surrounded
by newspapermen and the more important of his expedition associates, prominent among them the stocky, unstoppable Rosika
Schwimmer. The students included one from Barnard: Betty Hall.
An odd choice I thought. Her politics fitted but no one would have
rated her an activist. Whoever did the scouting for students must

have picked Betty for her blue-gray eyes and her blonde southern charm. Anyway I was glad she was there. Together we waved farewells from the ship's rail to mutual friends on shore.

It has been reported that former Secretary of State Bryan would be joining our party, as well as Senator Robert M. LaFollette, David Starr Jordan, Oswald Garrison Villard, Lillian D. Wald, and Jane Addams. None of them came. Some accepted invitations and later reneged. The best "names" we had with us were Judge Ben B. Lindsey, Denver Children's Court reformer, and Inez Milholland Buoissevain, who, although an outstanding pacifist, was best known for having ridden a white horse in a woman's suffrage parade. If Ford wanted the fulsome free publicity he got, it must have been on the theory that any publicity is good. Reactions ranged from abuse to mockery. Characterizing Ford "and his crusaders" as "impudent meddlers making fools of themselves." Asserting, variously: "The whole thing is a publicity stunt." "Ford is crazy." "Ford has a swelled head." "He thinks money can do anything." My own feelings on making the trip were mixed. I had no faith in the pilgrimage; it seemed hopelessly quixotic. But it provided an opportunity to get to know antiwar students from all over the country. And that was exciting. Also, the entire party would be met abroad by the veterans of the international struggle against militarism, campaigners of proved effectiveness. Including, in Scandinavia, parliamentary leaders who were socialists. That was exciting, too. I would have hated to be passed over.

Expedition members assembled twice daily. Heard pep talks and approved resolutions for presentation in Europe. Drafted manifestoes and addresses to neutral governments and their peoples. Always after discussion and heatedly debated amendments. We students remained silent at these "business meetings." We were expected to. We had meetings of our own. Betty and I got especially close to fellow students from Vassar, Johns Hopkins, Ohio State, Oberlin, and the University of Nebraska. Betty and I shunned hymn-sings and such, and after a time we tended to shun the "business meetings" as well. The decks were usually windswept and icy, and sometimes hazardous, but we found them a precious resource. When the combination of their slipperiness and the pitch and roll

of the ship made walking impossible, we clung to the rail, not mind-
ing a drenching, even enjoying it in the excitement of the advancing
and retreating horizon and the raging mountains of sea.

After a rough voyage—protracted by a long detour northward to
bypass the mined English Channel—the storm-battered *Oscar II*
reached Christiania (now Oslo) on December 19. Ford left us there,
returning home immediately on the steamship *Bergensfjord*. We
heard he was sick. So I never acquired any firsthand knowledge of
Henry Ford. Never had a direct word from him beyond "good morning" or "good evening" as, swaddled in blankets, he passed Betty
and me on one of his lonely walks on deck. After the first day's
greeting I never saw him at a meeting of expedition members. He
may not have attended any. I did not actually get to know Madame
Schwimmer either—then or later. She was too busy. And, in a sense,
so was I. (I mean after Christiania.) On shipboard the only fellow
passengers I talked with much were students. I did work up something of an acquaintance with two of the newspaperman: William C.
Bullitt of the *Philadelphia Public Ledger* and Tom Seltzer of the (socialist) New York *Call*. Bullitt, later U.S. ambassador at Moscow and
at Paris, was a 1912 Yale graduate, a sleek, sophisticated Philadelphia mainliner. Derisive about the expedition (like all the newspapermen) but professedly an antiwar liberal, he said he liked the
Masses, preferred it to *The Nation* and *The New Republic*. He
smiled easily, laughed at his own very good jokes, and was a free
spender at the ship's bar. An intriguing guy. I didn't know how to
take him.

Two lengthy communications, distributed aboard our special
train from Christiania to Stockholm, detailed how the expedition
would proceed without Ford. I gave little thought to these long documents. In fact I scarcely read them. The party had had five days in
Christiania. Greeted by radical members of the Storthing, banqueted
in the city's *Folkets Hus*, addressed at, and addressing, a number of
mass meetings. Our student group conferred with a deputation of
sympathizing Norwegian students. During the scanty hours of winter daylight we were free to roam the snowbound Norwegian capital. I loved the eerie quiet of traffic moving on runners instead of
wheels, though I shivered in two sets of long wool underwear! The
day before we entrained for the overnight trip to Stockholm, I met

Betty in the writing room of her hotel before breakfast as usual. (Male and female students were lodged in separate hotels.) She was sobbing. Betty sobbing? What the hell was wrong? Would she tell me, I asked. She threw herself on a desk and wailed. Then without stopping or looking up she mumbled that if I wanted to know what was wrong it was I.

"I? How?"

"You don't care for me. I might as well be a committee meeting."

I was stupefied. Could I really mean so much to that unreachable, lovely, adorable woman? She kissed me ardently, and a locked-up, unsuspected emotion broke loose in me. I knew in an instant I was in love, for the first time in my life. I dared not hope she would say that she loved me, but she did. She did! We spent the morning in Betty's room, fondling, making love. We talked, explaining ourselves to each other as if we'd just met. When she announced that she was hungry we reminded each other we hadn't had breakfast.

In the afternoon Betty and I hired a horse-drawn sleigh and arranged a ride in the country. We held hands under the bearskin lap robe. Incredibly, I got out and knelt in the snow at Ibsen's tomb. (Like a murderer caught in the act I can only plead temporary insanity.) Obliged to sit up all that night in the same darkened train compartment with six fellow students, we groped for each other in silence, talked in whispers. All at once I heard myself whisper, "Betty, when we get home let's get married." She squeezed my hand, nestled closer, and we kissed. "The nicest proposal I have received yet," she cooed. "I accept, honey, while I have you in my hot little hands." (No one else had ever called me honey. I don't think I had heard anyone called honey except on the stage or in novels of the Old South. It made me feel that we were really engaged.)

We skipped a scheduled early morning meeting at Stockholm to get some sleep. Refreshed after a couple of hours, I half ran from my hotel to Betty's, exulting. I slipped and slithered in the snow, bumped into things (litter baskets and whatever), hardly noticing. She came to her door yawning but with an open flask in her hand. "Brandy," she explained, tiny creases forming at the corners of narrowed eyes. We had breakfast sent up and celebrated all morning— with brandy and otherwise. Before we went downstairs the flask, of course, was empty. But Betty probably had a bottle in her suitcase.

She had been brought up on the stuff, literally suckled on it. Her mother in Virginia, like her mother before her, used to dab brandy on the nipples to keep the baby quiet. We skipped every meeting that day. And the next. And the next. The peace mission trans-shipped to Denmark with us practically a private party of two.

But at the door of her hotel room in Copenhagen she turned and said, "I'd rather you didn't come in. I'm tired, and not feeling very well." Next day at breakfast she remarked—offhand, like "pass the bacon"—that we had better forget about the marriage because she couldn't say when—or, well, if. By the time we boarded the ferry to Warnemünde (in Germany) she was openly avoiding me. I was crushed.

By permission of the Kaiser's government our company traveled through Germany to neutral Holland at night in a blacked-out train. Peeping through shuttered windows we got an occasional glimpse of spiked helmets. The pilgrimage halted for several days of organization and propaganda at each of the more important Dutch cities along our route. During all this time I was capable only of coddling my misery. The pilgrimage wound up at The Hague. Nearly everybody was shipped home then. Those selected to stay convened the Ford Neutral Conference at Stockholm and submitted mediation offers to the warring nations, which ignored them. We students sailed from Amsterdam on the *Noordam*, Holland-America line. Betty tête-à-tête with Bill Noble, my roommate.

Betty Hall was not the profoundest love of my life. I have that now. I forgot Betty, as I forgot others. And faster. I tell about her in *extenso* in part because she was the first. And in part to account for my shamefully wasted opportunities for work and contacts during the Ford Expedition.

5 Eleanor

I had expected the trip abroad to fit neatly into my Columbia Christmas vacation. But we were late everywhere and did not get back to the U.S. until the end of January. With the explanation (pretext) that I had been AWOL, I was denied readmission to classes for the balance of the term. I did not tell my parents. They never knew. I left the house every day routinely. The school situation troubled me, of course, but not greatly. It left more time for *Challenge* and the Socialist Club. And the Collegiate Anti-Militarism League. This was a new organization with Robert W. Dunn of Yale as president. I heard of it when I got back from my trip, joined it, and was made organizing secretary.[1] It seemed so exactly right for a person of my age, in this country, at that time. I took over editing a magazine called *War?*, the league's official organ (named from a book entitled *War? What for?* by George R. Kirkpatrick, later Socialist Party candidate for vice president of the United States). I induced Eleanor Parker to come into the league with me. Mrs. Henry Goddard Leach and others of like mind and like substance gave money. We rented office space on Broadway near 115th Street, opposite the Columbia campus.

I was sweeping out the office one day when a skinny youngster with the light-blue and white skullcap of a Columbia College freshman stuck on his head appeared at the front door and asked to be put to work for the cause. Owen Cattell (son of Professor James McKeen Cattell). He was only seventeen, and his wide eyes and full pursed lips made him look even younger. He had no political background. Apart from a passionate opposition to war, his main interest was zoology (in which he intended to major at Columbia). He was a godsend: willing to tackle whatever, unaffected and likeable, naive

---

1. I don't recall a League representative from City College of New York. Both Jay Lovestone and Bert Wolfe, who will appear prominently in these memoirs, were at CCNY about then—and around the Rand School, and in the Intercollegiate Socialist Society—but I did not hear of them anywhere. Including the Socialist Party when I joined it after the 1916 presidential elections. (My SP participation was confined to my small branch at 509 Eighth Avenue.)

but tough-minded, a fiend for work, unsparing of himself, fearless, tenacious, always dependable. Built to stay the course (like his father). In title Owen became secretary of the Collegiate Anti-Militarism League. With Eleanor as executive secretary and me as organizing secretary. Bob Dunn of Yale remained president, and George Hallett of the University of Pennsylvania had the title of treasurer, but Eleanor, Owen, and I ran the organization. For letterhead purposes, Columbia professors Harry Overstreet and Henry Wadsworth Longfellow Dana (grandson of the poet) lent their names as members of our advisory committee—along with Professor Emily Green Balch of Wellesley; Dr. Jessie Wallace Hughan of the (Socialist Party's) Rand School; Dr. Harry W. Laidler, National Secretary of the Intercollegiate Socialist Society, et al. Dapper, sprightly Professor Dana lent more than his name. He wrote for us, spoke for us, visited our office, and constituted himself a personal friend.

President Wilson achieved a major Preparedness breakthrough with the National Defense Act, adopted June 3, 1916. Together with significant industrial provisions, it vastly expanded the regular United States Army, authorized a National Guard of 450,000, and established a Reserve Officers Training Corps with units at universities, colleges, and military camps. The mailed fist now brandished here in America! A feeling of urgency enfiladed the antiwar movement, including the Collegiate Anti-Militarism League. We concentrated on opposing Reserve Officers Training. It proved a lively undertaking. The league had open supporters in many big universities and virulent antagonists in all. School authorities reprehended us; our propaganda was banned from certain campuses. Students who had signed up for the training camps provoked confrontations—sometimes violent. The work persisted. We suffered defections but at that point ours was decidedly a growing organization. We joined with other antiwar groups in demonstration trips to Washington. Appealing to congressmen in their chambers. Picketing the White House (I picketed with seven or eight others from Columbia).

We hired Dorothy Day to assist us in the league office. The uninhibited Dorothy, two years younger than I, had intrigued me at that Sunday brunch in the Dell-Karb-Rogers-Day apartment, and I had been out with her a number of times since, usually in "The Hell

Hole," the back room of a Greenwich Village saloon. I knew she was (as usual) broke. I don't remember what we paid her, but it couldn't have been over fifteen dollars a week. She would have worked gratis (part-time at least) because she was an enormously generous person and she liked us and believed in what we were doing and it was exciting.

Besides loving excitement, Dorothy created it. She was "game for anything unrespectable," the more outrageous the better. The typical putative Villager, but without the phoniness. Rawboned, square-jawed, white-faced, and flat-chested, she was yet compellingly sexy. And she had a rich offbeat infectious humor. She drew men. But she was so easily involved herself and so generous with herself (as with everything) that she was often hurt. (In a later period of our lives— in the 1920s—I actually watched Dorothy being hurt in a love affair. No, I was not the man in the case. I never had an affair with her.)

During the few months when Dorothy worked in the Collegiate Anti-Militarism League office, she formed the habit of taking lunch (whiskey and the excellent free lunch) at the good old Lion saloon on 110th Street. I sometimes accompanied her. She chain-smoked cigarettes and made friends with everybody in the place, especially the bums. She had a wonderful collection of funny stories, all supposedly true, many involving herself, invariably ribald. And she never failed to tell at least one obscene joke about nuns or priests or rabbis or the evangelist Billy Sunday. (She pronounced herself "a dedicated atheist.") In less than an hour she would be back at the office, sober and zealous, "working like hell for revolution and peace." After work she liked to talk about a Greenwich Village novel she was writing, to be called *The Eleventh Virgin*. (She finished the novel and a couple of years later got it published—with its title *The Eleventh Virgin*. I think it was considered trash. I never read it but I remember her telling me of one vivid scene she had written for it. About the heroine's chemise, draped over a chandelier to soften the light: "The damn thing caught fire at the most inauspicious moment.")

Chambers of Commerce, Kiwanis Clubs, and patriotic societies sponsored rallies, parades, and so on to popularize the Preparedness drive. Flags waved and bands played, with an unpleasant accompaniment: jingoism masquerading as Americanism; anti-militarism branded anti-Americanism. A tragic happening in San Francisco inflamed the situation. A bomb exploded during a Preparedness parade on July 22, 1916, killing ten persons and wounding forty. Who planted the bomb and why are still disputed. Detectives arrested Tom Mooney, a radical and militant labor "agitator," together with "his partner," Warren Billings. They were tried and convicted in an atmosphere of almost insane hysteria—on testimony later proved to be false (the witnesses confessed to perjury). Mooney was sentenced to hanging, Billings to life imprisonment. People and organizations of all beliefs (among them the Collegiate Anti-Militarism League) called for a new trial. I helped collect money for it. The courts denied it. But Mooney's death sentence was commuted, and eventually (after long years) both men were pardoned. Meanwhile the case was an international scandal. Our magazine, *War?*, reverted to it repeatedly.

The league and *War?* preempted so much of my time that I could not hope to continue giving myself to *Challenge*. I did not want to. *Challenge* had stopped being "my magazine." In fact it had stopped being *Challenge*. On Max Schuster's motion, and with me in the minority, the editors (all selected by me!) had decided to transform it from an organ of rebel nonconformism to one that spouted well-behaved blah. The magazine was to become an open forum, "entirely nonpartisan" and with "equal space for all points of view." It was my own fault. Why in hell had I handed them the right to decide such matters in the first place? Rather than confess idiocy, I blame inexperience. (I assumed that "democracy" ruled the *Masses*, but this was not so. Max Eastman determined its character. He consulted his fellow editors regularly, but the final word was his.) As soon as I quit, *Challenge* folded. For better or worse, the magazine could not get along without me.

November 7, 1916. Election Day. And my first vote. I voted Socialist of course: Allen L. Benson for president. My father declared for reelecting Wilson. (Because "he kept us out of war.") In the evening I asked if Pop had felt strange voting Democratic for the first time in his life. "Charlie," he said, "I couldn't do it. When I got into the booth my conscience stopped me." He voted the straight Republican ticket, headed by Charles Evans Hughes. I wonder how my brother, Harry, would have voted if he were old enough. Possibly for Wilson.

Although he and I slept in the same room and I was an almost irrepressible propagandist, I can't recall a single political conversation with Harry. His general outlook was a lot closer to Pop's than to mine. My sister, Anna, was no longer around. She was now Mrs. Sidney M. Green and a mother. Had been married in 1912—by Rabbi Stephen Wise. (Yes, Pop was still an unbeliever. Secretly. One Saturday when a neighbor was passing I saw him hide his cigar. He was increasingly anxious to be recognized as "belonging." Pop's main objection to my radicalism may have been that he felt compromised by it.) Anna's husband, Sidney, was in the textile business—and a salesman (what else?). I rarely saw them. They still showed up at the family's "Friday Nights," but I didn't.

After the 1916 elections, I joined the Socialist Party. But school and Anti-Militarism League work—less of school and more of the other—filled most of my days. Much of the time Eleanor Parker was with me—in and out of the office. We had progressed from comradeship to empathy and from empathy to something like love. (I guess what first attracted me was her singularly deep voice—the most mellifluous deep voice I have ever heard.) During the summer I had visited her every weekend at Asbury Park. Her mother operated a small hotel there and Eleanor was helping out. I looked forward to those weekends: the verve of her organ-toned shoptalk (the league's) and laughing gossip on the ride from the station, and the sneak visits to her room around midnight. To Eleanor's mother, a pinch-faced WASP of seedy gentility, mindful of her DESCENT(!) from a signer of the Declaration of Independence (James Wilson), I was non grata. Unmistakably. Mrs. Parker had character. She was dutiful, mettlesome, illiberal, and anti-Semitic. And she was tormented at her daughter's predilection for me. She would have denied me the house if she didn't fear that, doing so, she would lose Eleanor.

6 "Will You Be Drafted?"

Nineteen seventeen was a momentous year for the United States—and for me. The Entente allies were losing more ships than they were able to replace. How did that affect us? Americans now had over $2 billion invested in British, French, and Russian bonds, in addition to huge bank loans and business credits. Trade with the allies had risen from $800 million in 1914 to $3.2 billion in 1916, practically all on open account. A socialist comment: "American industry and finance could no longer afford to have the allies lose." Literally true or not, the economic pressure of the situation was inescapable. On February 3, 1917, when an American ship was sunk in the War Zone (after a warning), President Wilson broke off diplomatic relations with Germany. We were already halfway in.

Suddenly, in mid-March, marvelous good news. Nicholas II overthrown in Russia. The worst of absolutisms had been replaced by a provisional government proclaiming civil liberties and promising the election of a Constituent Assembly. At last something regenerative in the midst of the killing over there. "Darkest Russia" now had a regime headed by the liberal Prince Georgi Lvov—with Professor Paul Miliukov (leader of the Constitutional Democrats) as his foreign minister and Alexander Kerensky (a Socialist-Revolutionary) his minister of justice. This first Russian Revolution relieved the allies of the moral incubus of tsardom. To join them now would be to participate in a crusade "to make the world safe for democracy." President Wilson signed the declaration of war against Germany on April 6, 1917.

The American Socialist Party, far less powerful than its brother European parties, met its crisis more bravely than they had met theirs. An emergency convention of the party, arranged for earlier, assembled in St. Louis the day after the U.S. war declaration. The delegates adopted a resolution sponsored jointly by "Old Guard" socialist Morris Hillquit of New York and "New Left" spokesman C. E. Ruthenberg of Cleveland. It proclaimed: "The Socialist Party of the United States in the present grave crisis solemnly reaffirms its allegiance to the principles of internationalism and working-class solidarity the world over. . . . We brand the declaration of war by our government as a crime against the people of the United States and against the nations of the world."

Hillquit, it is generally agreed, was the dominant figure at the convention. The proclamation in its final form was largely his work, and his skillful maneuvering is given credit for its "coalition" sponsorship. One of the party's two or three top "moderate" leaders, and chairman of its National Executive Committee since 1900, he was also a highly successful New York lawyer. I knew little, as yet, of the internal ideological rivalries but was proud of my party's St. Louis proclamation. And prouder still when a membership referendum ratified it by approximately 21,000 to 350.

In spite of St. Louis and the referendum, there proved to be significant socialist apostasy in the country. Many—if not most—of the best-known socialists were emphatically pro-war. These sometime leaders bolted the party, among them Allen L. Benson, the Socialist U.S. presidential candidate for whom I had voted.

Apostasy among socialists paralleled more of the same in radical labor unions (except the syndicalist IWW), and in radical groups generally. (The conservative American Federation of Labor machine, under Samuel Gompers, was as chauvinistic as the Chamber of Commerce.) The liberal intellectuals flocked to the colors en masse—with Walter Lippmann, Herbert Croly, and the rest of the New Republic crowd showing the way. My Columbia comrades? "Let the old cat die," wrote Morrie Ryskind to the Collegiate Anti-Militarism League. (I published his letter in our magazine with a sarcastic reply.) "Let the old cat die" expressed a common and proliferating tendency. After May 18, date of the Selective Service Act, the league with all its branches was a skeleton organization. (The act required all men age twenty-one to thirty to register for military service classification. Conscription.) The exodus from our ranks astounded me, but it never occurred to me to join the stampede.

While the legislation was pending, a determined few of us got together in the league office to define our position. The meeting decided: (1) to assail the proposed conscription measure as "ordering compulsory sacrifice of young men for a war whose sole beneficiaries will be over-age profiteers"; and (2) to urge men twenty-one to thirty to defy it by not registering—if (as was already certain) it became law. (It became law that day.)

With the help of Eleanor and Owen, I undertook to get out a leaflet affirming this position. I worked up the thing that afternoon, Eleanor and Owen revised it with me, and the three of us rushed it to the printer—Max Siegel—a socialist who, we had been assured, would do a hurry-up job for us. He did. Within a few hours we picked up the printed leaflets (captioned in heavy black type: "Will You Be Drafted?"). We mailed a copy to every name in our files. Our stalwart friends distributed copies on street corners near Columbia, NYU, City College, Brooklyn College, and Fordham.

Attacks on protesters, pacifists, and radical labor multiplied. Socialist Party meetings were broken up. A mob threatened gentle David Starr Jordan (former president of Stanford University and a prominent pacifist) with violence. IWW organizers were tarred and feathered. And prosecutions under the Selective Service Act, and later the Espionage Act, aggravated the climate of harassment. To defend free speech, free press, and free assembly—and freedom of the rights of conscientious objectors—the American Union against Militarism converted itself into the National Civil Liberties Bureau with Roger N. Baldwin as director. Baldwin made the Civil Liberties Bureau (now the American Civil Liberties Union) a significant and enduring phenomenon of American culture. He was America's most devoted libertarian since William Lloyd Garrison.

People sometimes visited our office in search of advice—or to get the latest issue of *War?*—or whatever. One day two men of draft age came in at the same time. One asked Owen if he wasn't Charles Francis Phillips. Owen answered, "No. I'm Owen Cattell. Charlie's over there." I walked over and shook hands. "How can we help you?" I inquired. Just then I heard Eleanor tell the other guy who she was. End of dialogues. Our visitors flashed badges and arrested the three of us. We spent half the day huddled together in a police station before learning the charge: *conspiracy to obstruct the Selective Service law*. We weren't too worried; for we'd been treated considerately, never questioned, allowed to phone home, and were now finally released on our "our recognizance." We lived in a free country. There was no law against opposing conscription, and we were not conscious of having ever engaged in a conspiracy. This was June

1, 1917. I know it from newspaper clippings. Our case was the first one involving defiance of registration and the papers were full of it. On June 6, I was arrested again. It was the day after registration for Selective Service, and I had failed to register. Given a special opportunity to register (by the draft board), I refused. They let me go free pending settlement of the conspiracy charge.

Our trial was to begin two weeks later. Mrs. Parker invited my father and Owen's to a "council of war" with us at her house on West Twenty-third Street—but when Professor Cattell suggested calling Roger Baldwin, Pop walked out. Mrs. Parker wanted to get an agreement exempting Eleanor. Eleanor, humiliated and furious, insisted that her mother did not speak for her and that we three were in this together. Our "council of war" lasted less than ten minutes. Professor Cattell called Roger Baldwin from a telephone booth down the street. Baldwin knew about our trouble with the law; all New York did. He said if we hadn't called him he would have called us. He wanted to know if we had the right lawyer. The outstanding specialist on conspiracy was, he could tell us, Morris Hillquit. Hillquit was up to his ears and not easy to get but certainly would take this case. But did we want such a prominent socialist representing us? Professor Cattell asked each of us in turn. We were all for it. I said, "My father will jump out of his skin but I want Hillquit."

Hillquit, as Roger Baldwin had foretold, said yes immediately. He warned, though, that the trial was practically tomorrow. He would have to meet right away with us: the three defendants "and responsible elders." But he was tied up every business day that week. It would have to be Saturday or Sunday. Professor Cattell got an inspiration. Morris Hillquit and Winter Russell (assisting him), along with Eleanor and me, became weekend guests at the Cattell family home overlooking the Hudson in Garrison, New York. My father and Eleanor's mother had turned down invitations. The huge turn-of-the-century dwelling, with outbuildings, could have accommodated a convention. And in complete seclusion, for the Cattells owned the mountain. (The professor was an original. For a couple of years, beginning in early childhood, Owen and a twin brother were left alone on the mountain, segregated from all other humans except a tongueless nurse—for scientific purposes. To see if they would develop a language. They did not.)

Hillquit questioned Eleanor, Owen, and me all Saturday morning. Mostly about the "Will You Be Drafted?" leaflet—which, he had learned, was the basis of the conspiracy charge. How, when, and where did the leaflet come to be designed? Did all three of us work on the actual writing? How did it get to the printer? To whom were the printed copies delivered? Were we all involved in the distribution? In what way? Who paid for them? And so on. He informed us that violation of the conspiracy law was classified as a felony, punishable by up to two years in federal prison, a $10,000 fine, and loss of all citizenship rights. So it was a serious matter. "I just want you to know the worst," he said. He was crisp but kindly, gestures graceful and deprecatory, wicked black eyes smiling reassurance. Spoke precise English in a confidential foreign (probably Yiddish) accent. (Born in Russia, he landed in this country poor and alone at the age of seventeen.) At the time of our trial he was forty-eight years old, lithe, trim, and at the peak of his stubborn career. A few months later, as the Socialist Party's mayoral candidate, he would poll over 150,000 votes—at that time the most ever for a New York Socialist.

That weekend introduced me to the cordial Mrs. Cattell—a fiery-haired Englishwoman at least fifteen years younger than the wrinkled professor, and like him a staunch liberal and pacifist. She made me feel like an old and preferred friend. There, too, were Owen's eight-year-old brother Jack and his ten-year-old sister Quinta—fifth-born of seven Cattell children. Sunday afternoon, out on the mountain, the house party turned playful. Blindman's buff and hide-and-seek, with everybody, old and young, participating. Imagine a very undignified Morris Hillquit groping helplessly about the lawn, blindfolded, arms outstretched. Spindly old Professor Cattell, bones fit to creak, scurrying to hide himself behind a shrub or an outbuilding. Exquisite Mrs. Cattell in mad pursuit of Winter Russell or Eleanor or one of the kids. It was a fantastic, bizarre, riotous, and utterly delightful experience.

Two or three days later came a final (briefing) session with the lawyers in Hillquit's New York office. And on schedule, June 22, 1917, at 10 A.M., we duly appeared in court. Federal Judge Julius M. Mayer presided. The courtroom was jammed, then and throughout the five days of our trial. On a motion by the prosecutor, Harold A. Content, Judge Mayer dismissed all charges against Eleanor at the start. Perhaps not having an apple-cheeked American girl among the defendants would make a jury less reluctant to convict. Eleanor protested but they shut her up.

The government had only two witnesses against us—both of them surprises. The first was Max Siegel, the printer who had been so accommodating with our leaflets. We had gone to him because he was recommended as a socialist. He turned out to be a socialist pro-war style. He identified us as having together ordered the leaflets, and together called for the printed copies. He asseverated, apologetically, that he had given the material to his printers without actually reading it and did not know what was in it until copies were out on the street. Why did he have to give us away? Because, he declared, the leaflets might keep impressionable young men from answering the nation's call. I believe he may have been acting to save himself. Once the leaflets were traced to his printshop, the government "had the goods on him." The fact that he was a known socialist made his position worse.

When the prosecution's other witness took the stand, I gasped— and so did a lot of other people. It was my father. He sat upright, his head high, his thin lips compressed, very righteous. I tried to get him to look at me. Not a chance. As if he didn't know I was in the room. Mr. Content put the leading questions to him considerately, regardfully. The judge offered him a glass of water. He testified, with uncomfortable gravity, that I was reckless and uncontrollable; had contempt for authority, including the government; neglected my schoolwork and spent most of my time agitating against the war effort; would not hesitate to encourage violation of the most serious law if I didn't like it. My father! I can't imagine how the poor soul mastered his conflicting emotions to go through with it. Hillquit kept objecting that Pop was expressing assumptions open to question. And most of the objections were upheld. Hillquit cross-examined savagely, and Pop winced. He recovered himself though. What he was doing was disassociating himself from me. Before leaving the witness chair, he blurted out that he would disinherit me. (He meant it. He wrote me out of his will.) He must have been gratified to read in the next morning's New York Times, "The elder Phillips is known to have no sympathy with the propaganda of which his son was a part."

There is no reason to detail our defense. I was the "star witness." In a couple of days of testimony, I accepted responsibility for inspiring the leaflet, for its entire line of argument, and for the actual writing. I said I had had some help of course but denied that this amounted to a conspiracy. Unless any meeting where decisions were taken was a conspiracy. There was no suggestion here of undercover activity. My office had been open to anyone who cared to walk in. Which was the truth. When I left the stand I thought I had been an excellent witness but Hillquit told me I was terrible. He said I talked too damn freely and the prosecution loved it.

The jury was out a long time, which we took to be a favorable sign, but its verdict was guilty. The judge announced he would sentence us then and there. His demeanor had been stern throughout the trial and was stern now. We could expect no mercy. But his first words made me wonder. He was a father lecturing sons for misbehavior and at the same time explaining himself to all and sundry. We were college boys old enough to know better, but had no previous record of offenses. We had to be punished. But we were sensitive enough and our upbringing was such that the condition in which we now found ourselves was, in some degree, already punishment for us. We were, as he had said, still college boys, with the future still in our hands. He hoped we had learned our lesson, for our own sakes and for the sake of our families.

He then pronounced sentence. Owen Cattell to serve one day in prison and pay a fine of $500. Charles Francis Phillips to serve five days in prison and pay a fine of $500. In short next to nothing. I have no doubt whatever that if we had not been "college boys" of "impeccable" (upper-crust) families we would have gotten close to the maximum. My father paid the $500 and walked away without a word to me. I never saw him again until 1930 when he was dying. (Neither my mother nor sister nor brother attended the trial. They couldn't have been indifferent. It wasn't like them. I can't account for it. Harry may have been unable to get there—for reasons that will appear later. But not Mom or Anna.)

Conspiracy convicts usually go to the Federal Penitentiary at Atlanta, but my sentence was too short to warrant transportation. I served my five days in the Tombs, New York City. In a large dormitory with thirty or forty miscellaneous "roommates": drunks, and panhandlers serving overnight sentences; convicted burglars in for six months or more; men being held, in default of bail, for trial on charges like rape—even murder. Everybody was assigned work. I mopped the floor and made beds. After supper, before lights out, we played checkers. The food was slops but I got used to it. The worst thing that happened to me was that a guard had me write my name on a card, forced my thumb-print on it, and before I knew it I had been involuntarily registered for the draft. I told the s.o.b. that he knew what he could do with the registration because I would not obey any call.

I got mail in The Tombs. A letter from Eleanor every day. A long letter from Owen (who, by the way, had not even been locked up; "served" his day just hanging around the courthouse). A letter from Quinta Cattell, and one from little Jack Cattell. Here is what Jack scrawled:

Dear Mr. Phillips:

Everybody seemed to enjoy the article you wrote in my journal. Owen told me that while you are in jail I had a good chance to get an article out of you for the next number. I hope this letter is going to get to you before you come out.

Jack Cattell

The first thing I did when I got out was make sure the Collegiate Anti-Militarism League was in business. It was. At least the office was open, with Owen at a desk, stuffing envelopes. He and Eleanor, between them, had paid the rent and kept the name on the door. There was an invitation for me to speak at an antiwar conference at the Rand School (the Socialist Party's cultural center in New York) in September. I accepted. Meantime I had three urgent personal matters to attend to. Number 1: Find a place to live. Number 2: Look for a job. Number 3: See Eleanor. (She was helping out at the hotel in Asbury Park, for pay.) Number 3 took precedence. During an exciting Asbury Park weekend (dodging Mrs. Parker), Eleanor and I decided to marry. Soon. I would still have another year at Columbia but what of it? If we both worked we ought to be able to manage.

7 Confirmation from Afar

Morris Hillquit got me a summer job as a copyreader on the Socialist Party's New York morning newspaper, the *Call*. (Dorothy Day had told me she was once, briefly, a *Call* reporter. On a stunt. Got herself hired by proposing to live on five dollars a week—like many a factory girl those days—and writing what it felt like. Her salary: five dollars a week. She did it conscientiously, getting a room in a tenement and eating junk food. The experiment was supposed to last a month but her stories failed to catch on.) I did not have to report at the copydesk until evening and so was able to carry on at the Anti-Mil League uptown, mostly working on another issue of the magazine.

At the *Call*, Chester Wright was editor and Charlie Ervin city editor (or vice versa). Along with me at the copy desk was Irwin Granich, about my age, and like me filling in for a staff member on vacation. He had shaggy black hair, sleepy black eyes, and a dazzling white-tooth smile—and he could write like a wizard (though overfond of the lurid word). He was a friend of Dorothy Day's. I had met him previously at an ISS convention at the Rand School. I learned from him then that he was a product of East Side Jews without money. I learned it all over again now. (And would be reminded of it frequently in the future when I was no longer Charlie Phillips and Irwin Granich had become Mike Gold.) You weren't supposed to forget it.

Different as we were from each other, Irwin Granich and I had common interests. Besides feeling the same way about capitalism and war, we both loved Blake and Dickens and Dostoyevsky and Shaw and Samuel Butler. He had a basement room at 23 Christopher Street and needed someone to share the rent. At his invitation I moved in with him. On the floor above lived Louis Weitzenkorn, a New York *Call* regular, and his girlfriend, Lilly Winner. On the floor above that, Dr. Maximilian Cohen, a chubby, goggle-eyed dentist. I had what might be described as a waving acquaintance with him.[1] Weitzenkorn ran what he called "a proletarian-type F.P.A. column" in the paper, captioned *Guillotine*. Both Irwin and I wrote doggerel for it occasionally.

Besides sharing our room rent Irwin and I shared a bed. The bed was large and would have been comfortable enough except for the bedbugs. I mentioned the bedbugs to Owen and he said, interestedly, that he would like to sleep there some night. When I asked why, he said bedbugs fascinated him! He meant it. I don't recall if I have ever met another consecrated zoologist, but Owen was surely the only one I ever knew who liked bedbugs.

At Christopher Street I received a delayed (much forwarded) message from my missing brother, Harry, a note penciled in an army camp at Syracuse, New York. Harry, too young for the draft, had enlisted. (A second draft was to take kids of his age, but he couldn't wait.) "Dear brother," he wrote, "I believe in you for doing what you believe in like I am doing what I believe in. Think of me sometimes. Your brother, Private Harry Phillips." Short but great! At that moment I felt close to Harry, and loved him.

On October 31, 1917, having gotten our blood tests and a license, Eleanor and I were married in City Hall. Eleanor wanted our mothers to be there, and they both came. Mrs. Parker actually kissed me on the cheek. She and Mom stared at each other as if they were different species. Hardly exchanging a word, they separated quickly as we left for our honeymoon and I don't believe they ever saw each

---

1. Max Cohen was a somebody among the "most Bolshevik" elements inside the American Socialist Party: the party's formally constructed Left Wing, which soon seceded from the Socialist Party and broke into two schismatic entities: Communist Party (CP) and Communist Labor Party (CLP). Max Cohen became a top figure in the CP, whose membership was largely East European immigrant, 75 percent Russian, but recognized as its topmost leaders Cleveland-born Charles Ruthenberg and Italian-born but definitely American Louis C. Fraina. The CLP also had a largely foreign-born (non-Slav) membership but contained most of the comparatively few native and second-generation American Bolsheviks. It stressed the importance of its American location and was at least English-speaking. Its leaders included Alfred Wagenknecht, James Larkin, Ben Gitlow, and John Reed. Attempts to bring the CP and the CLP together failed, resulting only in an additionally schismatic United Communist Party (UCP). Eventually Moscow forced their unification. As indicated below, I was far away during these developments. Learned of them long after.

other again. Our honeymoon trip was, I rather imagine, unique: a hitchhike to Boston, and a subway ride under the river to Cambridge. Then back to New York by train. We had one day in Cambridge—where Harry (Professor) Dana gave us lunch at the grand old Longfellow house that was now his. Our home in New York was a tiny second-floor flat at 102 Third Avenue. With more than one visitor we were crowded. When we fixed the place up—painted it, put in bookshelves—it was quite attractive, though dark. After a while, we barely noticed the rattle of the El trains.

We got a warm letter of congratulations from Harry (this one from somewhere in France). Also letters from classmates of mine (I should say former classmates): Phyllis Perlman; "Bishop" Beuick—soon to be drafted; Bill Brown—driving an ambulance with the French army; Morrie Werner—with the British Expeditionary Force; Opie Swift—at sea (he was a petty officer in the navy). Morrie's letter informed me that "George Sokolsky, that arch-faker, has gone to Russia for the *New Republic*." He added: "This makes me lose some faith in the *New Republic*. Some day I expect to hear that he will be in Mesopotamia for the *New York Times*." (Morrie guessed Sock's direction but underestimated how far he would go. He wound up in postwar China publishing a newspaper financed by the invading Japanese!) Opie wrote: "George White is in training at Camp Columbia . . . Cramer is in a Canadian Regiment . . . Westwood has reached France. God—we never thought that our class would end like that a year ago. . . . I wonder what the next reunion dinner of 1918J will be like?"

Meanwhile, remote in New York, I was one of a comparative handful pouring out zealous though little-heeded propaganda to stay the war. For several years I had been obsessed with the idea of socialism, of a classless society in which men and women were delivered from subjection to capital. It was not just an idea, it was a promise, even though I didn't know exactly how and when it would come about. But now the abstract became concrete, and the remote immediate. On November 7 a second 1917 Russian Revolution, led by avowed socialists (Bolsheviks), set up a Workers and Peasants Government, with "The Internationale" as its official anthem. The liberation of the world had begun! (People who knew Russian explained that "Bolshevik" meant "majority." I liked that.) The first act of the regime was an appeal for immediate peace. The news reports mentioned two Bolshevik leaders: Lenin and Trotsky. They were unknown to me, and to most Americans—including socialists. (Max Eastman said in his autobiography that the *Masses* group first heard Lenin's name in 1917.) It did not matter. At my Socialist Party branch—509 Eighth Avenue—we comrades hugged one another. I yelled myself hoarse—with the rest of the audience—at a huge Madison Square Garden salute to the heroes of the New Russia. Our socialist fatherland. So regarded (in those early days) by practically the entire American socialist movement.

Max Eastman, a main speaker at the Madison Square Garden bedlam, read a fraternal message from John Reed in Russia. Reed had gone there on a newspaper assignment, had seen the thing happen, and had been caught up in it himself. He was riding around with the Bolshevik leaders, watching mass demonstrations, sitting in on "soviet" (workers' council) meetings. He was often invited to address meetings, and did, sometimes with an interpreter, sometimes without. Whatever he said, understood or not, the *amerikanets* was listened to with earnest faces and applause. The *Masses* soon began printing installments of Jack's story—later to be published by Liveright as *Ten Days That Shook the World*. (The *Masses* had barely gotten started with the installments before the magazine was suppressed.)

Eleanor was now a Barnard graduate. I ought to have been a Columbia S. of J. senior but wasn't. I had been kicked out—for repeated absences and unheeded assignments. My temporary job on the *Call* had ended, and I was again working part-time, this time at an apartment house switchboard. On Saturday afternoons I carried a spear (and swung an incense jar) at the Met—though music torments me—especially opera. My main work of course was Anti-Mil. Eleanor was earning a fair salary at I forget what.

8 Camp Upton

Early in February 1918 the mailman brought me a notice to report for military duty. We had expected it sooner or later. My course was clear. I ignored the notice. Reporters, apprised by the Draft Board, came to the Third Avenue flat. Was I deliberately disobeying the call? I said yes. What would I do? Nothing. I would be home every night. If they wanted me they would have to drag me away. The next day two husky plainclothesmen came for me. Six o'clock in the morning. We were dressed but not finished breakfast. I told them I wasn't going. They argued with me for five or ten minutes. Then put handcuffs on me and pulled and pushed me downstairs and into a car. Eleanor was coolheaded and supportive. Thoughtfully she had slipped a doughnut into one of my pockets and some reading material into another (an Everyman's Library edition of *The Way of All Flesh*). She followed us into the street and blew me a kiss as the car drove off.

They took me to Penn Station, and from there to Camp Upton at Yaphank, Long Island. At camp I was delivered to induction barracks, and a hairy-handed sergeant with a cracked voice asked me routine questions—name, birthplace, etc.—which I refused to answer. All I said was that I did not intend to cooperate in any way. The sergeant got up from his desk, grabbed my coat collar, shoved me away, and snarled, "You trying to shit me you fucking bastard?" A baby-faced lieutenant told him to lay off; I would be taken care of. Next, they put me through a physical examination. They had to take my clothes off. I wouldn't. I didn't struggle, just refused to cooperate. Then I was left sitting on a bench, naked. A long time passed. I was cold so I put my clothes back on. It was late. I had been sitting or standing in one place or another all day. Finally the sergeant came for me and I was issued a uniform. I could not accept the uniform. I let it drop to the floor. The sarge picked it up, stuck it under his arm, grabbed my coat collar with his free hand, and marched me out across the darkened parade ground. To a dormitory barracks full of inductees—some already in bed. He shoved me onto a cot, threw the uniform at me, and left me without a word.

It was nearly time for taps but they brought me supper. My only lunch had been the doughnut. Everybody in the barracks knew about me from the newspapers. Nobody referred to it. They were unconcernedly, uninquisitively compassionate—like the fellow inmates of The Tombs. The general attitude seemed to be, who the hell wants to be drafted but here we are so what's the use kidding? A few, at least, must have had strong feelings about the war, one way or the other. It didn't show.

Next morning's reveille got everyone out of bed but me. The sarge yanked me up. I refused to dress. The sarge had two or three men put the uniform on me. He called me son-of-a-bitch bastard or something more vividly vituperative and told me to get in line. Then he barked out an order to everybody. "Face right!" Everybody did. Except me. He walked over and spun me around so savagely that I lost my balance and fell. He waited until I picked myself up. Then: "Forward march!" They marched. All except me. This time he hit me so hard that I went down again. He gave me a fervent kick and left me there. The line marched out—presumably to the mess hall. An hour or so later I had a friendly visitor. The baby-faced lieutenant who had saved me from probable mayhem in the induction barracks. He positively exuded friendliness. Not officer to conscript but man to man. He offered me a plump white hand and sat down on the cot beside me. "Phillips," he announced familiarly, "you and I are ex-schoolmates. Different years, but the same great school."

"Columbia?" I asked.

"No. Mt. Pleasant Academy. I graduated from there, then went on to Harvard."

I didn't believe him. (And don't now.) But how did he learn about me and Mt. Pleasant? When he offered me a cup of coffee I accepted, warily. I needed the coffee anyway. Actually it was coffee and buttered toast—served in his private office—a cubbyhole with a desk and two chairs. Well it was a brief comradeship. He said he recognized I was intelligent, highly motivated, and no coward. But my course was wrong and, my intelligence ought to tell me, futile. "You can't beat the army." And so on. Repeated several times and in several different ways. He was telling me this for my own sake as an ex-schoolmate. (It was that corny!) All with the authentic Bostonian-Harvard inflection. (The Harvard part of his introduction may have been true.) I didn't discuss anything with him. I just said we saw things differently and I had to do what I had to do. He dismissed me with a sad smile.

I went back to the barracks and lay down on my cot and read *The Way of All Flesh*. I ignored mess calls. By evening my stomach began to hurt. I thought of hunger strikers, marveled at how they were able to keep up. I would have to do some foraging. But no. When the rest of the guys came back to the barracks, one of them—a gum-chewing kid from Brooklyn—brought me a sandwich and a piece of pie. I tried to talk to him about the war but he wouldn't listen. No one would. (Sneaking in food to some sucker up against it was only according to code. Talking was different.) Were they afraid to talk to me? Well I suppose they were. Perhaps not so much of the higher-ups (although that was certainly—and not unwarrantedly— latent in the situation) as of one another. And probably, in some cases, of themselves. If they talked to me they might become interested. And where would that lead them? Mostly, though, they were "just good Americans." Convinced, if unenthusiastic about being in the thing themselves, that somebody had to beat the pants off those Germans. I couldn't help being disappointed, but I was used to rebuffs by then. I assured myself that time was working for us; Russia had proved it.

The next day, the same routine. I obeyed no orders. They had to get me up, dress me, and so on; the sarge was very rough. My lieutenant friend paid me a second visit. What did I hope to accomplish as a CO? I was absolutely alone. Wouldn't find another CO in all Camp Upton. This went on for one more day. The lieutenant reasoned and the sergeant roughed me up. Sarge hit me again that day, but not hard. (He would have loved to knock all my teeth out.) Then they seemed to give up on me. I was to be transferred to a different barracks. A corporal came and invited me, very politely, to go with him. "Where to?" I inquired, wondering. He shrugged his shoulders. "You'll like it there," he said. In that case I decided I'd rather walk than be dragged. My new abode proved to be CO Barracks! The baby-faced lieutenant had lied to me; there were indeed COs at Camp Upton. Twenty. Twenty-one, including me. Ten Quakers, seven Holy Rollers, one nondescript pacifist, and three socialists (myself and two others). Interned indefinitely. We cooked our own food, did our own washing, kept our quarters clean. We could walk around outside but only a short distance from the barracks. We were allowed to send and receive mail. No visitors.

Maybe the very polite corporal had expected me to like the place because we were left pretty much to ourselves. But I could hardly have found worse company. The religious COs appalled me with their lack of concern for anything except themselves and their wonderful souls. True, they were unshakable war resisters. They refused to kill. But why? For the sake of humanity? No. To save their souls. To avoid a sin that would consign them to an eternity of uninterrupted torment. Hell was vivid to them. They lived in fear of it. They read their Bibles and prayed. Nothing else mattered. We three socialists did most of the work around the place. The religious COs shirked. Especially the Quakers. (Which was a stunner. I had thought of Quakers as kindly, considerate, large-hearted, community-oriented, selfless. Doubtless a great many are. Maybe most of them. I have never lived with any except those in Camp Upton at Yaphank, L.I.) At night the place was a horror. The Holy Rollers disturbed everybody's sleep with sudden shouts of "Help me, oh Lord!" Some of them jumped out of bed and rolled on the floor, screaming.

The mail—both getting and sending—afforded relief. Mostly the mail meant Eleanor. We wrote to each other nearly every day. I heard also from Owen, with news from the Peace Front. And various old friends, now renegades from the cause, were yet friendly and writing to me sympathetically. As in this from Al Seadler, postmarked Fort Logan H. Roots, Arkansas, March 5, 1918:

Dear Charles,

From Miriam, Si and Esther came the news of your trip to Yaphank, and the announcement that you would, in all probability, persist in your refusal to do service. I don't know that I blame you for sticking to it, for it's not so long ago that I believed as you do, but I'm oh, so very sorry that you have to get into this mess again. . . . I'm beginning to wonder whether I should have had the nerve to go through with it. I'm glad now that I came to see things differently. . . . You're wrong, Charles, dead wrong, and I wish you could see things differently. But regardless of how you come out of

49

this you have my best wishes. Please, if there is anything I can do for you, let me know. If you can't write from your camp, tell Eleanor and give her my address. . . . If well-wishes and good luck from a buck private to a C.O. are of any value, they are yours. As ever, A. B. S.

9 The Road to Mazatlán

By the time I got this letter I was no longer at Camp Upton. Early on March 3, an orderly escorted me to the office of the camp's commanding officer, one General Johnston. The general looked at me severely and snapped: "I have just discovered that you are a convicted felon. Unfit to serve in the army of the United States. You are unqualified, and we do not want you. You are dishonorably discharged. You are not to communicate further with anyone in this camp. The orderly will take you to the railroad station. He will give you a ticket. You will take the next train." So I was out of the army! I caught the twelve o'clock train. I had been permitted to phone from the Yaphank station, and Eleanor met me on arrival in New York.

My dismissal made headlines in all the afternoon papers. Within hours a one-word telegram reached me at 102 Third Avenue: "Congratulations." From Owen. I was soon receiving communications from strangers. Here is one postmarked New York, March 4, 1918:

Notice a little clipping in today's Tribune. It is a pity the Sergeant and the Lieutenant did not break your INFERNAL NECK. You are a FELON, a CRIMINAL, a LOAFER, a SLACKER, a PACIFIST and everything else that could make a MISERABLE DIRTY CUR. Of course they kicked you out of Camp Upton as nobody there would want to associate with such a miserable PUP, but they will get you yet, the sooner the better. . . . You are one of the VILEST, most DEGENERATE CREATURES

on the face of the Earth and are not fit for DOGS TO ASSOCIATE WITH.
Damn your Rotten Soul.

[signed] J. R. King

Here is a one-liner, undated and unsigned, the envelope of which I
have lost, so am unable to give the postmark:

You are a coward BASTARD.

The following message, penciled on a scrap of paper, was slipped
under our door at 102 Third Avenue:

You dirty looking cur at this very corner before many months is
gone you will get a damned good bullet put through your rotten
heart you are a danger to the country you rotten anarchists.

Not especially encouraging. Once again I reflected that the revolution in this country would be a long time coming. Still I had to do
my part. I would go back to what I had been doing before being
dragged off to camp. It seemed only logical. The Collegiate Anti-
Militarism League was dead, but I started a new war resisters organization called The Young Democracy, with an office at 70 Fifth
Avenue. All my time went into it. I got money, including a small
salary, through Rebecca Shelly, a well-known pacifist whom I had
met during the Ford Expedition. The Rand School provided a large
mailing list, nationwide in coverage, and we arranged a conference.
We got lots of publicity—welcome and unwelcome—because after
Camp Upton I was a marked man.

Item. March 9, 1918, editorial in the *New York Times* headlined
"MARTYRDOM WON FAR TOO EASILY":

One of our correspondents expressed yesterday, in a letter
printed on this page, the dissatisfaction shared by many others at
the lightness of the punishment inflicted on the young pacifist [sic]
who obstinately refused even to put on the uniform of his country's
army as the first step toward serving it in its hour of need. As a matter of fact Phillips was not punished at all when he was turned out
of Camp Upton on the ground that he was a felon and therefore

ineligible for association in the ranks with loyal Americans. To the only people for whose opinion he has any regard he was far from disgraced by this dismissal. On the contrary, in their eyes it put him on a pedestal and wreathed his brow with whatever may be the pacifist substitute for heroic laurel.

Not only has Phillips himself, for the present, at least, defied the Government and escaped the draft, but he has revealed to all of like mind the way to do the same thing and attain the same distinction among their fellows. It is reported from Washington that this strange product of American education may be returned to Upton, either to do his duty or to suffer a punishment entirely different from the dismissal he deliberately courted. And that our military authorities can be severe in the punishment of military offenses has on several occasions been revealed. It may well be, therefore, that the too interesting youth will soon undergo a "martyrdom" less enjoyable to him than mere denunciation by an officer for whose scorn he cares less than nothing.

Item. April 11, 1918, *New York Times* news story headed "COLUMBIA STUDENT WHOM CAMP UPTON REJECTED, ACTIVE AGAIN":

Henry MacDonald, director of the Mayor's Committee on National Defense, announced last night that the Department of Justice had learned that Charles Francis Phillips, the former Columbia student who was discharged from Camp Upton on the ground that he had been convicted of a crime, had issued a call for a convention of "The Young Democracy" on May 4 and 5 at the Mountain House, Valhalla, N.Y.

Inspector T. F. Pitch of the Post Office Department, according to Mr. MacDonald, declared the pamphlet in which the call appears unmailable, and, orders were issued to seize all literature and correspondence of the organization. . . .

The signers [of the call] with Phillips included: Devere Allen, Owen Cattell, Evans Clark, H. W. L. Dana, Robert W. Dunn, Elizabeth Freeman, Freda Kirchwey, H. K. Moderwell, Lella Faye Secor, Rebecca Shelly and Christian Sorenson.

Item. April 12 *New York Times* editorial, "HIS TRIUMPH GIVES HIM COURAGE":

After that interesting youth, Charles Francis Phillips, was turned out of Camp Upton. . . vehement declarations came from Washington that the authorities at the camp had erred. . . . We were told that Phillips would have to go back and obey orders or suffer the usual consequences of mutiny in time of war. The natural supposition was that this course had been followed, and, as nobody heard that anything had happened to young Phillips, it was generally assumed he had yielded, with or without grace, to the commands of the high powers. . . . But it seems Phillips did not go back to Camp Upton. . . . Instead he stayed at home and resumed the activities that led to his original conviction. . . . As they (the authorities) could not, or at any rate, did not, make him enter the army, the chances are that they cannot, or at any rate won't, make him stop trying to keep other young men from learning what he in his wisdom considers a dreadful trade and knows to be a dangerous one.

The succession of these and similar items revealed, and constituted in themselves, a mounting pressure. I could see I was not going to be allowed to carry on indefinitely. What would I do if I were redrafted? Nothing could force me into becoming part of the war machine. But to repeat the Camp Upton exercise with its failure to get a whisper of response from buddies looking on—to go through that disappointing experience all over again—made no sense to me. I would have to follow some other course. Eleanor agreed. We discussed the thing one night with confidants who were visiting us in our Third Avenue walk-up. Owen, his father, and Harry Dana. It was unanimous.

On April 15 I read that the War Department had disapproved General Johnston's discharge of me from military duty. On May 2 Secretary of War Baker announced in an interview that I would be redrafted. I was prepared. That night Eleanor and I left secretly for Mexico. (The Mexico idea had been put into our heads by Professor Cattell.)

Our first stop was San Antonio. Lewis Maverick, a Ford Expedition comrade, lived there. We wanted his advice on getting across the border. Maverick was sympathetic but nervous. He merely mentioned the name of the largest border city, El Paso. In San Antonio we bought a revolver, a compass, and maps of the southwestern states, and then entrained for El Paso. Registered there at Hotel Paso del Norte (Mr. and Mrs. I-forget-who), we toured the city. And—at dusk—an adjacent area along the Rio Grande. There was little water in the river. You could almost wade across. Well, we were exploring. A sharp "Halt!" interrupted our continuing tour. A soldier was pointing a gun at us. He marched us to a nearby military encampment, where an officer informed us that we were under arrest. We protested that we hadn't done anything.

"You were arrested at the border."

"We had a right to be there—without crossing into Mexico."

"You were caught crossing *from Mexico.*"

It was true. A small segment of the border near El Paso lies north of the river. We had wandered into and out of Mexico without knowing it, and were arrested for entering the country illegally!

We were all innocence. Entering the country? A great joke. Why, we were staying at the Hotel Paso del Norte. They could check the registration. The officer decided to hold us anyway. At least for the time being. If they had searched us we would have been lost. They didn't, God knows why. We were permitted to go to a restaurant for supper—under guard. While we ate and our guards waited I got rid of the revolver, the cartridges, the compass, the maps. Under the table. (Risky? Sure. But keeping the stuff would have been riskier.) I nudged Eleanor. We rose, half the meal still on our plates. Had to get out of there fast. (Whoever discovered the stuff may have appropriated it. Because we never heard anything of it.)

When we got back to the camp two charming southern gentlemen were waiting for us. Department of Justice. Young, soft-spoken, and evidently not too bright. What were we doing in that part of the country? We said it was a stop-off on a trip to Los Angeles. Our honeymoon. They melted (Eleanor looked very sweet), even invited us out for an ice-cream soda. One of them did ask to see my draft card. I told him it was in my suitcase at the hotel; I could go for it. He said it wasn't necessary. What was my draft classification? (That was a stumper. I didn't dare say 4F. Too healthy-looking.) I blurted out something, 4G I think. "Aged and infirm parents," he said understandingly. "I happen to be in that classification myself." As the conversation proceeded, one of the two remarked, "It beats me how you kids contrived to get yourself across the border and back without knowing it. In the entire length of the border there is only one other place where it could have happened: Douglas, Arizona."

That night we boarded a Southern Pacific train for Los Angeles but left it at Douglas, Arizona. The train, as a timetable had informed us, made a half-hour breakfast stop at Douglas. (In those days Southern Pacific trains carried no diners. Passengers ate in station dining rooms along the route.) Following a premeditated strategy, we wandered away from the station, then rushed back breathlessly—too late. The train had departed. (Our two suitcases went with it—checked through to L.A. We had to leave them on board for our pretended mishap to be convincing.) The stationmaster commiserated with us. There would be no other train before midnight. "To pass the time" we negotiated an hour's drive, which, naturally, took in the Mexican border. It was, as our driver confessed, not much to see, just a dirt road with a ditch on the far side and an expanse of open field. He pointed out the Mexican village of Agua Prieto—a blur in the distance. Two soldiers shouldering rifles patrolled the road from opposite directions—passing each other and later presumably reversing their steps.

Toward nightfall we hid behind a dilapidated shed twenty or twenty-five feet from the road. We crouched there till our knees ached—timing the approach and retreat of the soldiers. Satisfied at last that they would be back-to-back long enough for us to get across the road, we seized our moment, scurried over, and flung ourselves into the ditch. We were in Mexico! We waited until they passed each other again, then jumped from the ditch and ran like hell into the gathering dark—toward the distant lights of Agua Prieto. We still did not feel safe. The soldiers might, we thought, spy us before we got very far and chase after us, or maybe fire a shot across the border. But, Allah be praised, we heard no sound.

We arrived at the poky market town of Agua Prieto sweaty, dirty, and without a change of clothes—but exultant. The dusty plaza with its strolling couples appeared splendiferous in the evening haze. An illuminated hotel sign on a low adobe building told us how tired we were. We must have been a suspicious-looking pair and spoke not a word of Spanish, but a few dollars got us a room.

The Mexico we had entered so blithely was a country of some fifteen million people (as compared with today's eighty million plus) scattered thinly over a vast area (equal to the U.S.A. from the Mississippi east). With tremendous mountain ranges and long coastal lowlands, hot northern desert and hot southern jungle, and a great temperate central plateau cut by gorges hundreds of feet deep, it was thrillingly beautiful, and formidable. A land of arid agriculture. Of the lone horseman, the ox-turned treadmill, the hand-guided wooden plow, and (incomparable beast of burden) the burro. Peopled essentially by Indians and part-Indians, most of them poor, ragged, and illiterate—born to oppression. General Porfirio Díaz ruled Mexico for thirty-four successive years—allied with the country's historic exploiting trinity: feudal landowners, the Catholic Church, and foreign capital.

An uncoordinated revolution inspired by liberal reformer Francisco I. Madero, an aristocratic idealist, overthrew the Díaz dictatorship in 1911. But in 1913 Madero was deposed from power and murdered by his own commanding general, Victoriano Huerta. The reactionary Huertista regime was overthrown in turn. The revolution went from one phase to another and when we arrived (May 1918) was still far from over. The pompous graybeard Venustiano Carranza, proclaimed "First Chief" of the revolutionary forces, had established a measure of order and now sat in Mexico City as president of the republic. Although himself a landowner of full-blooded Spanish parentage, he had reaffirmed the Madero principles—and carried them further. A radically advanced democratic constitution adopted with Carranza's sponsorship was now, formally at least, the basic code of the land. It called for distribution of land to the peasants, progressive labor reforms, confiscation of church property, outlawing of virtually all public church functions. It nationalized the country's subsoil (mineral wealth, etc., including deposits of oil and natural gas), prohibited foreigners from engaging in Mexican politics, and restricted their business and property rights.

In Carranza's time there were no functioning political parties. Simply *Carrancistas, Villistas, Zapatistas, Obregonistas,* and so on. Carranza's regime enjoyed the allegiance of several state governors and military chiefs, but was contested hotly by Pancho Villa in the northern states of Chihuahua and Durango, by Emiliano Zapata from his Morelos stronghold in the south (close to the capital itself), and by nondescript guerrilla chieftans from one stronghold or another. Armed bands of revolutionists and bandits calling themselves revolutionists, the true heirs of Madero, roamed great stretches of the republic.

Very little of all this had penetrated the consciousness of New Yorkers—Eleanor and me included. We knew that the United States had recognized Carranza and that General John J. Pershing had failed to catch Villa after Villa's death-dealing Columbus raid.[1] As to more recent Mexican revolutionary history, we knew hardly anything, and Mexican geography we knew only in outline.

Our final destination was not Agua Prieto but the capital of the republic, Mexico City. We had no suspicion of how long it would take us to get there. There was a train south from Nogales in the Mexican state of Sonora—on the border fronting Nogales, Arizona—but to reach it from where we were required a long zigzagging trip through cactus country, first by ramshackle automobile, then by narrow-gauge rail. Our lack of Spanish did not facilitate the arrangements. The railroad from Nogales south (the Sud Pacífico de México) reached the Gulf of California town of Guaymas (now Ciudad Obregón), then hugged the coast for hundreds of miles to Mazatlán on the Pacific. From there one traveled farther south by boat to tropical Manzanillo. And from Manzanillo another railroad. First, inland to Colima; from there a few hundred miles back north to Guadalajara; then east to Irapuato, and at last deep down (southeast) to Mexico City. Each point an overnight stop. For fear of assault the train ran only during daylight hours, and then with military escort trains ahead and behind. The boats between Mazatlán and Manzanillo (mere tubs) took several days to cover the distance—

---

1. In an incursion into U.S. territory, Villa's men on March 9, 1916, raided Columbus, New Mexico, killing a number of American citizens and burning the town. President Wilson ordered a punitive expedition under General Pershing to capture Villa dead or alive. The expedition pursued Villa through the Mexican state of Chihuahua for eleven months without success. Carranza objected to the pursuit and notified Pershing that further invasion would be resisted by force of arms. Pershing had to withdraw—leaving U.S.–Mexico relations seriously embittered.

and came and went irregularly. People waited weeks for one. For Eleanor and me the boat and subsequent travel requirements, were academic—our money ran out at Mazatlán.

Arriving at Mazatlán with funds reduced to seven dollars (fourteen silver pesos),[2] we spent most of that for bullfight tickets and a leisurely dinner. The dinner—in a nondescript cantina exposed to the street like a stall—consisted, amazingly, of shish kebab, baklava, and Greek wine, all of it delicious. Nick, the Greek proprietor of the place, was both cook and bartender. He had worked in prestigious New York restaurants and spoke broken English, and we got to know him well. On our way out of the cantina we passed a trio of Americans, not much older than ourselves, on the way in. We went back. When we got close I recognized the two men: Robert Carleton Brown of the *Masses* and Alan Norton, whom I had met once at Webster Hall. We had no need to inform one another why we were so far from home. They got Eleanor and me a room in the same *pensión* with them and left Mazatlán the next day, bound for South America.

At the end of the week the señora demanded money for our board and lodging. We managed to pay—with some delay—by borrowing from a young American of draft age whom we had met in the plaza. But since we had no baggage and might not be able to pay next week the señora asked us to leave. And then we were on the beach, literally.

We slept on the beach, performed our morning ablutions there, bathed in the green and white swirl of surf, and scoured the neighborhood for food: coconuts knocked from tall palms, fruit from banana and mango trees—and a handout from the shrimp fishermen on the other side of the Mazatlán peninsula. Ours was the *Olas Altas* (High Waves) section—a broad stretch of glistening sand shut off by towering rocks and a *malecón* (sea wall). The loveliest spot for miles around, it made a lumpy bed, and we had to rely on our morning dip to get the kinks out. I left Eleanor standing naked, drying

2. No one would take Mexican paper money. Only silver and gold. People had to travel with huge bags of silver pesos and tostones (half-pesos). Sometimes they took someone along just to carry the money. Even the insignificant sum that, in course of time, I was able to get hold of used to weigh my pockets down. So that I'd find holes in them.

herself in the hot sun, and went clambering among the rocks. In a little while I overtook a young man of about my age idling along at random. He was unmistakably American, and I knew by the way he was dressed—even before I saw his gaunt face and heard his greeting—that he was Californian, a native son. Herbert Calvert and I understood our mutual status in Mexico immediately, but we had more in common than that. We discovered we were both socialists, both pro-Soviet, both readers of the *Masses*, both interested in literature. He had (I discovered later) peculiar quirks: Upton Sinclair—style food faddism, spiritism, arguments with himself out loud. But he was a likeable, ebullient, straightforward guy.

Meeting Cal in this remote part of the world proved a great good fortune. He took me home—a rented American-style dwelling, shabby but quite comfortable—and introduced me to "the other members of the Calvert household." His gray-eyed, level-headed, warm-hearted wife, Mellie. And Harold Herrick, a bluff, thoughtful, broad-shouldered giant from Utah. Cal, Mellie, and Herrick were University of California students together at Berkeley. Herrick and Cal skipped to Mexico in the summer of 1917. They and an older man, a German-American, grew tomatoes in a place near Mazatlán and by the end of the year had shipped a couple of carloads to the U.S. But then the American consul blacklisted them. That finished the venture. Mellie, who had come down separately, was now supporting the three of them. She worked as a stenographer for the Sud Pacífico de México (built and still partially staffed by the U.S. Southern Pacific); she was the only English-speaking steno in the Mazatlán office. We visited Cal, Mellie, and Herrick often. They were the center of our social life—practically the only social life we had—during our entire long stay in Mazatlán.

Yes, there were other war evaders in Mazatlán, some six or seven when Eleanor and I arrived. Singles, they used to hang around Nick's cantina so we got to know them all. They were not conscientious objectors, just malingerers, who really deserved the indiscriminate term "slackers." A dull, ignorant lot. The only one of any dignity or interest was the fellow who lent me money to pay that week's bill at the *pensión*. Diminutive, small-boned, fragile-looking, he probably was a homosexual. I was surprised to learn his vocation. Professional prizefighter. Incidentally, he was the only one of the bunch who had any money. The others were on the ragged edge, but none were more ragged than Eleanor and I. Our toes stuck through our shoes. We filched bread from Nick's tables. That, with the coconuts and the fruit and meals we got at the "Calvert household," constituted our diet. No "slacker" could get a job. The permanent American residents (about a dozen) would not go near us, while our inability to speak Spanish handicapped us with the natives. Openings were scarce anyway. Then, as now, Mazatlán was Mexico's largest west coast port. But largest is a relative term. The population was under 10,000. You could walk the (unpaved) streets in the morning and encounter no traffic but a plodding burro or two loaded with charcoal or milk. And hear no sound but the clip-clap of hands shaping tortillas indoors. In the midday heat nothing stirred.

10 Jesús Escobar

The serenity was misleading, apt to be interrupted at any time by a brawl in a cantina, an angry demonstration against this or that, a pistol shot. There were wailing beggars when the movie theater opened its doors, mutilated ex-soldiers outside the bullring. If, as I learned later, you got too far out of town, you could see bodies hanging from telegraph poles. You might hear a peremptory *Alto!* (Halt!) *Quien vive?* (Who are you for?) Meaning Carranza, or Villa, or Pelaez, or whomever. Much might depend on your answer. Mazatlán and its immediate surroundings were Carranza territory, loyal to the government of the republic. But the revolution still impinged, offering hope as well as fear. The peons were still peons, but the aristocrats were no longer masters. You had a feeling that things were tentative, that anything might happen. Still, being young and heedless, we weren't too conscious of danger.

But, as I guess I have made clear, it was no place for jobs. Aside from the fishing, Mazatlán had no industry to speak of. Just a brewery, an electric utility, an ice house, some harness making, and tiny *masa* mills, where corn was ground and mixed with other ingredients to form masa, the dough for tortillas. There were fifteen or twenty masa mills in adobe stalls all over the town. The ice house served only certain restaurants, the good hotel, the one American-style drug store (with soda fountain!), and perhaps the very rich. Most people simply filled a porous pottery container (an *olla*) with boiling water and kept it in a shady place. The water became cool and delicious. The utility company, on the other hand, served practically everybody. Even the poorest shack in town had one naked electric bulb hanging from the ceiling. Electric current powered the all-important masa mills.

Seated at a table in Nick's with hunks of bread in our laps, we stared innocently at the dinky pastel-blue Palacio Municipal across the street. It was near noon and the Greek cantina-lunchroom was filling up with paying customers. As we prepared to leave, Nick came over. He pointed to a grizzled Mexican across the room and whispered, "The mister there he like to talk with your wife."

"What for?" I demanded.

"I'm think he wan' offer her job."

"Do you know the guy?"

"Oh sure. Everybody know him. It's-a Jesús Escobar. Rich guy."

Nick explained that the Mexican had been curious about us and that Nick had told him we were very, very poor Americans with our feet coming out of our shoes and no place to sleep but the beach. And the Mexican had said right off that he might have some work for the lady. Would Nick bring her over?

I took a good look at this astonishing Jesús Escobar. He was middle-aged (I judged in his early fifties) and chubby. The absence of prominent cheekbones and his complexion proclaimed him to be more Spaniard than Indian. He had a receding hairline and, at least from a distance, his eyebrows seemed almost white. He wore a white, peasant-type shirt unbuttoned at the throat. Conferring briefly, Eleanor and I decided there could be no harm in her going over to the man's table with Nick. In less than five minutes she was back. Jesús Escobar had offered her a job. The money wasn't much: three pesos a day—barely double the wage of a peon (and equivalent to $1.50 U.S.)—but with it came a simple habitation for both of us. Rent free! Eleanor couldn't figure the guy out. He spoke to her in fluent, reasonably correct English, but with a Mexican accent. He did not know exactly what her work would be—would have to think about it a bit—but we could move into our house that afternoon. Hungry and homeless, we resolved to accept but be on our guard. Around three o'clock we picked up the huge iron key at the cantina where Señor Escobar had said he would leave it.

Our house proved to be a one-room adobe hut connected to one of the masa mills by an always locked door. It had a beaten-earth floor, and high in the front wall, near the corner, a small window-opening with iron bars. A single light bulb hung in the center. Placed against the wall by the front door was a rude side-table, and above the table hung a gilt-framed mirror. There were also a straight-backed chair and a narrow canvas cot (in which Eleanor and I slept, sweating). A lean-to shed off the rear half-wall contained a bricked charcoal stove arrangement, a dining table of rough boards, two benches, and some pottery: *ollas* and stuff. A big backyard, a common yard for our house and the masa mill, had a one-hole privy in a far corner—perhaps fifty yards away from us. Litter dotted the intervening stretch: bits of clay, shavings, rusty nails, broken tools. Add in some stunted vegetation of the cactus family and the not infrequent tarantulas and scorpions, and it's easy to understand why nighttime visits (barefooted!) to the privy required a certain amount of courage.

When we arrived that first afternoon, soapy lettering on the mirror spelled out WELCOME. Finding three silver pesos in a saucer on the table beneath it, we rushed to the tin-roofed open-air market which sold everything from victuals (cooked and uncooked) to clothing and cheap furniture. The fly-specked pork tasted great to us. The evening brought our first guest. Bernardo Domínguez, a clerk in the big hardware store, asked if I would be interested in teaching him English. He would pay monthly for lessons three nights a week. The sum was insignificant, but we were glad for anything at all to supplement the modest stipend from Eleanor's as yet undefined employment. So then and there I became a teacher.

Eleanor assumed she would have to start work the next day. She did not know where to go, however, so we stayed in the house and waited. About four in the afternoon a ragged Indian boy, not over ten years old, appeared in our open doorway. Now, we thought, we would find out. But he said nothing. When we questioned, he merely shrugged his shoulders, evidently not understanding us. He opened his fist to reveal three silver pesos, laid them on the table, and departed. The sequence was repeated the day after, and the day after that. Toward the end of the week the boy brought, in addition to the three pesos, a note requesting an invitation for our humble servant, Jesús Escobar, to have dinner at our house on Sunday. How could we refuse? Our answering note asked him, cordially, to come at two. We thought we'd have to finance the whole dinner by borrowing from the Calverts, but early Saturday morning my so lately acquired pupil, Bernardo, appeared and presented us with a live duck. We still had to borrow from Cal and Mellie, but not for the main dish.

Having no refrigeration, we had to keep the duck alive until Sunday morning. We tied it to the table in the shed, but when we awoke on Sunday the rats from the masa mill had torn it to bloody pieces. Poor helpless creature. And poor us! We had slept late and there was no time to see if anything could be done about a replacement. So, would anybody believe it, we used what was left of that obscene carcass! We washed it, "plucked" it, cut away the worst portions, chopped up the rest, and cooked and served it.

Señor Escobar arrived promptly at two in a big chauffeur-driven automobile. The señor was dressed like a Florida businessman: natty suit of Palm Beach cloth, four-in-hand tie, etc. He told the driver, a peon in a broad-brimmed straw sombrero, to come back in an hour, shook our hands formally, and followed us through the house to the shed, where the table was set for our feast.

As we ate, he took off his jacket and loosened his tie. Between the duck and the dessert (guava jelly with cheese), he remarked confidentially that he had been interested in us only because we were Americans. It didn't matter how or why we got to Mazatlán, he simply hated to see "good-looking" Americans in such straits. Eleanor explained she had failed to show up for work because no one had told her where to report. Did he want her to start on Monday? He said no, he was still thinking what he preferred to have her do. She needn't worry. He would let us know.

After dinner he invited us for a drive around town in his open touring car. He handed us a Japanese parasol to shield ourselves from the hot sun. During the drive we were treated to a candid monograph on Jesús Escobar. Born to privilege in "the good old days" of Porfirio Díaz, he had spent his youth idling, carousing, terrorizing the peasantry with his gun, and thieving (stealing from church coffers systematically). He was, in his own words, "the black sheep" of an aristocratic family. His father had been governor of the state of Durango during the Díaz overlordship. Nothing was sacred to our Jesús, "not even Don Porfirio." At one point he'd gotten a "stupid servant girl in a family way," killed her protesting father, and run away. The matter was hushed up and Jesús returned home, but then "the Goddamn revolution spoiled everything." He skipped to the United States, married a Mexican woman in Los Angeles, and at the time we met him still had a family there. He spoke unaffectedly of his exploits, without either bravado or shame. We just listened.

Jesús liked it in Los Angeles and lived there a couple of years until he ran out of funds. Feeling that he could rebuild his fortunes more easily in Mexico, he recrossed the border at Nogales. The railroad took him to Mazatlán. He brought with him a thin pocket notebook, a Los Angeles drugstore giveaway, paperbound, with a Bromo Seltzer ad on the front cover. Besides blank pages for jotting down notes, it contained miscellaneous reference material: weights and measures, a calendar, and so on—including a recipe for making soap. Jesús made a few bars of soap and peddled them house to house. Having sold out the first day, he kept at it. Soon he was operating on a wholesale basis, selling to Mazatlán stores. He made and packaged the soap in an adobe-stall "factory," where three or four girls worked for him. "Of course," he observed, "I seduced them all." (Once, as we were driving through a particularly grubby part of town, he interjected, "See that dirty little ragamuffin playing in the gutter? He's my son.") In the money, he went back to Los Angeles to show off to his family. He'd intended to become an American citizen, but went broke again and returned to Mazatlán. He "had to" come back, he said, "because, you see, Mexico is easy pickings." He started his soap business again, and again he made money at it.

In time he realized he didn't need so much space for his soap business. "Why can't I put in one of those machines that grind corn?" he wondered. "There's always a market for masa." But there was a masa mill directly across the street, owned by the man who owned every mill in town, and whose nephew was the *presidente municipal*. The utility company, not surprisingly, turned down Jesús's request for electric power. When Jesús demonstrated that he could grind the people's corn and sell them masa for half the price charged by "this son-of-a-bitch monopolist," the utility folks remained unmoved. He knew an appeal to the presidente municipal would be useless, but he persisted and finally made a deal with the local *jefe político*.[1]

So Jesús got the needed electric power, put in machinery, and gave the people masa at five centavos (two and a half cents) a liter. Rather than come down on the ten centavos he was charging at all his mills, the "son-of-a bitch monopolist" closed the one across the street from Jesús. When the town learned Jesús Escobar was providing five-centavo masa, he had more trade than he could handle. He opened another mill, then another, still another. Finally he forced the presidente municipal's uncle out of the business. "Then," he told us, "of course I raised my price to ten centavos. Then twelve, thirteen, and fifteen. Because, you see, I had the people by the balls. They had to have masa." He told us all of this as if he were describing the weather.

We did not get all this information in one drive. It came out bit by bit. In the meantime we pondered his intentions concerning Eleanor. When I questioned him, he said her work wasn't planned out yet. In fact, there never was any work. But every day the boy came with three pesos. And nearly every Sunday Jesús came to dinner. That was all he every asked of us. Sometimes we went for a drive, sometimes not. Occasionally he brought us a small present.

By the time we came into his purview, Jesús was Mr. Moneybags, involved in everything but ostracized socially. He had tricked, cheated, betrayed, despoiled, abused, and outraged so many people that he had a multitude of enemies and no friends. He was, in fact, the most hated man around. Once I had occasion to search him out.

1. (Literally, "political chief.") Under Porfirio Díaz every center of population had its own jefe político—usually a military man—side by side with, and independent of, the regular civil officials. This duality of function was also a feature of the unstable revolutionary period. The jefe político, not the elected presidente municipal, was the real boss of the town.

It Had to Be Revolution

He lived alone in a cramped hovel, with one barefoot, sombrero-shaded guard sitting out front and another in back, rifles across their knees. I heard he kept his light on throughout the night. It appears that in all his life he had never been good to anyone except his Los Angeles family and us. To us he was not only good but respectful. Eleanor and I often puzzled over it. This reprobate, this self-confessed criminal, who despised mankind and preyed upon all and sundry without a qualm, why should he have been so solicitous of us? We concluded he probably needed to feel he had done at least some good. That someone had reason to be grateful to him. A supposition. It may or may not be the answer.

The roof over our heads, the three pesos a day, and the monthly pittance from my pupil, Bernardo, left us still poor. We collected turtles' eggs on the beach and ate them, gelatinous shells and all, raw or scrambled. Not able to afford toothpaste, we brushed our teeth with charcoal. Pigs whose feed was street refuse wandered in and our of the premises, caked with filth. We had cockroaches as big as baseballs; if by accident you stepped on one it was like a gun going off. But on the whole, ours was a singularly easy existence. Too easy; we had not come to Mexico seeking a life of ease. We went swimming, visited back and forth with the Calvert household, and enjoyed the leisurely evening parade in the plaza. Poking around town, I discovered a small public library (open one afternoon a week, from four to six) with a few gnawed books in English: *Origin of Species*, *A Tale of Two Cities*, Lew Wallace's *Ben Hur*, and I think one more. I practiced my beginner's Spanish on the shy teenage librarian, practiced it with anyone who would let me. As soon as Eleanor and I were a familiar presence, people tended to accept us. Gringos were resented and hated in Mexico, but we were gringos with a difference. As refugees from the American war power, we were enemies of the American establishment, and consequently Mexico's friends.

In time the slow pace of Mazatlán life was interrupted by the state of Sinaloa's governorship campaign. (Mazatlán, though not the capital, is the state's "big city.") Sombrero-dwarfed country *peones* paraded through the streets, escorted by sweaty military bands and shouting "*Viva la revolución!*" Stopping frequently for rest and refreshment, they proceeded on their way amid answering *vivas* from assorted Mazatlán onlookers. The paraders wound up at our central plaza, where the bandstand was draped in broad red streamers proclaiming the candidacy of Ramón I. Iturbe (the one "official" candidate and sure winner). Standing before a massed audience of bobbing sombreros, politicians in business suits and military chieftans in uniform struggled to outdo one another in revolutionary-sounding exhortation.

Iturbe was a long-standing *Carrancista*. However, Carranza needed Iturbe more than Iturbe needed the pompous old Carranza. An Iturbe-controlled army of sorts kept most of Sinaloa firm for the federal government, but dissidents held sway in some parts of the state. Indeed, from time to time, partisans of Pancho Villa dominated a section close to Mazatlán. This was symptomatic of conditions throughout the republic. In the cities order was fragile, in the villages it was a sometime thing, and wide regions were swept by open civil war—always in the name of the revolution.

There were many wry jokes about this, and sly bits of song. A typical one parodied "Adelita," a popular lyric in which a lover avows that if his Adelita would only marry him everything in life would be perfect:

> Si *Carranza se case con Villa*
> y *Zapata con Álvaro Obregón*
> y *tu cases conmigo, Adelita,*
> *se acaba la revolución.*

> If Carranza marries Villa
> and Zapata marries Álvaro Obregón
> and you marry me, Adelita,
> the revolution will be over.

In spite of all that was dear to me in sunny Mazatlán, I was anxious to get to Mexico City, where there would be at least the nucleus of an organized labor movement and perhaps the rudiments of a socialist party. In order to acquire the wherewithal, I decided to start some small business (like Jesús Escobar with his soap). I remembered that people bought orange juice on the street in New York, and realized that, while the Mazatlán area lacked oranges, pineapples were plentiful and cheap. Eleanor and I went to Jesús with the idea. He arranged for us to have a juice stand alongside the Palacio Municipal at nominal rent, and instructed his versatile carpenter to build us the stand, paint it white, and design and build a wooden press for the pineapples.

It was a neat little stand, about five feet square, open on all four sides—with a peaked roof to shield Eleanor and me from sun or rain. Every Mexican emporium must have a name, and we hung Japanese paper lanterns at the corners and called ours *La Linterna*.

The stand was open from eleven in the morning until the movie house closed—rather late at night. Eleanor and I spelled each other and made a little money on our watered juice. It didn't taste as good as the pure stuff, but the Mexicans evidently liked it and the price was right. As soon as we were definitely in the black, Jesús' three-pesos-a-day stopped coming. In the meantime, Bernardo had quit taking English lessons, so we had only the stand. Soon *La Linterna* replaced Nick's as a gathering place for the unattached "slackers" in town. They would perch on the iron railing that fenced the Palacio Municipal and lament having to be "stuck in this two-bit country." Now and then one of them would buy a glass of our so-called juice. I don't know how they got the centavos, but think they did a little begging.

At about this time, my sister, Anna, wrote me a nice (careful) letter—relaying a greeting to Eleanor and me from Harry. I think he had just been made an officer (Harry and I, hardly ever in touch prewar, communicated directly and indirectly throughout our respective sojourns in France and Mexico). Anna also forwarded a letter addressed to me from Bill (William Slater) Brown, my very close S. of J. friend. As I remarked earlier, he had volunteered to drive an ambulance with the French army before the U.S. entered the war. Because of a letter written to me, he evidently became an object of suspicion. Bill had been penned up in the "enormous room" with e. e. cummings and the rest. He was now disenchanted with "this grotesque humanity" and demanded fiercely, "Why are little children beautiful?" When I saw him again, on Cape Cod in the thirties, he was an almost incoherent drunk.

In time, the wooden press designed by Jesús's carpenter broke down and defied repair. Eventually we acquired a second-hand metal press, but it gave the drink a disagreeable metallic taste. We now tended to water the juice more and more, it tasted quite awful, and our customers dropped away. We tried to compensate by selling pineapple slice, and pineapple candy (concocted by Eleanor with brown sugar), but that didn't amount to anything. Then, suddenly, the pineapple season ended. We had never considered such an eventuality. It made no difference. We were about finished anyway. We gave up the stand. It stood there for several days, a forlorn spectacle. Finally we were notified we had to demolish it and take everything away.

We were still in touch with Jesús. We still had his house, but not the three pesos. And still had him with us of a Sunday—though now less often. Shortly before the business folded, he came to the stand to tell us some news—bad news for us, he was afraid; good news for him. His Los Angeles daughter was coming to live in Mazatlán and he wanted our house for her. He didn't want us to think he was leaving us out in the street, however, and told us we could have another house, one that we could keep as long as we liked. It was smaller and lacked a backyard but otherwise was like the house we were giving up. There was even the familiar acrid smell of a masa mill next door. Almost before we were out of the old house Jesús had men tearing up the street in front of it and installing a broad sidewalk. The house itself was to be transformed. I don't know how things looked when Jesús's daughter arrived. By then Eleanor and I were no longer in Mazatlán. We heard the yard was a garden spot.

11   Byways Untouched by
the Mexican Revolution

We were really waiting for something that would get us to Mexico City. Making inquiries, we learned that teachers of English were wanted urgently at a private language school in Guadalajara. A

Mexicanized elderly American named Simeon Shefflow who owned and operated the school offered well-paying jobs and pre-paid transportation. It sounded like us. Guadalajara, to the south and in the cooler upland country, was well on the way to Mexico City. We had been in Mazatlán nearly six months.

After a four-day boat trip to Manzanillo and a slow train over the Sierra Nevada Occidental, we arrived in Guadalajara. Shefflow met our train and escorted us to the school—a magnificent old mansion. We were the only teachers. Since classes were scheduled for the morning and the late afternoon, we had a midday break of several hours and an opportunity to acquaint ourselves with cool and lush Guadalajara, second city of the republic, yet quiet as a museum except for the periodic sound of church bells. Impassive men with sandaled feet and a blanket over one shoulder tipped gray felt sombreros to priests on the street. Señoras and señoritas in black lace mantillas bowed to them. It always made me shudder. Carranza, Villa, Zapata—the Mexican Revolution seemed a distant dream.

The school wanted to find a third teacher and start evening classes. On my recommendation Shefflow hired Michael Gold (né Irwin Granich), who came on from the Gulf coast. (From Tampico, a popular wartime refugee haven: Maurice Becker was there, and later Owen Cattell. "Mike" had written me from there when I was in Mazatlán and we had maintained contact.)

From our first day in Guadalajara Eleanor and I had been reading help-wanted ads for Mexico City. We now decided Eleanor should quit the school and try her luck there. I would follow as soon as she found something. Not long after, Shefflow announced a week's suspension of classes and suggested that Mike and I take a vacation. I guess he needed a vacation himself—or more money. Mike and I passed the week as guests at a cattle ranch in the nearby mountain country which was owned by cousins of Jesús Ramírez, a *simpático* pupil of ours who had become a good friend. With a little urging (very little) Mike and I stayed a couple of extra weeks. We never returned to the school, which owed us quite a bit of back salary anyway.

Mike and I got along like alter egos at the ranch because we were writing a three-act play together—a travesty of American capitalism, with songs, for presentation in left-wing trade union halls. We worked on it several hours a day, and finished two acts at the ranch. Mike never worked on it after that. I wrote the final act myself—a couple of years later. (I was responsible for most of the lyrics, and I got an old socialist in Chicago to write the music. The Workers Party of America, Chicago section, produced the play, *The Last Revolution*, in 1923.)

12   Mexico City and
the *Cinco Gatos*

We said goodbye to a number of the ranch's peons. The ranch owners, Jesús Ramírez's cousins, escorted us to Guadalajara, where we caught the *mixto* (combination passenger-freight train) for Mexico City. Eleanor, already settled in a Berlitz School teaching job, had arranged for me to teach there, too.

Mexico City! Late night. And bitter cold. (Mexico City nights are coolish even in summer and this was mid-December.) We got some sleep in a fleabag near the station and headed toward Eleanor's place in the (remarkably warm) morning. Just to be at last in the Mexican capital was exciting. I had been warned that the altitude (8,000 feet) might be hard on my heart, but it wasn't (then or ever). In the crystalline air and silhouetted against the bluest of skies we saw, clear as spring water, the snow-covered summits of Popocatépetl (Smoking Mountain) and Ixtaccihuatl (Sleeping Woman), twenty miles to the south. These twin extinct volcanoes, both over 17,000 feet high, were a Mexico City landmark, visible in all their majesty from everywhere in the city.

Eleanor wasn't home. So we went in search of Henry Glintenkamp (who had given me the sensational first cover design for *Challenge*); he was a Mexico City refugee, and Mike had his address. We found him in his room at a downtown hotel, and there was my good wife as well. Quite a surprise. Not that there was anything wrong about it—Eleanor, heedless of protocol, might pop in wherever, and Glint was sort of an old friend. Still, I didn't like it.

Eleanor accompanied me back to the fleabag for my suitcase, and I moved into her furnished room above Fat Sing, a pocket-sized Chinese restaurant on Dolores Street. It was a Sunday, and Eleanor, with the day off, showed me something of the city. The broad Paseo de la Reforma, nearly three miles long, lined by trees and, at intervals, statues of Mexicans revered in the nation's history, is surely one of the world's finest boulevards. But on the Avenida Juárez, the thoroughfare leading into the Paseo, I saw hungry-looking urchins ten years old and younger hawking lottery tickets, an old woman in rags holding out two cigarettes for sale, and innumerable beggars. Indeed, beggars were everywhere in the capital, and many dragged a mutilated limb or had one sleeve hanging—mementos perhaps of the as yet unfinished revolution. Eleanor remarked that I'd see whole families sleeping on the cold pavement at night. We encountered no priests, no nuns, no acolytes. There was a great deal of traffic, and rickety little buses called *Fortingos* (Model-T Fords, adapted) whizzed along the Paseo with unprosperous humanity crowding the runningboards.

The Berlitz School had only a part-time place for me, a couple hours in the late afternoon. I sat through many of the always sunny mornings on a bench in the Alameda, the city's popular central park. People of all classes frequented the park if they had a moment or more to spare. (It had been off-limits for peons before the revolution. Now they could sit there all day, and shiver there all night.)

I hoped to meet someone who would put me in touch with Mexican labor organizations. Nowhere, it seemed to me, was the need to organize greater than among Mexico's betrayed masses, and nowhere, if independently organized, could the masses hope to accomplish so much so fast. The old overlordship had been overthrown. The (largely Indian) peons, miners, and city workers were still savagely exploited, but every general and politician had to pay lip-service to their latent power. Just what was this Mexican Revolution? It was, on one level, simply the effort of an uncoordinated new social oligarchy, a comparatively tiny element in underdeveloped Mexico, to establish itself in place of the old. It postulated the good life for the millions, and the masses responded. Aroused, inspired, uprooted, engulfed, the people were played upon, swirled about like dry leaves in the wind. Still, at every juncture, these same masses constituted the rank-and-file military force of the revolution. Moreover, conditions were fluid. A strong, independent, class-conscious labor movement could very well carry the upheaval beyond its "ordained" limits. And perhaps *(Quien sabe?)* such a movement could actually validate all the conscienceless socialist oratory of the politicos. I wanted to work for the labor movement, and so I spoke to everybody I met. (My Spanish was pretty good now.)

Naturally, all the American "slackers" in the capital gravitated to the inviting Alameda. Most had been around for a year or more, yet had no contact with Mexican labor or with Mexicans generally. Like the Mazatlán bunch, they lived only for the day when they could crawl safely back to "civilization." (The war was over now, but until there was an actual peace treaty conditions had to be considered "unfavorable.") A few of the "slackers" were different, however, real COs. Notable among them was our good friend Maurice Becker (down from Tampico), a man fascinated by the simplicity, wildness, cruelty, and kindness of Mexico and the Mexican people—and determined to stay on indefinitely. Then there was Carleton Beals (an assumed name), who may or may not have been a true CO. In any case, Carl was in no hurry to return home, for Mexico had launched his lifelong career writing colorful Latin-American travel books (they made him "Carleton Beals" for good). Also evidently planning to stay a while was a freak pseudo-socialist, a scarecrow with a pale face and a thin red beard called Linn A. E. Gale—accompanied by his adoring wife, Magdalena. Gale circulated *Gale's Magazine*, an obscurantist monthly combining Social Renovation and the cult of New Thought. He rented a room and advertised (in English) the Establishment of the New Thought Church of Mexico. He preached Sunday sermons there, wearing a black cutaway morning coat. The blond Magdalena stood at the foot of the pulpit, barefoot, in a white flowing robe. The show failed to catch on and had to be discontinued.

In the days of Porfirio Díaz, Mexico City had had a large English-speaking population, catered to by an English-language daily

newspaper. Much of the "Anglo-American colony" had now vanished. There was no English-language newspaper, and no government favor. Carranza was anti-American to the extent of being pro-
German. But *El Universal*, a big Mexico City daily, evidently found
it worthwhile to include a column in English devoted to local
American-society gossip—written by some rattle-brained American
society matron who claimed to hear it all. Since there were two
leading Mexico City dailies, *El Universal* and *Excelsior*, and since
they were archrivals, I saw my chance. I told *Excelsior* I could write
a livelier column than the matron's, and I was hired. In addition to
society notes, my column offered amusing aphorisms, quips, little
poems—much in the vein of F.P.A.'s "Conning Tower." I even res-
urrected my old byline, "Gulliver." After all, who could tell who
"Gulliver" was? Being, of course, without access to the "right people," I had to fake the society notes, cribbing them from the previous
day's *El Universal* and simply changing the wording. Once I cribbed
something that was later admitted to have been false. My opposite
number, who evidently suspected something, thereafter referred to
me in her column as "Gullible."

It was on a Sunday in Chapultepec Park that we encountered Genaro Gómez, the man who would introduce me to organized labor in
Mexico. Genaro was a baker by trade and president of an independent local bakers' union. And, I soon learned, a socialist—"a real
socialist," he added. Gómez was a member of the Socialist Party of
Mexico, which, despite its comprehensive name, had only a handful of members. They were the *Cinco Gatos* (five cats), as the dis-
paraging Mexican idiom had it, though the actual number was about
twenty. The party held its meetings in members' houses. Genaro
took me to a session presided over by Ignazio Santibáñez, a curi-
ously charismatic graybeard who wore a shabby black coat over a
white shirt with stiff collar and cuffs. Santibáñez was a schoolteacher, and except for Genaro and a shoemaker named Juan Bau-
tista Flores, everyone there seemed to be a schoolteacher. On further
acquaintance I found that the socialism of these *camaradas* was
half-anarchist. Nevertheless, they were committed anticapitalists
and independent of the phony socialist sloganeers. They were anxious to grow and, rather surprisingly, they had some promising

trade union connections—Genaro's bakers, Mexico City printers and brewery workers, bakers' organizations in Puebla and several smaller cities, and one bakers' organization in the important silver mining town of Pachuca. Eleanor was not particularly interested but I was. I joined the Cinco Gatos and became one of their leaders (it did not take much).

In early spring 1919 at Santibáñez's home I met a tall, slim, handsome Hindu Brahmin of twenty-nine known as Manabendra Nath Roy. Another pseudonym. (Mine, at the time, was Frank Seaman.) This Roy had consecrated his life to the overthrow of British rule in India.[1] Fervent, intelligent, resourceful, charming, self-confident, daring, and ruthless, he had joined a terrorist group in his native Bengal as a schoolboy of fourteen. He later served a prison term in India for robberies to buy arms. When the war broke out, he left India in disguise to conduct arms-buying missions in Burma, Indonesia, and Japan. A succession of smuggling deals—arranged with German intermediaries—miscarried. He did secure some German money and promises of a lot more to fund sabotage and propaganda in India. In 1916 he shifted to the United States, where there was a broad base of support for an independent India. Roy met with groups of his countrymen in San Francisco, Palo Alto, and New York, and spoke at public meetings with Lajpat Rai and others.[2] He carried a letter commending him to the German consul in New York, and there in 1917 he published his first book, *The Way to a Durable Peace*, an argument for the self-determination of peoples. When the United States was clearly about to enter the war as Britain's ally, Roy crossed into Mexico. With him came his new wife, Evelyn, who had been a student at Stanford University.

Arrived in the Mexican capital, Roy published a Spanish translation of his book, including a new chapter directed against the

1. Roy (Narendra Nath Bhattacharya), born in 1898 to a prominent Bengali Brahmin family, joined the Indian revolutionary movement at an early age and in time became one of the Comintern's leading spokesmen on the national and colonial questions.
2. Lajpat Rai was perhaps the most famous Hindu intellectual living in the United States at the time.

Monroe Doctrine. This stance certainly did not hurt Roy's relations with the bitterly anti-American Carranza regime. He met President Carranza personally at a state banquet in the German embassy and was invited to visit him at the National Palace.

All this happened while I was wondering if Eleanor and I would ever make it to Mexico City. Once we did, Roy impressed me as he impressed everyone. I relished his earnestness, the quality of his mind, and accepted him on faith. He shipped money to India regularly. He always had plenty, and I assumed he got it from rich sympathizers. Certainly, at that time, he didn't get it from Germany. What official German presence there was in Mexico represented a conquered (and penniless) land.

Roy had an open-door policy at his home in the Colonia Roma, and I went there often, every day or so after a while. The house was very grand, but Roy and Evelyn lived in Spartan style. His own personal expenditures were minimal. The guy was practically an ascetic, and understandably reticent about where the money came from—if only to protect his source. Roy and I became great friends (and co-workers), yet it was a long time before he said a word about his wartime dealings with the Germans.[3]

Politically, Roy was less of an influence on me than I was on him. When we first met he was an unreconstructed nationalist. He had sought out the Cinco Gatos with a resolution demanding independence for India—and a request that they send it to socialist organizations throughout Latin America with their endorsement. (Which they did.) Our early conversations were one long argument: nationalism versus internationalism, bourgeois notions versus the class struggle. I lent him a copy of the *Commu-*

---

3. For certain information I have relied on a Roy memoir compiled from loose notes found after his death. I have relied on these only where they jibed with the little he had told me. The memoir, however, contains glaring misstatements, such as the depiction of Mike Gold and me parading before President Carranza in Mexico City at a date when neither of us had yet arrived there. I never saw Carranza in person. In composing these autobiographical notes, Roy must have been relying on distant memory, reinterpretation, and supposition. I know very well how memory can lead one astray. On finding (in 1970 or thereabouts) a cache of my old diaries, postmarked correspondence, magazine articles, newspaper clippings, and so on, I was appalled at some of my own misrepresentations in interviews with Stanley Burnshaw (in 1962) and Theodore Draper (1964).

nist Manifesto (I had just read it myself), and introduced him to Mike, Glint, and Maurice Becker. He began to show up regularly at meetings of the Cinco Gatos, and his natural dynamism did the rest. Before long Roy was financing bigger, better-looking, and more widely distributed issues of the group's paper, *El Socialista*. He also financed a couple of trips I took for the Cinco Gatos (to the Pachuca mining area, and to the city of Orizaba—locale of a militant textile workers' union). Our group prepared to initiate and merge itself into what we hoped would be "a truly national" Socialist Party of Mexico.

13   Not Really a "Red" Newspaper

In the meantime there were developments in my own affairs. In May 1919, at work on my column for *Excelsior*, I read that General Salvador Alvarado was starting a new daily newspaper to be called *El Heraldo de México*. Alvarado, the richest of the nouveau-riche generals, had presidential ambitions. He had taken over a precious historic building, put in modern machinery, and hired a flock of talented editors—headed by a well-known intellectual named Modesto C. Roland. I decided to propose an English-language page covering general news, sports, and editorial comment as well as Anglo-American society notes. I prepared a dummy captioned "A Newspaper within a Newspaper" and made an appointment with Señor Roland.

He received me in a book-lined office next door to General Alvarado's. My proposition appealed to Roland's imagination. He got the general on the phone and told him about it. Excitedly. The general came in, took a quick look at the dummy, and—without knowing a word of English—hired me as English Section Editor of *El Heraldo de México*. They were willing to pay triple what *Excelsior* was paying me, and made allowance for a staff of four.

It Had to Be Revolution

Arriving for the first day at my new office, I was told to see General Alvarado immediately. His shrewd black eyes smiling, he put his arms around me in an *abrazo* and congratulated me. *El Heraldo's* announcement of its forthcoming English Section had brought in a flock of display ads for the first issue, and we had more after we got started. The announcement also brought letters from ladies offering to do the indispensable "social notes." I selected a Mrs. Godfrey Carter, pedigreed socialite, who sent in her (rather juicy) column every day about noon. I had had no trouble in lining up the other three staff members: Eleanor, Mike, and Glint. I put my salary into a common pot with theirs, making all four equal in pay ("like true socialists"). I did not, however, share control with them (I had learned one lesson from the *Challenge* fiasco), and proceeded to hand out their assignments.

Getting miscellaneous and sports news was easy. We had access to the stories filed by all *El Heraldo's* local reporters, and to everything coming in over the wires. *El Heraldo* subscribed to the AP, UP, and INS services in Spanish. All we had to do was translate. We took what we wanted from these and other sources such as the New York *Call, Soviet Russia Today,* and George Lansbury's *Labour Herald*. (Lansbury represented the extreme left wing of the British Labour Party.) Our feature stories had a deliberate class-struggle bias, subtle at first, then more and more outspoken. The stuff was not calculated to please our readers in the Anglo-American colony, but we continued to have plenty of readers anyway. Since a surprising proportion of the American and English residents never learned Spanish, ours was the only news they could read.

But the ads fell off. Canny though he was, the general never realized we were deliberately undercutting his policies. He heard complaints of something funny about the English Section, but didn't lose confidence in me. ("Frank Seaman" was not publicly identifiable with labor agitation until later.) Nevertheless, the loss of the ads disturbed the general, and he warned me against "offending." "I made one big mistake in my life," he told me. "When I was governor of Yucatán, I antagonized every Catholic. I'm still trying to get over that." For a while the salty general and I had a very nice relationship, but I knew it could not last. On the Sixteenth of September (Mexico's Fourth of July), I ran an editorial saying, "Mexico is not yet free. Uncle Sam is the reason." The next day we lost our last ad. And the day after that I was fired, and my whole crew with me. The English Section disappeared.[1]

During my time at *El Heraldo,* visiting Americans often drifted into our office. One summer's day came Jack Johnson, the first black man to win the world's heavyweight title. In Mexico City, Sanborn's, American owned, refused to serve lunch to him and his white wife. They left the place, returned with three or four Mexican generals, and got both service and an apology. We gave the story big space in the English Section. The stolid black giant was a popular hero in Mexico. When he fought an Argentinian in the Mexico City bullring, Mike and I were there. In fact we went there with him on the runningboard of his car. Aging, flabby, and punchdrunk, Jack was then a has-been in the U.S.; he knocked out his man, but took no joy in it and seemed depressed. On the way home from the fight, Mike prodded him: "Say Jack, you got anything against the *Bolsheviki?*" "Not that I know of," was the puzzled reply. We were, as we explained to him, collecting funds to publish the Constitution of Soviet Russia in Spanish. Jack gave Mike ten dollars.

It was a bad day for me. Eleanor and I had split up that morning. Actually she had left me for Glint. It was something that had developed over a long period. When Eleanor went solo to Mexico City from Guadalajara, the only Mexico City address she possessed was Glint's, the one I had gotten from Mike. I didn't like finding her in Glint's room when I got there—though at that time there was nothing between them. But later I realized that I'd more or less thrown them together. First by taking him on at the English Section. (Where he proved practically useless. He was an able, though uninspired, cartoonist, but we had no need for cartoons. Mike, who was really a gifted journalist, had to rewrite most of Glint's stories.) Second by encouraging Eleanor to spend evenings with him when I was busy with labor and political meetings— which meant almost every night. Eleanor had begun to lose interest in politics with the end of the war and never joined the Cinco

---

1. *El Heraldo de México* was an important and powerful daily for a number of years. It no longer exists. General Alvarado, contender for the presidency in 1920 and again in 1924, was assassinated during his second campaign.

Gatos. Glint gave her lessons in drawing, took her to art museums, and introduced her to some Mexican painters. He also took her to concerts and the opera. Eventually they were going to bed together. Theoretically libertarian in such matters, I was supposed not to care. But I did. Fiercely. When I insisted it had to be him or me, she went to live with Glint.

I thought I would never get over the loss of Eleanor. Yes, I had gotten over Betty, but this was different. Eleanor was my wife (legal considerations apart), my partner in joys and stress, my ever-loving and beloved. And now, as if nothing had happened, I had to face Eleanor and Glint every day at the office. The only alternative would be to fire them, which was unthinkable. They stayed with the English Section to the end. My only relief was work. I have never worked more obsessively—all day at the office, then half the night in labor halls and committee rooms.

And there were new developments to occupy me. Mexico had a liberal, anticlerical tradition dating back to Benito Juárez, the great reform president (a full-blooded Zapotec Indian) who had died in 1872. The Juárez tradition inspired Madero, and Carranza after him. But with Carranza something new was added: an overture to the working class. Under the Díaz dictatorship two sophisticated anarchists, the brothers Ricardo and Jesús Flores Magón, disciples of M. Bakunin, had created the embryo of a militant proletarian movement. Though the movement died with them, an indistinct memory of it lived on, and in Mexico City there was a workingman's clubhouse called Casa del Obrero Mundial (modeled after similar clubhouses in Spain) with a meeting room, a free lending library, and a cantina. In 1915 "First Chief" Carranza signed a pact with the handful of the Casa del Obrero Mundial. The offshoot was a "friendly" Confederation of Labor: Confederación Regional Obrera Mexicana (CROM). Thus was born the attempt to adopt antibourgeois rhetoric in the service of Mexico's bourgeois revolution. In 1917 it spawned a captive Socialist Workers Party headed by the CROM leader, a former electrical worker named Luis N. Morones. With government patronage the CROM grew fast. Its June 1918 conference at Zacatecas claimed affiliated trade unions with 70,000 members—a typical (not exclusively Mexican) exaggeration. The actual total may have been a bit more than 7,000.

Would Mexico ever have a true socialist party of consequence? Our Cinco Gatos invited all interested groups, parties, and factions to an organizing convention in order to launch such a party, and the invitation attracted a fairly sizable response. With fifteen or sixteen groups represented, a few from remote areas, the convention assembled in late September 1919. The gathering proved to be more miscellaneous than I had expected, or wanted. Among the "delegates"—and grotesque in this predominantly working class gathering—was Luis N. Morones, fat, perfumed, elegantly tailored, a diamond ring on his thumb. The credentials debate showed that some of his CROM accomplices were there, too. This struck us as ominous. It seemed as if Morones intended to capture the new socialist project for the government at the start. We of the Cinco Gatos opposed seating him and his henchmen. But they won—by one vote—and thus became executive board members of the United Socialist Party formed at the convention. It looked as though we had given birth to a monstrosity, and I knew we'd have to split if they got control. It did not come to that, however. On the next day, when the convention reconvened as the constituent assembly of the new party, I proposed that the party denounce worldwide socialist reformism and affiliate with the revolutionary Third (Communist) International.[2] Roy seconded the motion, and it passed—against the opposition of Morones. At that point, Morones rose to state that he could not allow himself to be identified with such an attitude and that, with no hard feelings, he and his friends would depart. And, professing that they nevertheless considered us "comrades," they left.[3] Our party later took the name Communist Party of Mexico and elected Roy and me its delegates to the Second Congress of the International, scheduled to meet in Moscow in the summer of 1920.

2. The new International (Comintern) had been proclaimed in Moscow in March 1919.
3. Morones was a labor politician with a future. In 1920 he helped General Álvaro Obregón spike Carranza's plan to handpick his successor in the presidency, and Obregón, on becoming president, made Morones head of the National Military Supply Establishment. When Plutarco E. Calles succeeded Obregón, Morones entered the cabinet as secretary of industry, commerce, and labor. A newspaper then reported him "the most important man in Mexico next to the president." Later he was reckoned a presidential possibility himself. In the end of course he was assassinated.

14 Borodin

At the convention just described I acted under a new and quite special influence. One August morning a dandy with equally polished black hair and shoes came into my office at *El Heraldo de México* and introduced himself with a lisp as "an Americanized Mexican," name of Rafael Mallén. I judged him to be a year or two younger than I. He came to say he had a friend who was anxious to meet me and whom I would enjoy meeting. Would I have lunch with them? This Mallén struck me as a phony but I thought there might be a story in it.

"I might want to bring a friend with me," I suggested, nodding toward Mike Gold's desk.

"Okay, I guess . . ."

"Mike," I called out, "we're invited to lunch."

Mallén led us to the Hotel Regis, once luxurious but now seedy and second-rate, and told us that his friend was a visitor in the city. The friend was waiting in his room. A large man, slow-moving but not heavy, he had deep-set eyes, a walrus mustache, and a face like a mask. He held on to my hand after shaking it. Speaking beautiful English in a subdued voice with a hint of a foreign accent, he explained that, traveling from the United States and knowing no Spanish, he'd had the good fortune to discover a Mexico City newspaper with a section he could read, and he wanted to express his appreciation to the people responsible for it. Who was he? "A businessman with an endowment of insatiable curiosity in all things human. Peter Alexandrescu. Rumanian." We did not go out to lunch; he ordered it sent up. He then proceeded to document his curiosity, asking for a comparison between Mexican and Spanish bullfighting, of all things. He drifted to food, Mexican painting, culture, and world affairs. Theater, literature, modern painting—and finally politics. Mexican politics. World politics. Revolutions. Soviet Russia. Where, I then realized, the conversation had been heading from the first. Engagingly, compellingly, in due course he extracted confessions of precisely where Mike and I stood on things. Yes, we were socialists, in sympathy with the new Russia. In truth he needn't have been so clever about it. We would have unburdened ourselves to anyone—point-blank. Our interrogator, though, had to make sure.

We talked all afternoon. Once sure of us, this pseudo-businessman confided that he was engaged on a diplomatic mission for the Soviet Russian government—a mission that, for the time being at least, required secrecy. He left it at that, not saying what the mission was, not suggesting what he wanted of us. The shadowy Rafael Mallén, who had been off in a corner with a newspaper, accompanied us downstairs.

We were tremendously excited, but puzzled. The story was too improbable. Well, we'd not gotten involved in anything as yet, so we'd just wait and see. Of some things we were satisfied. This excessively mysterious, somewhat pompous "Mr. Alexandrescu" was a person of consequence. He had dignity, authority, intellect, culture, personal magnetism. And he knew a hell of a lot about socialists and revolution.

A follow-up session next day dispelled our doubts, even as it fed our excitement. He produced unmistakably authentic credentials that certified him as Michael Stepanovich Borodin, Ambassador of the Russian Socialist Soviet Republic to the Constitutional Government of the Republic of Mexico. These credentials were to be presented only if it could be ascertained that Carranza would actually accept them—and recognize Soviet Russia. He also produced a credential as roving representative of the Organizing Committee for the Third (Communist) International. This one, signed "Angelica Balabanova, Secretary,"[1] was on a silk cloth that had been sewn into Borodin's coat sleeve. He told us something about himself. Although still in early middle age (probably around forty), he was an "Old Bolshevik" leader, a veteran of the famous 1903 Brussels Conference[2] and of the failed 1905 Revolution. After this rebellion

1. Angelica Balabanova was a Russian who spent much of her life in the Italian socialist movement. She became a well-known Bolshevik and the initial secretary of the Third International.
2. At this conference of the Russian Social Democratic Labor Party, held abroad because of constraints in Russia, Lenin and Martov split over qualifications for party membership. Lenin scored a temporary triumph. As a result, Lenin's adherents went down in history as the *bolsheviki* (majorityites) and Martov's as the *mensheviki* (minorityites). The split led to the formation of the rival Bolshevik

had been suppressed, he had endured the sequence, common to so many of his comrades, of prison, Siberia, escape, exile, and return to Russia upon the overthrow of the tsar. He knew the United States well. On his present assignment he had stopped off at Chicago, where Adolph Germer, secretary of the American Socialist Party, procured him an interpreter. This was Mallén.

Since he needed confidential surroundings to operate from, Borodin did not want to stay on at the Hotel Regis. We introduced him to Roy, and two or three days later he became a guest in Roy's house. (Mallén had by now disappeared.) Borodin remained in seclusion there while Roy undertook to reach and sound out Carranza. Evelyn kept strangers away from the house on one pretext or another, and no one got upstairs but Mike and me. Once we were no longer connected with *El Heraldo,* we went there constantly, and Borodin educated us—and Roy—in Marxism. Characteristically, he began with the intricacies of Hegelian dialectics. He also gave us our first knowledge of the Zimmerwald Conference and its successor at Kienthal.[3]

Carranza was still glad to see Roy, but the harried old man refused to meet Borodin even informally. He was not going to let himself in for anything like recognition of Soviet Russia at a time when Generals Obregón, Calles, and De la Huerta were openly threatening to revolt over the presidential succession.[4] For Mexico, an economi-

---

and Menshevik parties.

3. In the second year of the war—September 1915—resolute socialists from various nations met in the Swiss village of Zimmerwald. They represented different socialist tendencies, but all were antiwar. Among those present were Lenin, Zinoviev, Trotsky, and Martov, as well as Radek—who represented the Polish Left. Others represented groups in Germany, France, Italy, Rumania, Bulgaria, and neutral Norway, Sweden, and Holland. All recognized that the Second Socialist International had compromised itself hopelessly in the war and was in shambles. Some were for rebuilding and revitalizing it. Lenin proposed a new—Third—International, committed to world revolution. His proposal failed to carry there—or at a 1916 conference in Kienthal. But the Second International was beyond revitalization as an instrument of class struggle.

4. Reflecting the country's unfortunate history, Mexico's 1917 constitution prohibits a president from serving two successive terms. Carranza, unable to succeed himself, was attempting to force the election of a nonentity (Ignacio Bonilla), perhaps hoping to control him. Other candidates protested and "the Sonora trio," Obregón, Calles, and De la Huerta, threatened revolt. They did rebel, successfully, in the spring of 1920, entering the capital in May. Carranza escaped

cally backward country on the margin of world events, to recognize Soviet Russia at that time would have been premature, if not rash. "White" anti-Soviet armies still controlled large parts of the former Russian Empire. The assassination in Moscow of Ambassador W. von Mirbach (July 1918) had poisoned Soviet-German relations. Britain, the first of Russia's former allies to recognize the Soviet regime, did not do so until 1924; the United States would wait until 1933.

Borodin may have failed to elicit Mexican recognition for Soviet Russia, but his visit had its consequences: the "special influence" that had operated on me/us during the September 1919 convention called by the Cinco Gatos was of course Borodin's. His advice helped us get rid of Morones. And without Borodin we could hardly have thought of affiliating the enlarged party with the Third (Communist) International. Ours thus became the first party outside Russia to vote formal affiliation with the International. At that time, the International itself was still more project than actuality. Its "First Congress" had met in Moscow on March 2 of that year (1919). Nearly all the "delegates" were Russians, or foreigners who happened to be in Russia. The only true delegates were Hugo Eberlein of the Spartacus League of Germany, S. J. Rutgers from Holland, and miscellaneous Finns. The congress's proclamation, drafted by Lenin, had been radioed to the world by G. Chicherin, Soviet commissar for foreign affairs. In those days Soviet diplomatic and revolutionary activities were so closely related that the Commissariat took care of both. That "First Congress" did little more than issue a manifesto, and for all practical purposes the "Second Congress," scheduled for 1920, was really the first.

Borodin lingered in Mexico, waiting, as he explained, to receive a cable from "the Western European Secretariat" in Amsterdam. It was in early November 1919 that he called me to one side and asked to talk to me alone. He began by telling me he was Jewish. Borodin was his Party name, and Alexandrescu was the name he used for traveling. His real name was Gruzenberg, and during his exile he had been known as Berg. He had lived in the United States (as Berg)

---

but was assassinated thirteen days later. Obregón became president after a brief interregnum presided over by De la Huerta as provisional president.

for twelve years, studied at Valparaiso University in Indiana, and married a Russian-born fellow student. He and his wife had established "a progressive prep school" in Chicago. She still lived there, with their two sons. I appreciated these confidences but knew they were irrelevant to his purpose in getting me alone. He was, I had learned to believe, one of the world's most circuitous talkers. I could imagine him starting a conversation with Ping-Pong and suddenly having you swearing to an assassination. You wouldn't know how you got there. You could be sure of one thing, though: if he started on Ping-Pong he would wind up somewhere else. So I waited for him to come to the point. I knew he'd reached it when he asked me if I felt like taking a trip for him, one that would involve a bit of risk.

Nodding assent, I asked, "What do you want me to do in the dear old U.S.A.?" (I could get in across the border the same way I got out.)

"Nothing like that. You will be going on a sea trip. Cuba. Possibly Haiti. That will depend on circumstances. In Havana."

I assured him I was ready for anything but had no American passport, and even if I had one couldn't use it.

"Get a Mexican one. You look like a Mexican. Do you know some Mexican of the right age who would lend you his birth certificate? Someone not too close to the Party?" I thought at once of Jesús Ramírez, the friendly Guadalajara student who got Mike and me invited to his cousins' ranch.

The purpose of the mysterious sea trip? Well, it was this way. Borodin had departed on his Europe-America-Mexico journey with a suitcase containing certain blueprints best not discovered in his possession. A shipboard acquaintance (a Dutch commission merchant en route to Haiti, where he lived) had agreed to take the suitcase through customs for him. But they missed connections in New York. After futile searching, Borodin ("Alexandrescu") had to go on minus the suitcase with the evidently important blueprints. Haiti had no international phone service, and its cable service was not functioning.

Did I remember Rafael Mallén?

Of course I did.

Well, he had sent Mallén to Haiti for the suitcase and Mallén seemed to have disappeared. Since there was no direct transportation to the island, Mallén was to have gone via Cuba. He booked passage on a Ward Line steamer for Havana, but had not been heard from since.

So now it was Frank Seaman to the rescue. I was to go first to Cuba. If I found Mallén and the suitcase there, I was to make him give me the suitcase, by whatever means possible. Borodin handed me a small revolver. If I could not find him in three days, I was to cable for instructions. If I found him without the suitcase, I was to bring him back with me.

At this point, "Frank Seaman" ceased to exist. I sailed from Vera Cruz to Havana as Jesús Ramírez. Balmy Havana was filled with American tourists in 1919 and the casino was going full blast. I visited the casino but not to gamble. Luck failed me there and everywhere, for no one had seen my young polished-hair dandy. There was no Rafael Mallén on a hotel register. Or on any New York–bound ship's passenger list of recent date. In answer to my (not unanticipated) cable for further instructions, I was ordered to proceed to Haiti. At Port au Prince I was to travel up into the hills to suburban Petionville and ask for a Dutchman named Henrik Luders.

The small boat from Santiago de Cuba limped into Port au Prince with a busted engine. Port au Prince was a ramshackle capital with the stink of open sewers. U.S. Marines occupied the place (as they were to continue doing for many years), but I did not see them. The post office directed my guide to the Dutchman's very conspicuous house—halfway up a mountain. It was evening when we got there, and pouring rain. A woman opened the door slightly. I told her I had come from Mr. Alexandrescu. She let me in (not my black guide), said she would call her husband, and left me standing in the hall. After several minutes a short blond Dutchman appeared. He glared at me and without a word of greeting walked to a closet, flung open the door, and yanked out a battered leather suitcase. Its lock was broken and its lining ripped out. But, *mirabile dictu*, it was full of rolls of blueprints.

"You want it?" he snapped. "Take it. Take it. I could be in an American jail because of your Mr. Alexandrescu. 'A small favor' he asks me. He does not say he is giving me a smuggler's traveling bag with a false bottom. So please take it. Out. Out of my house. Goodbye!"

I didn't wait to hear more. Ecstatic at getting the blueprints so easily, I grabbed the suitcase and got out. I really was in luck—it had
even stopped raining—and my luck held. Boats between Port au
Prince and Santiago de Cuba did not come and go on schedule, but
the hotel informed me I could catch a boat in the morning. Arriving
in Havana, I had a day's wait for the return trip to Vera Cruz, so I
booked passage and prepared to get on a sightseeing bus. Then, just
because I thought, well, you never know, I decided to make one
more investigation of sailings to New York. By God there was a sailing that day—and on the passenger list the name of Rafael Mallén.

I was at the gangplank when the passengers arrived. When
Mallén saw me he almost collapsed. I pushed close and pressed his
hand against my coat pocket so he could feel the contours of the revolver. He could not go aboard, I told him; he was wanted in Mexico.
He let me lead him away like a baby, his nearest approach to resistance being a lament that he had paid good money for the ticket to
New York. I promised it would be refunded, and then sent off a cable: SAILING VERA CRUZ TOMORROW WITH BLUEPRINTS AND MALLÉN.

I brought him to my hotel and insisted he sleep in the same room
with me. Asked what he'd been up to, he said it had taken him
weeks to get to Haiti. There Luders had shown him a torn suitcase,
saying something about a false bottom. The Dutchman had yelled at
him, called him names, and threatened to have him arrested. He
had gone away too scared to face Borodin. But now, finding me on
his trail, he saw he could never escape an accounting. He was accompanying me back to Mexico so he could "have the thing out
and be through with it." I was inclined to believe him; as he described it, his experience of Luders and the suitcase dovetailed per-
fectly with mine.

Borodin and Roy were waiting for us at the railroad station in
Mexico City. I got the kind of reception an Olympic winner gets from
friends who have bet a fortune on him. They said they had a cham-
pagne dinner waiting for me, and hardly seemed to notice Mallén.

When we got to Roy's house Borodin took the suitcase into the
drawing room and shut the door. In a minute there was a howl of
rage. Out came Borodin, snarling, "There's nothing here but blueprints." What, I thought, did he expect?

"Where are the diamonds?"

I looked at him blankly. "Where," he repeated, "are the diamonds?" Suddenly he turned to Mallén, grasped his shoulder, marched him into the drawing room, and again shut the door. Borodin usually spoke quietly but this time he roared. He excoriated Mallén, verbally stripped the skin off him. He would be spirited to Russia, tortured—unless he came up with those diamonds. Where were they? In Cuba? Mallén had been gone long enough to have done anything with them. The poor guy swore he knew nothing about diamonds. If there had been any in the suitcase, they were gone when he got to Haiti. He told the same story he had told me.

When the Bolsheviks took power in Russia, they had little hard cash and no credit. In their extremity they began secretly to sell the prodigious Romanov crown jewels abroad. Borodin had been carrying some—they were expected to finance revolutionary activity throughout Latin America. Unable to break Mallén's story, Borodin searched him and let him go. And phoned to have him shadowed in the States. Did Mallén, in fact, take the diamonds—and perhaps arrange their disposal in Cuba? Or had the Dutchman stolen them? There was a report that they finally turned up in New York, but Borodin's comment to me was that he wished it were true. I don't believe they ever were recovered.[5] But the legendary mystery of Borodin and the crown jewels—a staple of Comintern lore—had begun.

There was little point in Borodin's remaining longer in Mexico. The Western European Secretariat cabled funds and probably suggested his next destination. He sailed for Spain December 1, 1919, and I went with him. He needed an interpreter with some general comprehension whose politics he could rely on, and I wanted the benefit of continued contact with him—and an introduction to the movement in Europe. Besides, I had been elected a delegate to the 1920 Congress in Russia and Spain was halfway there. I had my "Jesús Ramírez" passport.

Visas did not come easy across Europe in 1919, the year of revolutions. There had been a Spartacist insurrection in Berlin at the

---

5. There have been numerous versions of how Borodin tried to retrieve the suitcases from Haiti; but he sent no one there while in Mexico except Mallén and me.

beginning of the year, brutally recompensed by the murder of Karl
Liebknecht and Rosa Luxemburg; Bavaria had experienced a six-day
Soviet Republic; revolutionists headed by Bela Kun had seized
power in Hungary and ruled it as a Soviet Republic for four and a
half months before succumbing to a Rumanian army; general strikes
were endemic in Italy. Spain, which had profited from the war, was
calm, at least on the surface. The playboy king Alfonso XIII seemed
secure on his throne—even popular, it was said. But the watchdog
Civil Guards in their green uniforms and three-cornered patent-
leather hats were sometimes found murdered at their posts; the
overofficered army, humiliated repeatedly by the Riff tribesmen of
northern Morocco, was infested with plots and plotters; and the Cat-
alans and the Basques threatened secession. In 1917, a general strike
began in Barcelona and spread to other cities.

You had to show a reason for traveling. Fortunately, I possessed
letterheads from *El Heraldo de México*. I wrote myself a credential
as a foreign correspondent, with a roving commission for all of Europe. Also I had some "Jesús Ramírez" cards printed, duplicating
the bona fide ones. They served the purpose wherever I presented
them. Their effect on Mexican consuls and ambassadors, all happy
to oblige a leading Mexico City daily—and all conscious of General
Alvarado's personal power—was magical. My Spanish was prepos-
terously unfit for the role I sought to play: not colloquial enough,
not glib enough—and affected with a giveaway accent. I got along
by keeping my mouth shut, or—when speech was imperative—favoring the monosyllabic.

We sailed on the *Venezuela*, Hispanic-Atlantic Line, in a luxury
suite: sitting room, bedroom, and bath. The beds were king-size and
the appointments lavish. Such use of the funds in Borodin's care appalled me but he declared it necessary. If you want to hide revolutionary connections, he believed, you had better travel first class.
The theory was no doubt sound, but the fact was that Borodin liked
luxury. (He would not have stayed a single night at the deteriorating
Hotel Regis except that his funds had been running out and the diamonds were missing.)

The crossing from Vera Cruz to La Coruña in the northwest corner
of Spain took fourteen days (including a stop at Havana). On the
way Borodin carried my Marxist education further, placing special

emphasis on the need to combine theory and action. He held that the difference between the Bolsheviks and the Mensheviks was that the Bolsheviks took Marxism seriously. To them the class war was war. Had they believed otherwise, he argued, they never would have achieved power. This conclusion struck me as irrefutable. For the first time I realized what it meant to be a revolutionist. In that realization I felt recommitted to the cause I had embraced. I acquired a new respect for Borodin, too. (Having finished expounding Bolshevism, that multifaceted man turned directly to appreciations of Pushkin and Rousseau. He could quote Shakespeare to illuminate a concept. Once, when it was pertinent, he drew me a map of George Washington's retreat across Long Island.)

La Coruña was one broad cobblestoned street and a few cramped and muddy ones. In the broad street, husky women shouldered baskets, while men in gorgeous uniforms—military and other—strolled idly. I recall a line of cafés where a sprinkling of customers were drinking coffee, photographs of huge-nosed, huge-chinned Alfonso XIII, and at the station a crown-topped red mailbox. We were in town only until the wagon-lit left for Madrid. From the car window we got our first view of the starkly enthralling landscape of northern Spain.

Arriving in Madrid, we spent most of our first day in a suite at the fashionable Palace Hotel—reading the newspapers. Although Spain was nominally a constitutional monarchy, its elected Cortes debated in a power vacuum. Ministries rose and fell by royal favor. When we arrived in the country, the government was head by Antonio Maura, leading conservative statesman of the period. Yet the press was left surprisingly free, and Madrid had a dozen or more outspoken dailies. I studied them all, eager to ascertain their political line and to learn more about Spanish attitudes on organized labor, international relations, and Soviet Russia. Borodin, dependent on me in this, took notes on my observations.

15 Revolutionist by Profession

I knew a bit about the Spanish labor movement from what I'd read in Mexico. It had two main divisions: the UGT (Unión General de Trabajadores), a trade union organization allied with the Socialist Party, and the CNT (Confederacion Nacional del Trabajo), a syndicalist body dominated by anarchists. The anarcho-syndicalist organization—the only powerful one of its kind in Europe—was pretty much confined to Catalonia and a section of Andalusia. We knew we'd find support for the Third International only among the socialists, yet we confronted a problem there, too—the Spanish Socialist Party was quintessentially Second International. Its grand old man, Pablo Iglesias, had always been reformist, no revolutionary, and the active leaders whose names I knew—Julián Besteiro, Indalecio Prieto, and Francisco Largo Caballero—were all extreme right-wingers.[1] I scoured the newspapers for any clue of a left-wing opposition within the SP but found none. I did find an announcement of a Socialist meeting to protest the high cost of living, and assumed that if I attended somebody would lead me to the opponents of the "opportunist" leadership. But I had no luck there, nor at the Casa del Pueblo, where some of the crowd went after the meeting.

The newspapers often referred to a famous semipublic literary-political club called the Ateneo, which was said to be the focus of the country's intellectual life. It occupied a three or four story building not far from our hotel, so I went to investigate. A very young man, blondish and bespectacled, was seated at a table in the club's vast library. I spoke to him because the books in front of him were in English, and found that he was John Dos Passos. Although we had had acquaintances in common and he had written for the *Masses*, I really did not get to know Dos Passos, and didn't see him again until many years later. But he introduced me to two eminent

1. Late in life—during the Spanish Civil War of 1936–39—Largo Caballero, then approaching seventy, moved sharply to the left and became known as "the Spanish Lenin." He became premier of the Spanish Republic with two or more prominent Communists in his cabinet.

Spanish intellectuals sitting at nearby tables, both of them Socialists sympathetic to Soviet Russia. One, a gracious Professor Fernando de los Ríos, explained in flowing Castilian that he was more humanist than socialist, and not really a party man.[2] The other, Mariano García Cortes, a black-bearded giant in his early fifties, was prominent in the party, a representative in parliament. Yes, he was sympathetic to the Soviets, and had said so in the party. He did not propose to say more, but said that some of the kids in the Juventud (the party's youth auxiliary) would. He was busy now, but if I wanted to learn more I could see him almost any night at such-and-such café in the Puerta del Sol (the big central plaza that was then the heart of downtown Madrid life). He held his *tertulia* there, usually arriving about midnight and staying until four in the morning.[3]

García Cortes was surrounded by more or less like-minded cronies at his tertulia. Everybody was talking at once, but when García Cortes talked most of the others stopped and listened. Actually, the talk seemed to be mostly gossip, but I didn't really stick around long enough to find out. I left with a young enthusiast (about my age) who had been introduced to me as "the brightest kid in the Juventud, but impatient." His name was Ramón Merino Gracia, and he observed, scornfully, that the whole café gang was more interested in saving capitalism than overthrowing it. I brought him to see Borodin at the hotel.

Ramón, pale, hollow-cheeked, and sickly-looking, was a disappointed medical student. He had been expelled from the university and now worked as a waiter in the café where García Cortes and cronies met to talk. He convinced Borodin that he was intelligent, had something of a following, and would fight to affiliate it with the new International. In short, he was our man. Energized by contact with

---

2. Some time later, however, the Spanish Socialist Party sent the professor to Moscow to look the regime over. "But where is liberty?" he is reported to have asked Lenin. The reply: "Liberty? What for?" During the Spanish Civil War he became for a time the republic's ambassador at Paris, and after that at Washington—where he appealed unsuccessfully to Secretary of State Cordell Hull to permit the republic to buy arms.

3. Café tertulias—nightly all-male talkfests assisted by periodic sips of coffee, sometimes brandy or *anís*—were common in Madrid. Bankers had them, physicians had them, poets had them. Politicians of all persuasions. Bullfighters, newspapermen, chess fiends. Even stamp collectors.

a real-life Russian Bolshevik who was, moreover, intimate with Lenin and Trotsky, Ramón worked fast and effectively. Before long we were meeting with a cohesive group pledged to achieve Socialist endorsement of the Third International in defiance of the party leadership. We met in the grubby second-floor flat near the Plaza del Carmen which was the home of Ramón's elder brother Carlos. ("Carlitos," a shoemaker whose shop stood below the flat, had no interest in the movement but was trustworthy; he would have risked torture for his beloved brother.) We knew that there was no hope of winning over the Spanish Socialist Party; there would have to be a break. At Borodin's insistence, the group undertook to break in time to be represented at the approaching Second Congress in Moscow.

As soon as the determination to split was reached, Borodin departed for Amsterdam; he had been in Spain less than three weeks. Taking most of the travel money with him, he left me to carry on as his proxy.

Ramón arranged for me to stay at his brother's, in the front room ("our" meeting room) next to the tiny kitchen. Carlos, his wife, Felicia, and their eight-year-old daughter, Lupe, lived in one room in the back. The toilet was downstairs in the shop. They were a sweet, considerate family, uncomplicated and unprying. Felicia served me a bowl of thick Spanish hot chocolate (thick as a pudding and eaten with a spoon) in bed every morning. The only time I ever saw Carlitos lose his quiet good nature was when little Lupe was sent home from school (for "indecent exposure") because she was wearing socks instead of stockings. The neighborhood was very quiet at night. All the doors in the district were locked after ten, and if you were out without a key and got home late, you had to stand in the street and wait for the *sereno* (the peripatetic watchmen who called the hours). He shouldered an assortment of immense brass front-door keys—one for every house on his beat. You gave him a couple of pesetas for letting you in. I considered myself well off in the low second-floor flat, but Madrid in winter is colder than New York and our only heat source was a portable charcoal-burning brazier. If you left it in the room very long with the windows closed, you could suffocate.

I met regularly with Ramón and the group. They reported progress and I encouraged and advised them. They thought I was more experienced than I was, probably because I represented Borodin, and accepted me as an authority. I counted heavily on Ramón and two others: Juan Andrade and the horribly ugly but adroit Virginìa González. We made headway—slowly. Though we detached one rather important trade union and party leader, Daniel Anguiano, the older members generally refused to listen. As a result, we looked to the young Socialists of the Juventud.

Borodin sent me instructions—and a little money—from Amsterdam. Ramón brought me exchange copies of socialist papers from all over the world. Feeling a desperate need to increase my knowledge of the movement, I gave myself a crash course. Among the books I read were a history of the First International and the 1871 split between Marx and Bakunin (whose anarchist influence persisted in Spain as nowhere else), Lenin's *Imperialism, the Last Stage of Capitalism,* and his *The State and Revolution* (all these in Spanish). In English, I read Trotsky's *The Bolsheviki and World Peace.* In Mexico Borodin had taught me Marxist theory as a guide to socialist action. On shipboard he had convinced me that, in a country like Russia, serious socialists had to be prepared to use arms. The two books of Leninist theory persuaded me that capitalism could not be overthrown peacefully anywhere. Lenin had issued a call for "professional revolutionists," and I now determined to regard myself as a revolutionist by profession.

Sometime in February I realized that a lack of funds was handicapping our work in Spain. Most of the Amsterdam money went to Carlitos for my board and lodging. I was sure Borodin would advance something for the work—if I could see him. He had left Amsterdam for an undisclosed address in Berlin, a way station for Second Congress delegates on the road to Moscow. (Many of them had to be dispatched secretly, for revolutionary Russia was practically blockaded. Its only open border was with the tiny Baltic country of Estonia, and anyone bound for there was automatically suspect.) I couldn't pay for a trip to Berlin but I could manage one from Madrid to Paris. Hoping to get help from sympathetic comrades there, I went directly to the office of a great socialist newspaper. Not the French party's official organ, *L'Humanité* (at that time right-wing and anti-Soviet), but the slightly leftish *Le Populaire,* edited by Jean Longuet (Marx's grandson). The rather elegant Longuet listened impassively and advised me to see Pierre Loriot, who headed a Committee for the Third International. I visited him and his chief lieutenant, Boris Souvarine—in jail. I think they might have helped me a lot, but I was a young unknown and my story sounded phony. As it was, they let me have the railroad fare to Zurich, third class, and suggested that I try to raise more there and go on to Berlin.

Near the station in Zurich I noticed the word *Arbeitersaal* on a store window. The men lounging inside directed me to a very rich socialist named Rosa Bloch, who, they said, was "practically a Bolshevik." She was a sour-looking spinster of fifty or so, an intellectual. I begged her not for an outright gift but for a loan. She laughed and said that if she gave me money she would never see or hear from me again. Then, surprisingly, she opened her purse and gave me not just the railroad fare to Berlin but enough for a week's living expenses, equal, I figured, to about twenty dollars.

Rosa Bloch must have been dumbfounded when the money came back to her by mail a few days later. I got it from Roy. I knew he had planned to stay with a Frau Lustig on Kurfürstendam while en route to Moscow. Though the congress was still five months off, it seems he had decided to spend a lot of time in Berlin. I found him installed in a very superior rooming house. Evelyn was with him—as later in Moscow—and Frau Lustig gave me a room next to theirs.

The Roys had an address for Borodin, and he took all of us out to dinner—at the most sumptuous restaurant in Berlin. Borodin promised me the money for Spain, after I explained that I wanted it in order to start a weekly paper and to establish a travel fund that would enable our people to cover the country. Leaving the restaurant, he patted me with his soft hand (affectionately, I thought), said "Goodbye until Moscow," and got into a cab alone. Two hundred dollars in American money was delivered to me, care of Roy, in the morning. A message said that the rest would be waiting for me (Jesús Ramírez of course) at a bank in Madrid. I caught a train for Madrid, via Paris, that afternoon.

In the Paris arrival station a husky fellow in the uniform of an American colonel grasped my arm and a familiar voice cried, "Well I'll be damned! What the hell are you doing here?" It was Herman Mankiewiez—Mank—the sometime friend of my Columbia days whose *Dynamite* spoofed our S. of J. radicalism. I told him I was just enjoying Europe, taking advantage of the cheap European currency. "Me too," he said. And then, "Charlie, the ambition of my life has been realized. I'm keeping an ex-*Follies* girl." Since I was in a hurry to catch the Paris-Madrid train at the Gare du Midi, he drove me there. On the way he informed me he was going back to the States soon to marry a sweet little Jewish girl in New York, Sarah something or other.

The weekly paper and the travel fund made a big difference. I promoted a Spanish Committee for the Third International, and our Juventud comrades built it into something of a force—with branches as widespread as Bilbao and Malaga. The party leadership maligned us, harassed us, and expelled Andrade and Merino Gracia. These expulsions served as our pretext for splitting the party. Although our group was tiny and made up almost entirely of youth, it was the basis of the Communist Party of Spain. In the meantime Merino Gracia was selected to attend the International congress as an "observer." The Catalonian CNT also sent an "observer" to the congress: Angel Pestaña, a strict anarcho-syndicalist.

By mid-June I had to get going myself. Rather than proceed by way of Paris as before, I started by sailing from Barcelona to Genoa. Exciting things were happening in Italy; militant workers were seizing factories, and I hoped to get a feel for the stituation *en passant*. Carlitos and Felicia gave me a *boina* (beret) as a going-away present; no well-traveled Spaniard could think to board ship without one.

Arriving in Genoa in June 1920 I found the city paralyzed by a just-declared Italian general strike. You had to get around on foot. At the city strike headquarters I was "a comrade from abroad." It was the same at Milan. The Italian "capitalist government" seemed powerless. The socialists were the largest group in parliament, and at the opening session they had shouted "Long live socialism!" instead of hailing the king. (Mussolini's first *Fascio di Combattimento* had surfaced but evidently no one took it seriously. I did not hear of it.)

In Berlin the comrades put me in touch with "Comrade Peter," the "transportation man" for delegates going to the Russian Soviet Federated Socialist Republic (not yet the "Union of Soviet Socialist Republics"). Every delegate to the Second Congress had to check in with this brushy-haired man with the tobacco-stained fingers. He took my Mexican Party credential and provided me with another, written on silk in Russian, and sewn into the sleeve of my jacket. Then he gave me travel money (pounds sterling) and discussed with me, in a mixture of German, French, and English, the best way to proceed. At his suggestion I decided to travel to Moscow via Stockholm.

I had to wait a week in Berlin for a Swedish visa. During that time I met Wilhelm Herzog, a leading intellectual of the USPD. The German Social Democratic Party (SPD) had been loyal to the Kaiser instead of to socialism during the war and now led the German government. Radical and revolutionary socialists had broken away from it, beginning in 1915 when the dispute over war aims led to the formation of the Independent Socialist Party of Germany (USPD). Later came the Spartakusbund of the martyred Karl Liebknecht and Rosa Luxemburg, and its more or less direct descendant, the Communist Party of Germany (KPD). Herzog and his movie actress wife introduced me to Hilda Kramer, nicknamed *Dubiner* (Russian for lamppost), who had been secretary to the *Stadtkommandant* of Munich during the short-lived Bavarian Red Republic. A tall, statuesque beauty, she certainly did not deserve the nickname lamppost. Hilda and I had a convulsive three-day affair, which we resumed during my next visit to Berlin. Among other things she taught me quite a bit of German; I wish I could have remembered it all!

The problem of course was to get into Estonia, where nobody went but spies, speculators, and the big-city newspaper correspondents stationed at Revel, the capital. (At that time newspapermen were generally not admitted to Russia.) Estonia granted few visas, even from Stockholm, and did so only after one had waited weeks, or months, for Revel's okay. My *Heraldo de México* card got me an immediate interview with the Mexican minister to Sweden and, claiming to be a Mexican citizen on special assignment, I asked him to persuade his friend the Estonian minister to Sweden to issue me a visa without formalities. Obviously this was an astonishing request, all the more so because I had made it in rehearsed Spanish and evaded every attempt at superfluous conversation. The average Mexican in my place could have achieved nothing, but the power of the press—plus General Alvarado—was mesmeric. The minister might have checked up on me with Mexico City, but he didn't. While I sat there he telephoned the Estonian Legation and implored a hurry-up visa for an old friend for whom he could vouch personally. I had my visa in an hour and was sailing the Baltic for Revel that day.[4]

In 1920 a Soviet Trade Mission and a Soviet Diplomatic Mission, with innumerable auxiliary personnel, inhabited a converted warehouse in the ancient capital. I produced my silk credential and immediately found myself the center of excitement. Comrades came running from all over the place to embrace me. Not just a foreign comrade but a delegate, and one who had come all the way from remote Mexico! It was a great day for them as servants of the summoning power; my presence there seemed proof that this Third International thing was real! As for me, the greeting I received in Revel was a confirmation of my faith in Soviet Russia as a socialist homeland. We drank vodka, then tea, then vodka again. They taught me to sing (!?) "The Internationale" in Russian. The silk credential was sewn back into my sleeve, and I was informed that Petrograd had okayed me (by wire) for travel.

For obvious reasons my passport showed no visa for Soviet Russia, but one needed an exit visa to leave Estonia in any case. When the Estonian Foreign Office turned down my request, I boarded the through train to Petrograd anyway. When we arrived at the border station of Narva, however, an inspector made me get off, and the train went on into Russia without me—hauled by a Soviet engine. The Estonian locomotive and tender had been detached at Narva and the Estonian crew replaced. Standing beside the barnlike station of unpainted logs, the inspector told me I would have to return to Revel. While he was talking to me (in German), I noticed on a side track a locomotive marked with a red star and some Russian letters, evidently preparing to back away toward the border. Its wheels moved a bit, then stopped, then moved again, then seemed to hesitate. A fireman was feeding it fuel from a tender loaded with logs. Handing my suitcase to the

---

4. Revel is not an Estonian but a Russian name. Peter the Great conquered the country in the early seventeenth century, incorporated it into the Russian Empire, and tried in vain to Russify it. In 1918 it had declared itself an independent republic, and while I was there Revel resumed its ancient name, Tallinn.

inspector and remarking that I was hungry, I walked to the station's restaurant. Inside were tables and chairs and a long counter, and on a shelf behind it stood a samovar and a huge pyramid of hard-boiled eggs, miscellaneous cheeses, fresh rolls and butter, hot and cold meats, fruits, cakes, nuts. An amazing and significant display of Estonian plenty. I took it all in with half an eye as I walked slowly past, going in one door and out the other. Then I ran as fast as I could to the Russian locomotive and jumped on. It was traveling backwards. A flagman on the cowcatcher held out a hand to me, laughing. We crossed the bridge over the Narva River and were in Soviet Russia.

After a few hundred yards the locomotive stopped. The flagman turned me over to two smartly uniformed border guards who wore red star armbands. Without a word to me, expressionless, they conducted me to a log-built shelter and delivered me to their commandant. He was seated at a small table with a telephone and a rusty samovar on it. Soldiers with red star armbands lounged about. Portraits of Lenin, Trotsky, and Marx ornamented the otherwise bare walls. The officer plainly did not know what to think of me. He knew nothing about me except that I had jumped on the locomotive. Neither he nor any of his men spoke any language other than Russian. In this emergency I pointed meaningfully at my sleeve. They took my jacket off and found the credential. At that the commandant got up from the table, put his arms around me, and kissed me. He made a telephone call—a long one—while an orderly served me weak tea.

16   In Soviet Russia

The commandant interrupted his telephone conversation and handed the phone to me. A high-pitched voice addressed me in German. It was *tovarishch* Grigori Zinoviev, no less, speaking from

Petrograd.[1] After a few businesslike inquiries—how I got to Estonia, who gave me the silk credential, and so on—he said simply, "*Sie können fahren*" ("You can travel"). In less than an hour, my head in the stratosphere, I was on my way to Petrograd.

At last I was going to see firsthand what it was like to live in a country where the dictatorship of the capitalist class had been displaced by the dictatorship of the working class, as a prelude to the liquidation of all classes. Moreover, I was going to join with anticapitalists from all over the world in building an international revolutionary alliance to supersede the broken and disgraced Second International. Clearly, then, the trip was critical to me.

The commandant sent me off on a freight train, the only transportation available, with an orderly, the brisk young Comrade Stepan. Along with a detachment of soldiers, we squatted around a samovar on the floor of an open box car. They immediately offered us tea, and we got along beautifully in sign language. The train traveled slowly through forest country. Stops were frequent, and the soldiers always took the opportunity to find hot water to replenish the samovar. At one stop the train crew got out to chop down trees for fuel. Everybody helped carry the logs.

When we arrived, finally, at Petrograd's historic Finland Station, my solicitous orderly hurried me past the armed sailors patrolling the platform and through a packed waiting room to a one-horse open carriage (*droshky*) in the cobbled front plaza. Among the mob in and overflowing the station I noticed many off-duty soldiers. Unlike the natty soldiers encountered at the frontier, they wore shoddy, ill-fitting uniforms—and for some a red armband was all the uniform they could muster. Civilians were even more dowdy, but everywhere there was a wonderful air of good humor and friendliness.

Since the eighteenth century, Petrograd had been Russia's political, cultural, and social capital. A glittering modern city with

---

1. Grigori Yevseyevich Zinoviev, born Radomylsky, joined the Bolshevik Party before the Revolution of 1905, was elected to the Central Committee in 1907, and was close to Lenin in his years of exile before 1917. He and Kamenev would unite against Trotsky in the 1920s, only to be defeated by Stalin late in 1925. Zinoviev was removed from the Politburo in 1926 and expelled from the Central Committee in 1927. In August 1936 Zinoviev was tried, convicted, and executed in the first of the Moscow Trials.

industrial suburbs, it had seen the first act of what soon became a vast social and political revolution. As a result, the solidly organized Petrograd section of the Bolshevik Party had disproportionate influence throughout both the party and the new Soviet state. A few months before I arrived the political capital had been moved to Moscow because Petrograd was exposed to invasion. A strong German army (encouraged by the Entente allies) was still entrenched in nearby Finland, and the White army of General N. N. Yudenich had penetrated to the city's southern suburbs in the summer of 1919.

The prewar Petrograd population of over two million was much depleted. The wooden pavement of the famous Nevsky Prospekt had been torn up in many places, and the luxury shops and palatial homes were boarded up and closed. But our droshky soon entered an area vibrant with life and stopped before a large rectangular building draped with red bunting. This was the Smolny Institute, the former finishing school for daughters of the nobility that had been requisitioned for soviet headquarters during the revolution. Now it was a labyrinth full of scurrying figures in well-worn leather jackets and blouses, many of them unbuttoned at the throat. Soldiers were everywhere, and I was struck by the atmosphere of the place, which combined the informality appropriate to a proletarian regime with the strict discipline of a revolutionary dictatorship. You needed a *propusk* (pass) to get in and you had to show it on each floor.

Stepan, with propusks for both of us, swept me up three flights of stairs and direct to Comrade Zinoviev, head of the Petrograd Soviet, and Comrade Angelica Balabanoff, a tiny woman with a lined face and graying hair who had been named acting general secretary of the new Third International. They welcomed me unceremoniously, examined and kept my credential, and gave me a identity card, a special propusk, and a ration card. Also a stack of newly printed rubles—in denominations of 10,000 and up! (The presses were working overtime and if, as was said, the Bolsheviks intended to destroy the value of money, they were certainly succeeding.) Zinoviev, in his mid-thirties, was pudgy, puffy, and womanish in appearance. With his squeaky voice and limp handshake, he seemed disappointingly unimpressive. Nevertheless, he was one of Lenin's closest collaborators.

We did not "do" Petrograd. Stepan had orders to deposit me in Moscow safely and fast, and he wasn't taking any chances. We got on the overnight special, a crack train with wagon-lits and a prewar luxury dining car. Though the setting was ornate, supper was a dish of soup and some black bread, which Stepan paid for with meal tickets. In Moscow he delivered me to the comrade manager of the Hotel Delovoi Dvor, then saluted, embraced me, and departed. I had become fond of Stepan in our wordless companionship. I never saw him again.

Deep in the Russian heartland, Moscow may have been secure from invasion, but it had been the center of feudal power in the country, and was a backward place, both socially and culturally. The medieval walled city of the Kremlin was the most incongruous of sites for the headquarters of the Workers and Peasants Republic. The Kremlin itself, a fortified city within a city, had been built up over the centuries by the grand princes of Muscovy and the first Romanov tsars. On its south was "the moat" of the Moskva River; to the east stretched the great Red Square. When I was there, the mighty bell in the Kremlin clock tower sounded the music of "The Internationale" three times a day. The song resounded throughout Moscow, and hearing it was an overwhelming experience. (In 1942 the bell stopped playing "The Internationale" and began to ring out Stalin's new *national* anthem.)

The Delovoi Dvor, which had once catered to rich merchants and their families, was now reserved for Second Congress delegates, special guests, and auxiliary personnel. Propusks were required—both coming and going—and two sentries guarded the entrance. The comrade manager assigned me an octagon-shaped room as vast as a meeting hall. The ceiling was maybe eighteen feet high, and six tall casement windows with thick, dusty drapes lined its walls. Furnishings included a built-in mahogany wardrobe, double bed, sofa, numerous chairs, and family-sized round table covered in red felt. On the table lay a shiny leather briefcase stuffed thick with pamphlets, news bulletins, notices of various kinds, and writing materials and supplies.

This was my first "free" moment in the RSFSR (Russian Socialist Federal Soviet Republic), and I took advantage of it to go out for a leisurely look around. Even "downtown" and on important avenues like the broad Tverskaya, there was a curious stillness, the effect of the almost complete absence of vehicular traffic. Like everyone else, I found myself walking in the middle of the cobbled street. The commercial buildings looked uncared for, uninhabited, and store windows had nothing to display. But the street was full of people—sauntering, plodding, striding, pushing. Leather jackets accompanied by briefcases, peasant blouses and cloth caps. Shoes and boots were invariably scruffy, and feet were sometimes wrapped in rags. Unadorned and without makeup, women were nondescript in coarse old clothes. Despite the drabness of the scene, however, its universally "proletarian" quality was somehow reassuring. At a crossing I saw a battered trolley car so crowded that passengers were hanging from the windows. I joined a line waiting for the next car. It was a long line, and I waited nearly an hour. The crowd's patience, orderliness, and good fellowship impressed me. Nobody complained, nobody tried to get ahead of his neighbor. Eventually I squeezed onto a platform and rode the length of the route. And there was no fare to pay. Amid all the discomfort a foretaste of the millennium!

Although I had been given rubles, their function as a means of exchange was very limited. Fortunately, I did not have to rely on them. My *delegat* (delegate) status procured me a requisition of clothes at one of the government's priority warehouses, and I outfitted myself with underwear, boots, Russian blouses—thereby replacing what I had left behind in Estonia. The general population could buy at fixed (low) prices in government stores, but only on ration. Indeed, the true medium of exchange was the ration allowance. People with work cards received free meal tickets, lived in their (admittedly cramped) quarters rent-free, had access to free medical and dental clinics, free admission to amusement parks and theaters, and so on. Private industry, recognized as such, existed only in the rare shops run by self-employed artisans. Here and there in the street peasant women sold cucumbers or cherries brought in from the country, and little boys (disturbingly ragged) peddled cigarettes made from a harsh tobacco substitute called *mahorca*. Otherwise, except for a certain amount of barter, "trade" meant "speculation." A severely punishable offense, it was nonetheless tolerated in a petty way in places like the open-air

Sukharovka Market—where shadows of men and women offered old clothing, jewelry, family silverware, icons, and whatever—one of a kind.

This was the economy of rationed scarcity which Lenin later characterized as War Communism. Though the Civil War was all but won, the RSFSR was an embattled citadel. Baron P. N. Wrangel's White army still held on in the Ukraine. József Pilsudski's Poles, with French weapons and France's General Maxime Weygand, were making serious inroads on the Soviet western front. Inside the country counterrevolutionary plotting and sabotage persisted. The revolution had had no chance to begin creating a new and productive society. From my first day in Moscow I saw things that disconcerted and appalled me, but I told myself that they were a temporary anomaly. Overall, I thought, things looked great: the evidence of purposeful, shared hardship exhilarated me.

Our meals at the Delovoi Dvor were not very special. We used to reiterate with the hotel staff: "*Sevodnia kasha, zavtra shchi*" (Today we'll have kasha, tomorrow cabbage soup). We received an allowance of black bread, occasionally some dried herring, and sometimes there was a bit of meat in the soup. I always got up from the table hungry.

Except for the staff and auxiliary personnel I was practically alone in the hotel at first, but Roy and Evelyn showed up a day or two after me. Thus "Mexico" was represented early, well before the end of June! We three hunted up Borodin and found him living in the elegant mansion of a former "sugar king" directly across the river from the Kremlin. With him were Lev Karakhan, Soviet vice-commissar of foreign affairs, and Jacques Sadoul, a charming French army captain who had defected and was now being entertained as a distinguished guest of the Soviet state. Borodin, mysterious as ever, was apparently doing important work in Moscow. I was told he had a private telephone line to Lenin. He greeted us warmly, commended us particularly to Karakhan and Sadoul, and gave us much of his time before, during, and after the congress.

Delegates began arriving in batches early in July. From Germany came the aged and revered Klara Zetkin, who had known Engels and was closely identified with the martyred Rosa Luxemburg and Karl Liebknecht. From Hungary came Bela Kun, hero of the 1919

Revolutionary Proletarian Government, and his top associates: Mátyás Rákosi, Georg Lukács, Eugen Varga. From Italy there were Antonio Gramsci, the man who had inspired numerous factory takeovers, and Palmiro Togliatti (using the pseudonym Ercoli), destined to become undisputed leader of the most powerful Communist Party in Western Europe. There were dissimilarities, even antagonisms, within the various groups. The large German delegation was typical, it included Reichstag and ex-Reichstag members, trade union leaders, Marxist scholars, representatives of the KPD, KAPD, and USPD, nonparty street fighters—and at least one anarchist!

The heterogeneous French delegation included two big fishes who had originally opposed the formation of a new International: Marcel Cachin, editor of *L'Humanité*, the official organ of the Socialist Party of France, and L. O. Frossard, the party secretary. Both boasted long records as right-wingers (Cachin, in fact, had been a "war socialist"), but now, to my bewilderment, they declared themselves champions of the Soviet revolution. At the opposite end of the ideological spectrum stood Pierre Loriot and Boris Souvarine, founders of the French Committee for the Third International and my reluctant benefactors of a few months back. Contrary to expectations they did not play much of a role at the congress.

Spain, to my chagrin, was essentially unrepresented. Angel Pestaña, the Barcelona anarcho-syndicalist "observer," arrived during the sessions, but our Communist Party delegate, Merino Gracia, failed to make it in time. (When he did get to Moscow he was invited to meetings of the International's newly established Executive Committee.) I gravitated toward English-speaking delegates: John (Jack) Reed, Louis C. Fraina, and Jimmy Gilday among the Americans, Jack Murphy and Willie Gallacher among the British. We used to congregate, pre-congress, in Roy's room. Evelyn poured the tea, and Borodin sometimes dropped in. Another guest was wrinkled old Sen Katayama, the legendary veteran of Japanese labor who had journeyed to the United States and stayed there for twelve years. He was active with the American Socialist Party's left wing in 1917. Once Borodin brought big, burly Vladimir Mayakovsky, then the darling poet of the Soviet regime, in 1930 a disillusioned suicide.

The American delegation was a hodgepodge of four delegations. Louis Fraina headed one group from a body that called itself the Communist Party of America, while Jack Reed represented the rival Communist Labor Party. Actually the Communist Labor Party had by now merged into a United Communist Party (UCP), but both Fraina and Reed arrived in Moscow unaware of this development. The UCP sent a representative of its own named Edward I. Lindgren. Jimmy Gilday represented the IWW (Industrial Workers of the World).

Reed and Fraina were personal opposites. Jack was a hulking and adventurous American glamor boy out of the Pacific Northwest via Harvard and Greenwich Village. A crack journalist and emotional radical, he had been half socialist, half anarchist until November 1917. His firsthand experience of the "ten days that shook the world" crystallized his political stance and made him an idol of the emerging American Communist movement. Jack remained boyish to the end, whereas undersized, astigmatic Louis, born near Naples and transported to the New York slums at the age of three, seemed never to have had any boyhood at all. Stiffly intellectual (but self-taught), he was essentially a dogmatist—a gifted one, however. In his teens he'd been a redoubtable revolutionary Marxist; at twenty he led the Socialist Party's prewar left wing. The outstanding antecedent figure of American communism, Fraina was now somewhat under a cloud. Shortly before leaving New York for Moscow, he had been accused of being an agent provocateur in the pay of the U.S. Department of Justice. A Communist "court" exonerated him, but news of the charge preceded him to Moscow. Two investigating committees now exonerated him again, one just before the congress opened, the other after it had closed. Their decisions were unanimous, and Fraina's status was finally assured.

On arriving from abroad, each foreign delegate found in his hotel room a thickly stuffed briefcase like the one I described. Among the contents was a new pamphlet by Lenin which was destined to prove as important as anything he ever wrote. The English version bore the clumsily rendered title *The Infantile Sickness of Leftism in Communism*, which has since been variously rendered as *Left Communism: An Infantile Disorder*, *Left Communism*, and simply *Ultra-Leftism*. In its pages Lenin ridiculed two tactics common to the revolutionary labor movement, tactics that many counted as articles of faith: abstention from "bourgeois parliaments," and abstention from work in such established "reactionary labor organizations" as the American Federation of Labor and the British Labour Party.

Delegates were open-mouthed, almost scandalized as they read the pamphlet. Any author but Lenin—the expounder, organizer, and engineer of revolution—they would have proclaimed an arrant opportunist. Throughout the world the Bolsheviks stood for "direct action" as opposed to the bread-and-butter tactics of trade unionism, and for workers' councils (soviets) as opposed to parliaments. In country after country revolutionists had been encouraged to split and again to split, rather than remain minorities within "backward" labor organizations. Wasn't the Second Congress itself the result of a split within the Second International?

If ultra-leftism was a disease, then a lot of the arriving delegates had caught it—myself included. We had never dreamed it was possible to be "too left." The idea was to be as far left as you dared. That was the way to the revolution.

17 Lenin, Trotsky, and a Historic Congress

Lenin assailed our cherished "left" principles unmercifully, and without advance warning. His timing was significant. The Bolsheviks had believed that the October Revolution would be followed by successful proletarian revolutions throughout Western Europe. Lenin had predicted them in 1918, in 1919, and even in early 1920. Had he been right, *The Infantile Sickness of Leftism in Communism* would never have been written. Seeing that he had been wrong and realizing that the majority of workers everywhere still followed their old leaders, he concluded that Communist policies had to change, to adapt themselves to a slower world revolutionary tempo. This was classic Lenin: though stubborn, he could reverse abruptly when he felt the situation demanded it.

Maintaining that the reactionary labor organizations must be treated as enemies, the Americans and the British resisted. Willie Gallacher (who was eventually to become the first Communist MP) protested: "You cannot demand from us that we should work against and speak against that which we have spent years struggling for." But that was precisely what Lenin now demanded, with irrefutable logic. The nub was that serious revolutionists belonged among the mass organizations of workers, ipso facto, the Labour Party in Britain and the conservative trade union federations both there and in the United States. Eventually we were convinced—all of us except John Reed. In love with the small but militant IWW, Jack could not bring himself to accept the A.F. of L., not even in order to bore away from within and eventually capture it. Against all pressure, he maintained his position to the end, writing home to say that "nobody in Russia or Europe seems to understand industrial unionism."

The Russian population worked five and a half days a week, taking a half-holiday on Saturday. In late 1919, as I recollect, some miner or metalworker, on his own initiative or in response to suggestion, volunteered to give up his half-holiday and to work that Saturday afternoon, without pay, as a donation to the Proletarian Fatherland. The Soviet press lauded him and exhorted others to follow his example. They did, and *Pravda* and *Izvestiia* carried prideful reports of voluntary Saturday workgangs, *subbotniks*, that carried out specially assigned tasks. Someone organized a subbotnik of the RSFSR's various foreign guests, including Second Congress delegates, and we marched off with fanfare to work on road repair outside Moscow. I walked between Jack Reed and Jacques Sadoul. At the head of the line Nicolà Bombacci, an exuberant Italian with a long curly beard, began to sing "Bandiera Rossa" ("Bandiera Rossa trionferà, Bandiera Rossa trionferà, evviva il socialismo e la Libertà . . ."). The rest of us joined in as well as we could. We all sang "La Carmagnole" in French ("Rase, Rase, Rase,

Rase, tous les bourgeois . . ."); "Hold the Fort" in English; and "The Internationale" in a mélange of languages. Our subbotnik turned out to be a token affair; after ten minutes we were dismissed with thanks and bussed back to the Delovoi Dvor.

The congress convened on July 17, 1920, with a ceremonial opening in Petrograd, "the cradle of the Revolution." The arrangements were calculated to impress the local population on the one hand and us on the other. There were special trains, and a parade from the Finland Station through cheering crowds to the Winter Palace, the Field of Martyrs of the Revolution, and finally the Tauride Palace. The route was protected by long lines of workers holding hands. At the Tauride Palace, we had lunch with Lenin, Zinoviev, N. I. Bukharin, Karl Radek, and Maxim Gorky, followed by picture taking. (One of the pictures—with me in it—hangs on my wall today.)

The opening session of the congress was held in Petrograd's Opera House auditorium, today's Kirov. A 200-piece band played "The Internationale" as we marched to our seats on the deep stage. The session consisted of addresses to the (no doubt carefully selected) audience by Lenin and Zinoviev in Russian and by Marcel Cachin in French. Everyone rose for Lenin. He was a short, stocky, bald, slant-eyed man of fifty, a reddish bit of beard on his jutting chin. He spoke simply, unaffectedly—almost without gesture—but with mesmeric concentration. His short legs spread and his almond eyes sharp, he was an intense, vigorous, earthy, confident, utterly compelling figure. Without understanding a word, I was moved. The faces in front were shining.

Back in Moscow, regular sessions began in the Vladimir Throne Room of the Kremlin's Imperial Palace. Both Lenin and Trotsky participated, along with Bukharin, Radek, M. P. Tomsky, M. I. Kalinin, A. V. Lunacharsky, A. I. Rykov, Christian Rakovsky, G. Y. Sokolnikov, and some twenty other top Soviet leaders.[1] The Russian delegation, far larger than any other, had sixty-four delegates in all.

---

1. Stalin was not among them. During all my time in the RSFSR I would not have known of Stalin's existence except for one mention of his name. We used to speculate on the possible successor to Lenin if he should die. Nearly everybody said Trotsky. But an English-speaking Russian delegate at the congress (not an important one) remarked to me, "It just might be a comrade called Joseph Stalin." He may have been lining up his support even then.

Lenin with group of delegates and adherents outside the Tauride Palace, Petrograd, July 17, 1920, a few hours before the ceremonial opening of the Second Congress of the Third (Communist) International. Group includes Radek (3d from left), with Bukharin; Gorky (just behind Lenin), and (next to him) Zinoviev. Behind Zinoviev and to his left are the two delegates from the Mexican Communist Party: "Jesús Ramírez" and "M. N. Roy." Next to Roy is Lenin's sister, Maria Ulianova.

Zinoviev acted as temporary chairman of the congress, and a first order of business was to select a permanent chairman. One of the Italian delegates proposed Lenin, but he declined. Trotsky, nominated next, declined also. At that point I thought one of the illustrious delegates from Western Europe should be chosen. Others thought so too, but while we were weighing various names a Russian delegate rose to nominate Zinoviev. Another Russian delegate seconded, and a third moved that the choice be made unanimous. With the Russians obviously solid for Zinoviev, no one was disposed to object, but it was an unpopular choice. Zinoviev was

111

practically unknown outside Russia, and what we delegates had seen of the shrill and arrogant bureaucrat was hardly to our liking.

Zinoviev owed his Bolshevik status to Lenin's indulgence. He had been with Lenin at Zimmerwald and Kienthal and was his right-hand man throughout the prerevolutionary period. But in the fall of 1917 when Lenin called for the insurrection that was to bring the Bolsheviks to power, Zinoviev, along with L. B. Kamenev, had proved a backslider. They had termed Lenin's plan "adventurism" and written to oppose it in a non-Party paper. Lenin denounced them then as traitors, but readmitted them to the Party leadership when they regretted their "mistake" after the success of the October insurrection. Zinoviev was now again apparently the closest to Lenin of all the Old Bolsheviks. (But on his deathbed, in the secret document known as Lenin's Testament, Lenin warned that the Zinoviev-Kamenev "mistake" in 1917 had been "no accident.")

The only Bolshevik leaders known abroad in the summer of 1920 were Lenin and Trotsky; indeed, people spoke of them as a unit: Lenin-and-Trotsky. They symbolized the revolution, personified the Soviet state. Inside Russia—particularly within the Party—one spoke of Lenin alone. At every turn of its extraordinary career, he and he alone willed the Party, indoctrinated it, conditioned it, energized it, rallied it, and commanded it. Lenin's authority was unique and indisputable. But second place belonged unquestionably to Trotsky.

Trotsky was not an Old Bolshevik. At twenty-six he had been a great mass leader—chairman of the St. Petersburg Soviet during the abortive 1905 Revolution. In his years of exile he proved a stubbornly individual Marxist disputant, and periodically aspired to reconcile Bolsheviks and Mensheviks. He aligned himself with the Bolsheviks in the midst of the postwar revolutionary struggle—in July of 1917—when their position was desperate and the risk extreme. And in the fall of that year he emerged as the on-the-spot leader of the victorious October insurrection. In the uncertain months that followed he was the architect of the four-million-man Red Army, the strategist of its victory in the Civil War, and the wizard who brought order from the chaos of the Russian railroad system. Trotsky always lacked Lenin's realism, and Lenin's acute sense of the popular mood.[2] But he had an ability to inspire masses, a brilliant intellect, great oratorical skill, courage and dedication, and a remarkable talent for organization. He was now at the zenith of his power, popularity, and fame.

None of the pictures I had seen of Trotsky showed him as he was. I found him much taller than I'd expected, with a superb martial bearing, a powerful chest, and eyes that were incandescent behind his pince-nez. He was forty-one years old (nine years younger than Lenin) and had jet black hair and a small black goatee. He attended only a few of the sessions, speaking briskly, always to the point, in elegant French or German. Though he knew English well, he never used it because his speech would have had to be translated, by himself or an interpreter, three times; the three official languages of the congress were German, French, and Russian. Lenin, too, used French and German; for few delegates from abroad understood Russian and he wanted to speak to as many as possible directly. Zinoviev and Radek used German; Bukharin, French, but nearly all the other RSFSR delegates spoke in Russian only. Most of the Italians made their speeches in Italian, the Poles in Polish, and so on.

---

2. Trotsky, then People's Commissar for Foreign Affairs, headed the Russian delegation in the 1917 Brest-Litovsk peace negotiations. Believing the moral effect of the revolution had been such that the Germans would be unable to force their troops to move against Russia, he met the harsh German demands with the statement that Russia would not sign a treaty on such terms, but that she considered the war at an end and would demobilize. This was on February 10. A week later, with the German troops advancing, a bitterly divided Central Committee voted to inform the Germans that Russia was willing to conclude peace on the terms previously rejected. On February 23 the committee met to consider the German reply—which was an ultimatum containing still harsher terms. Trotsky, backed by Bukharin and others, then proposed fighting "a revolutionary war." Lenin said this would amount to "waving a pasteboard sword," and declared he would leave the Central Committee and the government if the terms were not accepted. Stalin suggested they could "refrain from signing but reopen peace negotiations." Lenin replied: "We can't refrain. Those terms have to be signed. If you do not sign them you will sign the Soviet regime's death warrant in three weeks." Lenin's motion passed by a vote of seven to four—but with four abstentions. Lenin announced that the Russian soldiers were voting for peace. To the objection that there was no voting, he replied: "They are voting with their feet; they are running away from the front."

Since there was no such thing as simultaneous renderings via earphones, the congress—sometimes in recess for one reason or another—lasted nearly three weeks.

At the very start of the proceedings, Jack Reed got the floor. Speaking for himself and twenty-nine others, he made two proposals: that the official languages include English, and that "the trade union question" (he was thinking of IWW versus A.F. of L.) be placed near the top of the agenda. Zinoviev overruled him on both counts and he lost in a defiant appeal from the chair. (It was the only appeal from the chair throughout the congress.)

Since a new, presumptively worldwide organization would emerge from this congress, we needed to make a declaration of principles and to formulate the rules and regulations that would guide the new International in practice. This, then, was our first order of business. Most of us had come to Moscow with no well-thought-out notion of the shape of the new organization. Perhaps it would be like the Second International in structure (a loose association of independent organizations, one or more from each country), but truer to the international commitment to oppose both capitalism and all forms of "social patriotism." What came out of the congress was very different from that. The new organization was designed to be, as the Russians liked to say, "the general staff" of the international class struggle. The program incorporated the revolutionary concepts of the Bolshevik Party, lately renamed the Communist Party; and the Third International became the Communist International, or Comintern.

The new rules stipulated that the International would contain but one group or party per country, and that each would be accepted only if it adhered strictly to the so-called Twenty-one Conditions. Perhaps the most fundamental of those conditions (no. 16) held that "all the decisions of the congresses of the Communist International, as well as the decisions of its Executive Committee, are binding on all parties affiliated to the Communist International."[3]

---

3. For the complete text of the Twenty-one Conditions, see Helmut Gruber, ed., *International Communism in the Era of Lenin* (New York: Anchor, 1972), pp. 241–46.

Of course there were objections, some of which I shared, and confrontations, too. Marx was quoted to justify and oppose, and accusatory labels were traded back and forth: "Kautskyist," "Bakuninist," "Centrist," "Conspiratorialist." Individual members of some delegations differed with one another, but the Russians always spoke and voted as a unit. They were tremendously—overwhelmingly—effective, and in the end most of us were convinced that the Twenty-one Conditions were essential.

Events have shown that, for better or worse, the results of this first debate would alone have made the Second Congress a historic one. But it was only a beginning. The agenda included the Question of Parliamentarianism, the Trade Union Question, the Colonial Question, and so on. Then there was the matter of electing an Executive Committee for the Communist International, and the question of where it should make its headquarters. Everything was discussed exhaustively, on and off the floor. A neophyte among these veteran protagonists of the labor struggle, I assayed the floor only once—and then in Spanish.

We saw less of the charismatic but sternly aloof Trotsky than we would have liked; for he was called away after the vote on the Twenty-one Conditions and returned only toward the end of the congress. Undoubtedly the war with Marshal Pilsudski's Poland claimed his attention. Despite all the demands upon him as head of the government, however, Lenin signaled that the congress had a high priority by participating pretty much throughout—arguing, insisting, smiling, and screwing up his eyes in his characteristic way. Now and then he climbed down from his seat on the dais, scurried up the aisle, whispered something in a delegate's ear, and then slipped back to his place. Throughout, he was completely unself-conscious.

While separate interpreters were repeating long speeches in different languages (with varying fidelity to the original), half the congress drifted into an adjoining reception room to smoke, to confer, and, when snacks were available, to eat. There I got to know a number of Soviet leaders fairly well, especially N. I. Bukharin and Karl Radek. Both were young and both were fluent in English. Bukharin was a diminutive, disarmingly sportive man, "the darling of the Party" and its most respected theoretician next to Lenin. Always a charming conversationalist, he was full of anecdotes from his days of exile in Vienna, Zurich, Paris, and New York. He had lively blue eyes, a slightly turned-up nose, and a high forehead. Prematurely balding at the temples, he was only thirty-two years old in 1920.

Radek, thirty-four, was a tall, thin Polish Jew. He had grown up in the socialist movements of Poland, underground Russia, and Germany, and—on Moscow's instructions—he had gone to Berlin in 1919 and helped to direct the Spartacist rising (chance saved him from the fate of Luxemburg and Liebknecht). He was daring and nervous, staccato in both speech and walk, and famous for his devilish, sometimes savagely sarcastic wit. The RSFSR's most sophisticated pamphleteer and propagandist, Radek had myopic eyes rimmed by thick-lensed glasses in a tortoise-shell frame. With his thick lips and the outlandish fringe of brown beard that rounded his chin from ear to ear, he might well have been (probably sometimes was) called "Monkey-face."

The reception room featured a large wall map studded with movable pins which kept delegates up-to-date on Russia's war with Pilsudski's Poland. After a series of severe Soviet defeats, the tide had turned and the Red Army was in Polish territory, expecting soon to capture Warsaw. A Polish proletarian dictatorship was already being assembled in Moscow, and Radek was to be its commissar of foreign affairs. When Louis Fraina and I entered the reception room one day and saw Radek briefing admirers, Fraina called out, "Hello, Machiavelli!" Radek thanked him for "the compliment" and said he'd just put a copy of Machiavelli's *History of Florence* into his suitcase "for ready reference in Warsaw." He never got there. Backed up onto their own soil, the Poles rallied to Pilsudski en masse, and the first Soviet attempt at "revolution by conquest" ended in a rout.

Like every delegate, I longed for a personal interview with Lenin. Chances of getting squeezed into his awesome schedule seemed slim, but I requested an appointment anyway in a note written on September 11 (see Figure 1). Eventually I got a message that named a time for our meeting. A Kremlin automobile called for "Comrade Ramírez," whisked me through the Kremlin gates without being stopped for the customary propusk examination, and deposited me at an ancient but renovated building that stood off by itself. I had to show my propusk to the armed guard in front, and to others at var-

From the Delegate of the
Communist Party of Mexico

Moscow, Delovoi Dvor Hotel,
No 216,
11 September 1920

Dear Comrade Lenin!
Next week I must leave for home, and before my departure I would
like to discuss with you the situation in Mexico and Spain. Would
this be possible?

With communist greetings,

Jesús Ramírez
delegate of
the Communist Party of Mexico
at the Second Congress of
the Communist International

Figure 1. Note from "Jesús Ramírez" to V. I. Lenin. From *Pis'ma V. I. Leninu iz za rubezha* (Moscow: Mysl', 1966), p. 146.

ious stages along my escorted progress inside: in and out of the elevator, down long halls, through numerous busy workrooms. I was
asked to wait at a heavy oak door while my escort disappeared inside. In a minute he opened the door and led me into an office, obviously Lenin's. He left me there alone, closing the door after him.
It was a spacious, airy office, but businesslike. I saw a battery of tele-
phones, a neat pile of papers on a polished desk, a wall map of the
world, pictures of Marx and Engels, a bookcase, chairs for visitors;
near a window sat a short "love seat" sofa.

Lenin came in through a side door. He shook hands warmly,
and we sat down together on the sofa. As he leaned toward me,
his largish domed head very close, I was struck by the contrast between his fair, freckled skin and his Tatar-like cheekbones and
slanted eyes. (Lenin's family came from the Kazan region where

117

there was much Tatar blood.)[4] One of his eyes closed from time to time, suggesting that he may have been having trouble with it. Wasting no time on conventional preliminaries, he said he was seeing me because I was from the Mexican Party. He knew that Mexico had had a bourgeois revolution and that the peasants were demanding land, but was vague on the role our Party was playing—or not playing. What could I tell him? Could he be of help? His information on the country was—frankly—fragmentary. He had not known that much of the peasant population was Indian. Did we have any literature in the Indian dialects? (No. The Indians were illiterate.) Then we would have to recruit Indian speakers. Those Indians, he said, should be your number-one objective in the countryside. (This was a wise observation, and I relayed it to Alfonso Santibañez and José Valadés in my next letter.) The rest of his remarks emphasized Mexico's strategic location in the Western Hemisphere. Everything he said made a contribution, and it all revealed the same simple, forceful logic. He was unself-conscious, concentrated, obviously concerned; it was easy to see why people who did not hate him fell in love with him. I think I did.

He had started the conversation in French, explaining that he had never learned Spanish. Then he recalled that Borodin had told him I was American, and switched to English. He said his English was rather poor—and it was. But it was better than my French. He told me about a book of his on American agriculture, which he had written some years back. It was currently available in Russian only, but if I was interested he would ask someone to go through it with me. He believed it probably should be translated, unless I thought it was out of date.

Casual though he appeared, Lenin had trained himself to conserve his energies and his time. He was quite un-Russian in being invariably punctual. (Trotsky was too.) My interview lasted fifteen or twenty minutes. When the time was up Lenin shook my hand

4. The region is now called Ulianovsk, as is the former Simbirsk, his native town on the Volga. Lenin was born Vladimir Il'ich Ulianov. When he first took the name Lenin he called himself "Nikolai Lenin." Sometime after the seizure of power, people began to refer to him as "Vladimir Il'ich Lenin." In the late years before his death, he was sometimes referred to simply, with implied affection, as Il'ich.

[1920, September, after the 11th]

Comrade Ramírez (Delovoi Dvor No 216)
Please get and send him a book, my book
  "The newest facts about the development of capitalism
  in agriculture. United States of North America."

Figure 2. Note from V. I. Lenin to Sh. M. Manuchar'iants, librarian of Lenin's personal library. Lenin refers to his work "New facts about the laws of capitalism in agriculture. Vyp. 1. Capitalism and agriculture in the United States of America" (see Polnoe sobranie sochineniia, 27, pp. 129–227). From Institut Marksizma-Leninizma pri TsK KPSS, Leninskii sbornik, 37 (Moscow: Izdatel'stvo Politicheskoi Literatury, 1970), p. 239.

and pressed a button on his desk. An aide escorted me to the street where the car waited. A copy of the agriculture book (see Figure 2) was at my hotel when I returned.

18   Goodbye to John Reed

The congress continued its relentless course. After debating Parliamentarianism and the Trade Union Question, it adopted Lenin's "Left Communism" postulates. Most of us had become convinced in advance, and the discussion was essentially over before it began. Some British comrades still gagged at the notion of affiliating their party with the opportunistic Labour Party, and some Americans still had doubts about working with the A.F. of L., but protests from the floor were few and easily disposed of. When Jack Reed conducted a one-man filibuster, Fraina disassociated himself from his countryman and Radek hinted savagely that Reed was not worth listening to. The fact is Jack had much sympathy but little real influence in the congress, where many considered him a political lightweight and reserved their respect for Fraina.

It Had to Be Revolution

The British Communist Party never achieved Labour Party affiliation, though in time it became a factor with a section of the Labour leadership. Similarly, though the old trade union federations disavowed them, both the British and American Communists acquired footholds in local—and several national—constituent unions (the dockworkers, the miners, the needle trades). In this way, the tactic approved by the Second Congress had significant consequences. It was in effect the embryo of the "United Front" tactic (elaborated in 1921 by the Third Congress) that was responsible for the multiplicity of insidious "front organizations" that later appeared throughout the world.

Finally, the Second Congress made history with the theses it promulgated on the Colonial Question. Empires and colonial rule have existed throughout history, but in the nineteenth century the urge to establish imperial possessions became (literally) a life-and-death contest among the "advanced nations." By the time World War I broke out, latecomers had been enjoined to recognize that "Africa was already divided up." According to such theorists as J. A. Hobson and Rudolf Hilferding, this new imperialism was the attempt of "finance capital" to escape from the limitations, contradictions, and working class pressures that characterized the now "mature" capitalist countries. Lenin, carrying Hilferding a step further, maintained that in those countries capitalism and imperialism had become one. He summarized his views in *Imperialism, the Highest Stage of Capitalism* (1917), one of the most influential of all his writings.

Lenin's theorizing was never idle speculation. He concluded that proletarian revolutionists at home had a common interest with independence movements in the colonial and semicolonial lands. While such movements had always been viewed more or less sympathetically by "enlightened" people, he saw them as a dynamic element in the revolution against world capitalism. The National Liberationists usually had no working class sentiments. More often than not they wanted to substitute some sort of local capitalism for that of the foreigner. No matter. Whatever their motivation they were part of a process calculated to destroy world capitalist imperialism from within and without.

In conformity with Lenin's view, the Second Congress resolved (my summary):

(1) To proclaim the absolute right of peoples everywhere to freedom from imperialist domination.

(2) To forge a link between the colonial and semicolonial peoples on the one hand and the revolutionary working class movements in the home countries of imperialism on the other.

(3) To require every constituent party of the Communist International to establish an Anti-Imperialist Department to work with the National Liberation forces in its assigned area.

(4) To encourage and assist all National Liberation movements, including wars of national liberation, with finances, equipment, expert advisers, and in any other way possible.

These sessions on Imperialism and the Colonial Question were among the most animated of the congress. Most of the important delegates participated and the debate was of course Roy's great opportunity. He was the only "native colonial" and thus the only delegate able to speak with experience and intelligence from the standpoint of the struggle in the subject countries, and he made a tremendous impression on everybody, Lenin included. He became a leader of the permanent Far Eastern Bureau of the International and developed mightily in the process, for both good and bad.

There was no intention of allowing the anti-imperialist program to become a dead letter. Sun Yat-sen, then the great hope for eliminating the foreign concessions in China, was brought to Moscow, shown every respect, and assured of material support. In India, Jawaharlal Nehru was cultivated assiduously. Revolts were actively promoted in the Dutch East Indies, in Africa, and in the various French Protectorates of the Near East. At one stage, much later, Russian emissaries, military and otherwise, virtually took over the conduct of the Chinese Kuomintang struggle against Japan. Borodin was dispatched from Moscow to head the operation, and for all practical purposes he ran the show there. He became world-famous. The Kuomintang accorded him the official title of National Adviser.[1]

---

1. In the long run he failed. When in 1927 General Chiang Kai-shek engineered a coup d'etat, slaughtered Chinese Communists who had been cooperating with the Kuomintang, and shipped the entire Russian contingent home, Borodin

It Had to Be Revolution

The congress, as already noted, also battled over the plaguey Trade Union Question. There existed an International Federation of Trade Unions (IFTU) which was headquartered in Amsterdam. Most of the world's important national labor federations were affiliated to it. It was now proposed to supplement the Communist International with a so-called Red International of Labor Unions in opposition to the "reactionary" IFTU.[2] The proposal, presented to the congress in the name of the Russian delegation, directly contradicted the previously adopted "anti–dual union" policy and provoked consternation in the hall. Members of one delegation after another attacked it, castigated it, ridiculed it.

But the Russians prevailed—as they had on every issue from the outset —and I suddenly understood that it had all been planned that way. Instead of sitting down to compare views with comrades from France, Germany, or wherever in a spirit of give and take, the Russians had determined everything beforehand. Indeed they had "packed" the congress. Side by side with the sixty-four Russian "delegates" sat a sizable "Polish delegation" composed of such prominent Bolsheviks as Felix Dzerzhinsky, A. S. Yenukidze, A. A. Yoffe, and even A. Zorin (at that time secretary of the Petrograd Soviet). Similarly, there were Bolshevized "Finnish," "Ukrainian," "Belorussian," "Georgian," "Armenian," and other such technically independent delegations, in which everyone acted as a disciplined member of an organized Bolshevik caucus. I was of course no stranger to the idea of caucuses aimed at hostile groups; we'd had our own caucus directed against the Spanish right-wingers. But in this gathering I found the expedient offensive.

In fact the tactic was unnecessary. The prestige of the Bolshevik leaders, who had carried out a proletarian revolution, assumed the government of a vast nation, fought off the great capitalist powers of the world, and still sang the "The Internationale," would alone have carried their program through the congress. Moreover it was a

---

returned to Russia in disgrace. He never had an important assignment after that.
2. Incidentally, the "trade unions" of Soviet Russia, being for all practical purposes organs of the state without independent bargaining power or coercive power of any kind, were ineligible for membership in the IFTU.

wonderfully adept program and, with comparatively minor doubts (as in the feasibility of a Red International of Labor Unions), I was all for it.

The result, of course, was an encompassing Russianization of the new International, a process accentuated by the environment of the Kremlin, the helpfulness of Russian auxiliary personnel, and the commitment of Soviet state resources. The Russians used to say the world revolution's "center of gravity" would inevitably shift to Germany or some other great industrial country, but for now it had to be the RSFSR. It was decided as a matter of course that the Executive Committee of the Communist International (ECCI) would be headquartered in Moscow. Every important country represented at the congress had at least one member on the Executive Committee, and the Russians exercised some pressure in their choice. Once the committee was elected, the Russian contingent (including "Poles," "Ukrainians," etc.) dominated it. Zinoviev, the only Russian candidate, was elected president of the Communist International—unanimously.

Of all the American delegates to the congress, Fraina was the only one who impressed the Russians. Yet when it came to electing an American to the Executive Committee the choice was Reed. No doubt the desire to see a native-born and quintessentially American exemplar on the Executive Committee was a factor.

The persistent political controversy between Reed and Fraina had little noticeable effect on their personal relations in Moscow. I was very friendly with both, and the three of us used to enjoy evening walks together along the Moskva River. Louis was present with me at Jack's bedside when he died. Nevertheless Jack had asked the ECCI to keep Louis away from American affairs after the congress, citing the spy charges against Fraina. Admitting that the charges had been discredited, Reed averred that since they had been made repeatedly and circulated widely in the United States, it might take several years of "untroubled leadership" in the American party "to lay the ghost." The formal proposal that Fraina not return to any leading position in the American party was voted down, but Reed had his effect. Fraina was assigned to conduct a prolonged mission in Mexico, with Sen Katayama as co-director and myself as general accessory. Mexico City was to become the organizing center of the Red International of Labor Unions for all Latin America. According to Roy, the idea of solving "the Fraina problem" in this way originated with Borodin. He said Borodin was also responsible for naming Katayama and me. I was the only one acquainted with the territory and the only one who could speak Spanish.

It took months for the plan to be fleshed out, final approval secured, and technical arrangements (financial and otherwise) completed. Moscow's "white nights" gave way to gray days, and fierce heat was replaced with even fiercer cold. (I got a requisition for warmer attire—including a Persian lamb headpiece—in which I thought I looked very smart.) The congress over, I had time to learn more about the life around me and to organize my thoughts about all I had seen and heard since crossing the frontier of the RSFSR.

A sine qua non of the transfer to socialism had been completed: the former class rule—of both capitalists and landed gentry—had been destroyed irretrievably. But the cost was dreadful. In 1920 the country's industrial output was 30 percent below 1913's. The food problem went from bad to worse, and in spite of the population's remarkable stamina the system could be maintained only through strict compulsion. The Left Socialist-Revolutionaries who had fought side by side with the Bolsheviks and participated in the original 1917 Soviet government were now in jail. They had attempted a revolt—in response to the "betrayal" that the Brest-Litovsk settlement represented—among other things. A young Left S-R, Dora (Fanny) Kaplan, had made a near-fatal assault on Lenin's life in late summer 1918. Dora Kaplan was not sent to jail; she was shot without a trial. Emma Goldman protested to Lenin about this and other shootings. He replied that the Soviets were struggling for survival and at the same time straining to advance the world revolution— "while I," as she quoted him in her book, "was lamenting over a little blood-letting." When she lamented the absence of free speech he told her, "Free speech is a bourgeois prejudice, a soothing plaster for social ills. . . . In the present state of Russia all prattle of freedom is merely food for the reaction trying to drown Russia." She reflected at the time that "Lenin might be right." I would have said flatly that he was.

Marx had envisioned a temporary dictatorship of the proletariat, and all truly revolutionary socialists—Bolsheviks and non-Bolsheviks alike—accepted it as a necessity from the first. But now the dictatorship of the proletariat had become the dictatorship of the proletarian "vanguard" (i.e., the Russian Communist Party). This was regrettable but, I and others assured ourselves, necessary. There were injustices, evil but unavoidable. And one noted that some received special favors. While our hotel food remained deficient, it improved—both in quantity and quality—in comparison with what was available to the mass of the people. In the Kremlin we sometimes got fresh gray caviar—the best. Excuses? Well, supplies were too scanty to go far anyway, so why not? Why not? I considered it scandalous, indecent (but was human enough not to turn anything down). On the other hand I knew of repeated instances of Bolshevik self-sacrifice for the sake of the cause. Though offended by the Russian tactics at the Second Congress, I had reason to believe that the outstanding leaders I had met were sincere, devoted, and basically incorruptible. And their dynamism, fortitude, and political know-how were well established. I had no doubt that soon a way would be found to ease the extreme shortages—and with it the tightness of controls. (This happened less than a year later with abandonment of War Communism and the introduction of NEP: the New Economic Policy.) In the longer run we could count on industrialization and, above all, the proletarian revolutions in other countries. Social barriers would then disappear automatically. I felt confirmed in my Communist faith, ready for any assignment.

(On later reflection I realized I still had inner misgivings. As when I learned that the so-called Workers Opposition was being attacked in *Pravda* day after day and not allowed to reply. The Workers Opposition was a group *within the Party* led by A. G. Shliapnikov. It shocked me that free speech was denied among Communists! Dictatorship of the proletariat interpreted as dictatorship of the proletarian vanguard was something I could defend—though I disliked the phrase. But did "vanguard" now mean "vanguard of the vanguard"? This possibility evoked similarly disturbing questions about the real meanings of the grandiose phrases we were using. Such doubts formed at the back of my mind and remained practically buried there.)

It Had to Be Revolution

Applying the Second Congress theses on colonial and semicolonial peoples, the energetic Russians called a Congress of Oriental Nations right after ours adjourned. It met at the end of August in Baku, on the Caspian Sea. Roy, naturally, played a prominent part in it. John Reed attended (on assignment) as a revolutionary spokesman from a leading imperialist country. While he was away his wife, the vividly attractive Louise Bryant, arrived in Moscow. I never knew Louise long enough to have much of an opinion about what kind of person she was. I think she was deeply in love with Jack and, for the time being, with her partnership in his life. She had style, an ivory complexion, and darkly shadowed eyes. Jack returned from Baku buoyed by the experience there and happy to see Louise. But he looked weak. Before September he was too sick to stand on his feet. First thought to be influenza, it was discovered to be typhus—picked up at Baku. He got preferential medical care, the best available. At first he seemed to rally and talked about soon "becoming a nuisance again" on the Executive Committee. But by mid-October he was dead. He was conscious most of the time, though with lapses into delirium, until the end. I went to the hospital every day, sometimes taking Fraina with me. Louise was there all the time. Jack had other visitors but only the three of us (and the nurse) were in the room when he died. His body lay in state for seven days, guarded by Red Army soldiers. He was buried in the Kremlin wall, with eulogies by Bukharin, Alexandra Kollontai, and others.[3]

Louise remained in Moscow for some time after Jack's death, but I rarely saw her. She seemed—surely was—inconsolable. (Eventually, of course, she got over it and married William C. Bullitt, whom I had met as a convivial Philadelphia newspaper correspondent with the Ford Expedition in 1915. He had since become a distinguished establishment figure, and was to become even more of one: ambassador to several countries, and so on.)

The "auxiliary personnel" around the Delovoi Dvor included a bevy of highborn young Russian women who had been educated in fashionable girls' schools. They were not expected to be Commu-

3. Stories that Jack had lost faith in communism at the time he died—some of them attributed to Louise—are false. During the days of his illness his reaffirmation of commitment to the movement—and to Soviet Russia—was unequivocal. Fraina and I remarked on it together.

126

nist, and probably none of them was; they were there to assist Second Congress delegates with clerical work. I often employed one of them, for she spoke perfect English and had good handwriting. Moreover, she was a thing of beauty, with stormy eyes set deep in her ivory face. Her name was Natalia Alexandrovna Mikhailova and she was eighteen. Her parents, both dead, had despised the revolution. Natalie (known among the American delegates by this English equivalent of Natalia) cared little about it, but she performed her assigned tasks conscientiously. She was surprisingly ignorant (credit the finishing-school education), but the Delovoi Dvor job was undemanding and she liked being among foreigners. After the congress I asked Natalie to help me translate some of Lenin's book on American agriculture. Although it was over her head (and sometimes mine), we got what we needed. As Lenin had feared, the material proved hopelessly outdated, and he never followed me up on it.

In idle hours Natalie guided me here and there about the city. I took her to see R. Gliere's famous *Red Poppy* ballet at the Bolshoi Theater. As might have been predicted, we began to sleep together. Jokingly, I asked her if she would like to go to Mexico with me. She said yes so fast that I gasped. She said it in earnest. Later the idea intrigued me, and we acted on it—all with the indulgent cooperation of the Soviet government!

19   A Frustrated Mission to Mexico

In order to travel Natalie first had to become *la señora de Ramírez*. So we married at a Moscow registry office. Four witnesses attended: Bukharin, Tomsky, Fraina, and Jack Murphy of the British delegation. With the wedding I became an official bigamist; for I was still married to Eleanor. Though I never had any deep feeling for Natalie, nor she for me, we enjoyed each other, she wanted to get out of Russia, and I trusted her. It was an adventure, and she proved a staunch, undemanding companion—for longer than either of us had any reason to expect.

It Had to Be Revolution

We left in November, as soon as the "technical" (chiefly financial) arrangements for the Latin American Bureau of the Red International of Labor Unions (RILU) had been completed. In our pockets were enough pounds sterling (from Soviet Russia's tight hoard of foreign exchange) to travel first class and a bit extra (not much). We traveled on "legal" passports, duly visaed, via Estonia, Berlin, Antwerp, New York, and Laredo. Fraina and Katayama left separately—Fraina having been entrusted with thousands of pounds (there is dispute as to how many thousand) to finance months of RILU bureau activity. We were to meet up in Mexico City. Both Fraina and Katayama were to break their journey in New York for a goodwill mission to U.S. Communist leaders to promote party unity. In Berlin, Natalie and I split up for a few days. I stayed in a pension run by a German comrade, a Frau Hötschel, all of whose boarders were Communists. Jack Murphy was stopping there on his way home to England. To my surprise and joy, Hilda Kramer (my *Dubiner!*) happened in for a night, and I promptly became "unfaithful" to my recent bride. (Several members of the German party were staying at Frau Hötschel's, more or less permanently, engaged in "hush-hush" work. I learned from them how a block of soap transfers visas, police permits, etc., from one document to another.)

I had another unexpected one-day reunion in Berlin. There on Unter den Linden was Herman Mankiewicz, fresh from the U.S., married to his super-Orthodox betrothed and living with her in Berlin. Why Berlin? "Because," in that wretched, frustrated, humiliated city, "dollars could buy anything." I had dinner with them in their showy apartment. It was a Friday night: candles burned on the table, everything was kosher, and Mank told smutty jokes! "Poor Sarah," looking lovely (and somehow smug), said hardly a word. I got away as soon as I could. In the street I was shocked to my gut when a ragged newsboy called out, "*Antisemitische Wochenschrift! Antisemitische Wochenschrift!*" (Anti-Semitic Weekly). (This, many years before Hitler.) Berlin in 1920, with winter approaching, was spectral. Hilda told me of mutilated beggars in frayed uniforms with cardboard breastpieces that proclaimed, "I fought for the Fatherland."

Inspectors at New York admitted us as Mexicans in transit. We remained in the country only long enough for me to pay a surprise visit to my brother and new sister-in-law, then on their honeymoon in Atlantic City. Harry's bride, née Edith Engel, was a sweetie from his teenage days. I had, and have, a special admiration for her—perhaps something more.

We rented a small dark adobe house in a working class section of Mexico City—two rooms and a cookshed. I had little money left and, in any case, no ritzy cover-up was needed for the business we'd be transacting here! Katayama arrived soon and moved in. He, too, was practically out of funds, and for the time being the old man (in his seventies), seasoned leader of a hundred labor struggles in his own and other countries, could do nothing but keep house with Natalie. He did the cooking on our charcoal stove, while I went about my contacts with the Mexican movement. I brought Valadés, Genaro Gómez, José Allen, and Manuel Ramírez (no relation to Jesús) home to meet the kindly Japanese comrade. They could converse only through me as Spanish-English interpreter. Fraina arrived about a week after Katayama, bringing with him a new Russian wife. Like Natalie, Esther Nesvishskaya was a "refugee from the Delovoi Dvor." The house now seemed cramped, and Natalie and I moved to a one-room arrangement nearby.

Our "bureau" was expected to acquaint trade-union organizations throughout Latin America with the Red International of Labor Unions, and interest them in sending delegates to a RILU congress that was tentatively scheduled for March 1921 in Moscow. With the arrival of Fraina and the money, we launched a weekly newspaper, El Trabajador (The Toiler). I edited it in consultation with Fraina and Katayama, and with the help of our comrades in the Communist Party of Mexico.

At that time (January 1921) a so-called Pan American Federation of Labor happened to be forming at a convention in Mexico City—a joint undertaking of the A. F. of L. and the Morones-owned CROM (Confederacion Regional Obrera Mexicana). I managed to get into the hall, and found that old Samuel Gompers himself had come, bringing some of his top people: Dan Tobin of the teamsters, Matthew Woll of the photo-engravers, and Mary Harris Jones ("Mother

Jones"), substituting for John L. Lewis, of the miners. It was a love feast between them and the Morones clique. The A. F. of L. gang could talk in Mexico the way they could not in New York, Chicago, and Washington. White-haired Mother Jones, 91 years old, shrieked, "They call us *Bolsheviki*. We are *Bolsheviki!*" Gompers and company applauded uncertainly along with the Mexicans, while Morones, in turn, assured the A. F. of L. crowd of his essential moderation. But enthusiasm lagged. One CROM delegate rose with an objection to the name "Pan American." When he tried to explain his reasons, Gompers, in the chair, ruled him out of order. Loud outcries erupted from the Mexican audience, which detested "Pan Americanism" as a concept that reeked of the Monroe Doctrine— which of course it did. (The Gompers-Morones Pan American Federation of Labor remained a paper organization, and faded away altogether within a few years.)

The Morones-Gompers entente displeased the CROM-affiliated trade unions, some of which became disaffected. We seized the occasion to invite them, and existing independent Mexican unions, to an anti-CROM labor convention. A surprising number accepted. In opposition to CROM, the assembly started a militant CGT (Confederación General del Trabajo), sent a fraternal greeting to the Communist International, and designated Genero Gómez to represent it at the scheduled congress of the Red International of Labor Unions (which actually met in July 1921). The CGT was an immediate factor in Mexico's day-to-day labor struggles—wage demands, strikes, and so on. I participated openly, once again under the name Frank Seaman. The CGT grew in size and importance until it outdistanced the CROM. In the 1930s, under the leadership of Lombardo Toledano, it became Mexico's main labor-union organization. By that time, however, it no longer professed Communist inclinations.

Neither Fraina nor Katayama appeared in public, but I reported to them every day. In a practical sense I was the Latin-American Bureau of the RILU, such as it was. The fact was that Mexico City could not be an expeditious working center for the Latin American movement as a whole. It lies farther from Buenos Aires, Sao Paolo, and Montevideo than from New York. Fraina announced he would go to South America and look things over, and the next day he was gone. His departure handicapped us in Mexico somewhat, for the bureau's treasury went with him. We were, of course, eager for the first word from him, but nothing came, ever.[1]

We continued our work at the CGT. It was a busy summer morning (1921) at CGT headquarters when the police barged in and picked up two members: Sebastián San Vicente (a husky, beetle-browed native of Barcelona, Spain) and me. We were held all day at the *jefatura*, incommunicado and without explanation. The police confiscated everything in our pockets, including my dog-eared Jesús Ramírez passport, which I never got back. (It had served me well enough to have accumulated some twenty visas of one kind and another!) At nightfall two plainclothesmen took us to the Buena Vista railroad station and put us on board a departing train. To the U.S.? Still no word of explanation. En route the conductor handed our custodians a telegram, and at the next station they hauled us off the train. We found ourselves in Querétaro, the town where Emperor Maximilian had been executed in 1867.

San Vicente and I spent a week or more in a cell of the local military prison. Without beds or bunks, we spent the nights on the cold cement floor. Querétaro is high up and since we got no blankets, we covered ourselves with newspapers. Here again we were held incommunicado, but at least we could talk to each other. San Vicente (I never called him Sebastián) was a semianarchist metalworker with broad muscular shoulders and big hands. An organizer rather than an ideologue, he liked people and you sensed it immediately. In spite of his strong Catalonian accent (a mark of disdain in Mexico), he was a popular speaker. I got to know him very well in Querétaro. We argued constantly—about anarchism, Carranza, the Spanish labor movement, the hour of the day—but always with mutual respect. A turnkey sometimes stole into our cell to smoke marijuana, and San Vicente coaxed him into bringing us the Mexico City newspapers. From them we learned that we were not the only

---

1. Fraina returned to the U.S. in 1923, having resigned from the Party. (He claimed, among other things, that he'd applied only $5,000 to his personal use during his life abroad.) Under the name Lewis Corey he began a career as an author and economist, writing two widely noticed books, *The Decline of American Capitalism* (1934) and *The Crisis of the Middle Class* (1935). By 1940 he had repudiated Marxism. From 1942 to 1951 he taught economics at Antioch College. He died in 1953 of a cerebral hemorrhage.

comrades who'd been arrested. The police had picked up every foreigner prominent in the left-wing politics-labor movement—under an order signed by President Álvaro Obregón. We were all being deported—"thirty-threed." (Article 33 of the 1917 constitution prohibits foreigners from taking part in Mexican politics. It had been adopted to protect against the subjection to foreign financial interests which had been one of the scourges of the prerevolutionary regime. Now, for the first time, the law had been applied to the labor movement—doubtless on a hint from Morones.)

When San Vicente and I were being taken from CGT headquarters, someone there called my home and told Natalie. She got to the CGT leaders right away, and a committee of them got to Obregón. He promised that if I was "thirty-threed" it would not be to the United States—thus our removal from the train at Querétaro.

From the prison of nightly cold in Querétaro they transported us to a cell in always steamy Manzanillo. The lockup in that then picayune Pacific coast port had only one cell and it was crowded, mostly with drunks, petty criminals, and other nondescripts whom the local *cacique* wanted out of the way. These inmates didn't remain long, and could hardly have stood it in any case. The heat and the stench were sickening. There was no toilet, and we were left to excrete in a corner. Vermin crawled over us all night. With the first daylight you joined the press for the cell door, just to stick your nose through the bars. Wives and daughters brought tortillas, tamales, fruit; the prison itself supplied no food.

Natalie appeared on our first morning, perspiring but a refreshing sight in her starched white. She informed me I was being held in Manzanillo until I could be deported by boat to Guatemala. San Vicente was to go, too, and Natalie would accompany us. The Mexican government had agreed to let her leave the country with me, and was paying the costs! She appeared regularly during our two remaining days of incarceration, bringing edibles for San Vicente and me. She was waiting with a small suitcase when we were released. A guard escorted us to the boat, and then we were free.

Though we tried, we could accomplish nothing for the RILU in Guatemala. The virtually feudal Central American "republic" lacked even the beginnings of industrial development. Guatemala City, where we established ourselves, had been devastated by an earthquake a couple of years back and was still in terrible shape. With our money all but exhausted, we rented a furnished room for three. Until I found a customer for English lessons and San Vicente took occasional work with a blacksmith (a matter of weeks), we lived on peanuts and bananas, which were cheaper than beans. (I couldn't stomach a peanut or a banana for years after.)

A large restaurant on the edge of town offered decaying meat at low, low prices. It enjoyed terrific business and teamsters and mule skinners patronized it regularly. San Vicente and I went out there to talk socialism to them, while Natalie wandered the streets or stayed home, patiently waiting for time to pass. (Books in a language she knew thoroughly were not available, and she wouldn't have read them if they were.) The teamsters (like everybody out there) were Quiché Indians. Though illiterate, they were relatively skilled workers. They ordinarily spoke Quiché but could manage to communicate in Spanish. We found them very approachable, and they listened to our propaganda, which we put to them in the simplest terms. One or two expressed mild interest—very mild. We also talked to the waiters, first in that restaurant, then in others, trying, in vain, to start a waiter's union. After two months of this, San Vicente still hoped, but I felt that at best we were wasting our time. I was determined to slip back into Mexico, whereas San Vicente, who now had adoring friends, preferred to stay. He arranged for a waiter named Manuel Gómez to give me his birth certificate. It was as "Manuel Gómez," then, that I remarried Natalie and obtained a Guatemalan husband-and-wife passport.

The passport was for some unforeseeable emergency, not for the return to Mexico. Guatemala borders on Mexico, and every day nationals of both countries traveled back and forth between Quetzaltenango, Guatemala, and Tapachula, Mexico, without having to show papers. Natalie and I took that route, both of us dressed in the heavy veils common to mourning women in that region. I worried that a border guard might have my picture; for if found again in Mexico I was subject to a term in prison and then to being turned over to U.S. authorities. And who knows what awaited me there?

In Mexico City, undisguised but "underground," I kept out of sight. Natalie negotiated a room and kitchenette for us, did the shopping, alerted comrades. A committee of three (José C. Valadés,

Manuel Ramírez, and José Allen) visited us regularly. They said Katayama had disappeared. In these circumstances, I decided to accept responsibility for the RILU bureau, recognizing that my contact with the broader movement was necessarily second-hand. With the cooperation of my three visitors I reestablished *El Trabajador* and edited it from my room. I left the house only at night (without Natalie), for exercise. When Valedés announced that he was being followed, we moved. This happened twice. Then Allen reported that a stranger had asked him what the hell had ever become of Frank Seaman. By the spring of 1922 there was no question of further effective RILU service in Mexico; I mailed a final report to Moscow.[2]

With a three-week tourist visa obtained at the U.S. consulate in Vera Cruz, "Manuel Gómez" and his wife sailed first class on a pleasure tour to New Orleans. (Credit CGT generosity—and the loyal go-between committee of Valadés, Ramírez, and Allen.) In New Orleans we melted into the local population.

20 Manuel Gómez and Wife
in Chicago

Right away, Natalie's good looks got her a job as a receptionist in a dental office. I tried the newspapers—*The Item* and *The Times-Picayune*—but had no luck. Well? We hadn't intended to settle in New Orleans. My objective was industrial Chicago and its section of the American Communist Party. Natalie, though fearful, agreed to be left behind, and I took the Illinois Central north.

2. The RILU itself never got very far anywhere (though notables like William Z. Foster and Harry Pollitt, future chairmen of the Communist parties in the U.S. and Britain, respectively, were associated with it). It was active during the 1920s and the first half of the 1930s.

South or north I had to have a job. A newspaper or magazine job in Chicago would be ideal, but I could get hungry looking. First thing, then, prudence took over and directed me to Chicago's enormous Sears Roebuck headquarters, reputedly an "assembly line for white collar workers." I became a mail order correspondent (chiefly a selector of form letters) and rented a "hall bedroom" on Kedzie Avenue.

Finding the Communist Party meant doing a bit of probing, but Borodin had taught me how. A newsstand on West Madison carried, half-hidden, a weekly tabloid full of Communistic lingo. This was the *Voice of Labor*, "official organ of the Workers Party of America (WPA)." I introduced myself to the editor, Jack Carney, and to a waggish columnist, Tom O'Flaherty, as Manuel Gómez, a comrade from Mexico (I was Manuel Gómez at Sears, too). Questions and counterquestions followed, after which Manuel Gómez was certified a member of the Workers Party. At my first meeting my rhetoric prompted a guy sitting next to me—a scrawny Scandinavian called Andy Overgaard—to invite me to a meeting of "the real party," the Communist Party.

It turned out that the Workers Party was a "legal" instrument of the then clandestine Communist Party; raids and wholesale arrests in 1920 (masterminded by Attorney General A. Mitchell Palmer) had forced the Party underground. It organized the Workers Party in 1921, in the wake of Lenin's strictures on "infantile sickness." Its official program called for the establishment of a workers' republic, but stressed day-to-day class struggle objectives. Nowhere was there any mention of soviets, the dictatorship of the proletariat, or armed insurrection. They called the Communist Party "Number One" and the Workers Party "Number Two," though their leaderships were virtually interchangeable. I soon belonged to both parties and was accepted as an expatriate Mexican. I told my new comrades nothing of my history in the international movement. (Having served as a representative first of Borodin and then of the RILU, I wanted to enter the American movement "on my own," to be a rank-and-filer and develop real roots.)

At the time I seem to have taken on certain Hispano-American mannerisms. Wearing a broad-brimmed black hat, I actually looked like Gómez. More than once somebody stopped me on the street and asked in Spanish for directions. For many years I was Manuel Gómez and nobody ever questioned my Mexican origin. I remained interested in the Mexican labor struggle, wrote to Valadés, and picked up exchange copies of the Communist *El Machete* at the *Voice of Labor* office.

In those days, Wally Carmon, whom I had known in Mazatlán, was living in Chicago. He and his wife, Rose, old Cleveland sweethearts, had a North Side flat at Clark and Fullerton. I learned of it in a letter from Mellie, my old friend in Mazatlán, and went to see them. I marveled at Rose, a dumpy, pumpkin-faced woman—unlettered, but hardly stupid—of extraordinary unaffected warmth and contagious good humor. Wally was working at Marshall Field and Rose, a trained bookkeeper, had a job with some picayune loan company. I took to visiting the Carmons several nights a week, for by now we were neighbors. I had moved from the hall-bedroom on Kedzie to a somewhat larger room on North La Salle and written Natalie to join me. When she arrived we made a foursome.

Had I not felt responsible for Natalie, I might not have sent for her. She was beautiful to look at, a satisfactory bedfellow, but dull to talk to. But she relied on me, asked little for herself (despite a half-concealed taste for finery), kept confidences, and was fiercely loyal. It was hard to tell what amused her. Certainly not gossip, which was a disappointment to Rose.

The American Communist Party had originated in the left wing of the Socialist Party, which had been inspired by the initial triumph of the Bolshevik revolution. The Socialist Party included a relatively large proportion of foreign-born members, many of whom belonged to semiautonomous foreign-language federations. Thus there was a German Federation, an Italian Federation, a Polish Federation—even a Jewish Federation—each with its own newspapers and meeting places. The Finnish Federation, based in Duluth, controlled a vast network of cooperatives and published a dozen newspapers, two of them dailies. The federations responded variously to the world-shaking events in Russia. Some stayed put in the Socialist Party, some split, some went Communist in a body. Thus the American Communist Party was born of a babel of foreign-language federations that were capable of drowning out the small English-speaking membership.

Among the sibling federations the East Europeans were especially clamorous: the Russian, the Ukrainian, the South Slavic, and others—especially the Russian. It had grown in members and self-importance as a result of the successful revolution, and its leaders thought themselves surrogate Lenins, qualified to dominate the American Communist Party. For a time they did dominate it.

While relegated to the underground, the Communist Party ("Number One") had little to do but decide how the Workers Party ("Number Two") should act. In 1922 the seasoned C. E. Ruthenberg proposed liquidating the underground party and transforming the Workers Party into an open Communist Party. Most English-speaking members, including "the Chicago trade union group" represented by William Z. Foster, William F. Dunne, and Earl Browder, favored the proposal. The political climate had changed significantly since the Palmer raids: the Workers Party could hold public meetings with impunity, it was publishing newspapers, and it was free to participate in elections for public office. Thus, the proposal made sense, but it met die-hard opposition, notably from the foreign-language forces led by the Russians. Conceding the logic of making "Number Two" an open Communist party, they nevertheless insisted on maintaining "Number One" as the "directing and controlling body." They denounced Ruthenberg and the rest of the "Americans" as "Liquidators"—a deadly epithet in the Leninist canon. In turn the "Americans" called their accusers "Geese." The Geese had a majority in the tiny Communist Party (five or six thousand members), but the Executive Committee of the Communist International ruled against them. They could not defy Moscow, and the dissolution of "Number One" was therefore approved unanimously.

The ECCI ruling on "Number One" destroyed the pretensions of the Russian Federation in American communism. The federation's membership eroded; some of its members drifted back to Russia, others just quit.

Throughout my Communist experience the "International" ordered and the brother Communist parties obeyed. Moscow made and unmade majorities, toppled and exalted leaderships, expelled whole sections of membership, reversed policies and tactics from one day to the next. The parties submitted out of Leninist discipline—and because their members had more respect for Moscow than for their local leaders. In the case of Geese versus Liquidators, Moscow's intervention proved a blessing; in other cases it was anything but. On balance, in the United States as elsewhere, subservience to Moscow was baleful and corrupting. (It had its amusing aspect in the wholesale aping of Bolshevik procedures and the parroting of Bolshevik jargon. National Executive Committees had their *Politburos*, with candidates (*kandidaty*) instead of alternates, and Congresses had *Presidiums*. Resolutions were *Theses*, Committees on Organization became *Orgburos*, the Communist International became the *Comintern*, the RILU, the *Profintern*.)

A final (Liquidating) underground convention of the American Communist Party, held at Bridgman, Michigan, broke up when police arrived. (The Department of Justice was said to have had a secret agent in the Party's Executive Committee.) Most of the delegates escaped but some thirty were arrested—including Ruthenberg, Foster, and Browder. Ruthenberg was convicted of "criminal anarchy" but, released on appeal, remained free until his death years later. Foster's trial ended in a hung jury. None of the others was brought to trial. Very new to the Party at the time, I had attended one secret meeting during the "liquidationist" debate, but learned about Bridgman only from the *Chicago Tribune*.

Now we had only the Workers Party. Unlike the Socialist Party it did not pretend that a socialist society could be achieved through piecemeal reforms, but linked its revolutionary purpose to the struggle to satisfy labor's immediate demands. We sought to win adherents who had been unreachable from the underground, but, alas, we weren't winning many. The Socialist Party's Jewish Federation and the important Finnish Federation—neither of which had ever joined the underground—came over to us. But "the broad masses" eluded us in droves. This was the 1920s of "silk shirts for everybody," "two chickens in every pot," and "two cars in every garage"—the decade presided over by Harding, Coolidge, and Hoover, each with large-scale working class backing. Actually the frothy postwar prosperity of the twenties was selective and precarious. The farmers had no part in it. Indeed, having been encouraged to overproduce for a huge export demand that no longer existed, they had now sunk into depression. A farmer sold (what he could) cheap and paid (for what he could) dear. In the meantime, urban areas had their slums and skid rows, unemployment and want. Itinerant workers, Negroes, and some of the foreign-born suffered badly. Among the farmers and a section of the labor movement there were anti-establishment stirrings.

What of the Workers Party? Our membership, practically nonexistent outside the East and Midwest, never got above 10,000 in these years. And not over 5 percent of those members were English-speaking. We assured ourselves that in the last analysis we were the hope of the exploited. But what would it take to assure *them*?

Today, the pretensions of an isolated and minuscule Communist Party in the world's strongest capitalist country—with that country near its peak of power—must seem absurd. But consider the matter in perspective. The Bolsheviks, a tiny force in the vastness of the ultra-reactionary tsarist empire, had proved that nothing is forever. And the Europe of the 1920s was a field of fierce contention between communism and several varieties of fascism.

Our Party's Central Executive Committee (inherited from the underground) resided in New York City, which had the biggest concentration of party members. Chicago, second in membership, had far fewer. The two cities' memberships differed strikingly: most of New York's Communists were Jews who worked in the needle trades, though there was also a sprinkling of Second Avenue intellectuals; in Chicago, the members were immigrant Poles, Lithuanians, South Slavs, and Italians employed in the stockyards, the railroad shops, and the steel mills of South Chicago, Gary, and Indiana Harbor, plus first- and second-generation Germans and Scandinavians, and the nucleus of seasoned American trade unionists grouped around Bill Foster, Bill Dunne, Jim Cannon, and Earl Browder.[1] Though formally united in the solidarity of the struggle, the Communists of New York and Chicago were also rivals. In Chicago, we deprecated our New York comrades as sectarians, while they described us as trade-union idolaters and inferior Marxists.

---

1. Foster had been an A.F. of L. giant, organizing 200,000 packinghouse workers in 1918 and leading a nationwide steel strike in 1919.

Moreover, the Central Executive Committee, the Party's highest authority, took the same view of us. Headquartered in New York, it naturally had a New York coloration. In our opinion the committee should have moved out to Chicago, the traditional center of anticapitalist movements where both the Socialist Party and the IWW had their national offices.

Having joined up as a rank-and-filer—doing "Jimmy Higgins work" (passing out leaflets, etc.)—and being heard at meetings not from the platform but from the floor, my Chicago comrades and I soon knew one another like family. I really belonged. We were organized in neighborhood branches and a City Central Committee. I was a member of the North Side Branch, which Jack Carney chaired. I made a Communist of Wally Carmon and he too wound up in the North Side Branch. When I succeeded Carney as chairman, I nominated Carmon for secretary and he was elected. He became chairman after the branch elected me to the City Central Committee.

Jack Carney and Tom O'Flaherty inspired the City Central Committee to raise funds by sponsoring a show called *The Last Revolution*—"a humorous proletarian operetta in two acts; plot and lyrics by Michael Gold and J. Ramírez, original music by Rudolf Liebich." This was the play Mike and I had collaborated on in Mexico. Produced in a large labor hall with a sizable cast (including "Natalie Gómez") and a seven-piece orchestra directed by Comrade Liebich, it raised $4,000, far more than anticipated. The play is set in a lonely capitalist land called Morganville. Elsewhere, in country after country, Communist revolution has occurred. Morganville, always on the hunt for trade, and because, after all, "business is business," has helped put each new republic on its feet. Now, the rest of the world remade, Morganville lives on as a preserve of capitalist concessionaires in a Communist world. With concessions no longer needed, Morganville languishes. The underfed, previously compliant workers ("Henry Dubbs") rise up and initiate The Last Revolution.

Although Mike had written his fair share of the story, most of the accompanying lyrics were mine. The City Central Committee published and sold *A Proletarian Song Book* made up entirely of the play's lyrics. I retain a copy.

Here are some snatches from typical verses:

Cover of songbook sold at the 1923 Chicago production of the musical travesty concocted in Mexico by " J. Ramírez," in collaboration with Mike Gold.

It Had to Be Revolution

NOBLE, NOBLE PLUTES
(Sung by Bishop Bunk, Senator Bunk, Judge Bunk, and General
Bunk)

See the plutes at their noble task
Guiding with God our tangled lives;
Reward in Heaven they do not ask—
Only this world for them and their wives . . .

Refrain
O, noble, noble, beneficent Plutes
Competing so dutifully every hour . . .

THE LAW OF SUPPLY AND DEMAND
(Sung by the Capitalists)

Attila when araiding was a bold if heartless thief
But nowadays we've civilized such things beyond belief.
We take the people's bread away, but Oh, for reasons grand;
It's all because of the Economic Law of Supply and Demand.
We soak them with the Economic Law of Supply and Demand.

THANK YOU KIND MASTERS
(Sung by the Dubbs)

Thank you kind masters for all you have done
To make our lot easier under the sun.
You've left us our arms and legs; flesh, bone and sinew.
And failing these royal gifts could we continue
To labor and live and bring you the mon?
Refrain
O, Gawd no, how could we?

I'VE NEVER BEEN A BOLSHEVIST
(Sung by Labor Misleader)

I've been a crook,—it's easy to abuse me.
There's not a crime my miserable soul has missed.
But the good Recording Angel will excuse me,
For I've never, never been a Bolshevist . . .

142

Manuel Gómez and Wife in Chicago

Refrain
Hibernism and nepotism and euphemism and aphorism:
These are the only isms that for me have had a lure;
Aneurism and helotism and rheumatism and priapism.
But as to naughty Bolshevism I'm pure, pure, pure.

MATRON OF THE BOURGEOISIE
(Sung by Mrs. Hawkins-Pierpont)

It seems that from my very birth
Creation recognized my worth . . .
For when at first I opened wide
My tiny mouth to breathe the air
A silver spoon was lying there . . .

Sears Roebuck, while boring me desperate, barely yielded a sub-standard living for Natalie and me. After a month or so I quit for a reportorial job on the half-century-old *Chicago Economist,* a weekly, where I ran a column of inane gossip concerning officers of small banks. ("The cashier of the Northwest Side Trust and Savings boasts a brand-new nine-pound son. Congratulations, Ed.") As a member of the venerable and prestigious *Chicago Economist's* "editorial staff," I was able to move to assistant editor of a slick-paper magazine entitled *Investment News*—with a pretty good hike in pay. It took nerve to apply; for my acquaintance with the world of finance and investment was limited to the personalities of certain out-of-the-way bank officials. I wrote about the grain market without understanding my words: simply a guesswork rephrasing from Board of Trade circulars. No doubt I would have acquired some familiarity with the field in time, but *Investment News* had me for only three weeks before I answered the Party's call. George Maurer, secretary of the City Central Committee, put me to work full time as local agitprop director. ("Agitprop," which meant agitation and propaganda, was part of our Russianized shorthand—like "Comintern.") My salary was set at ten dollars a week. Lowly yes, but then it wasn't drawn on capitalist profits.

One Sunday on West Madison Street, I noticed a vaguely familiar face among a group of women being bundled out of a patrol car. It

It Had to Be Revolution

was Dorothy Day. She'd been arrested on suspicion, in an all-night bar frequented by whores, and was now being let go. She was very drunk, and I took her home and put her to bed. Natalie and I (and the Carmons) saw her several times. (I remember us all going swimming together in Lake Michigan at Oak Street Beach.) Dorothy was living with a dark-browed bruiser named Lionel who used to beat her up. (She had been almost unrecognizable getting out of the patrol car because her face was a mess of swellings and discolorations—left there, she said, by Lionel.) She waited on him like a slave. When we visited her she was ironing his shirts. He had lots of women, and eventually he threw Dorothy out. She disappeared, and the next I heard of her she was an inspired Catholic.

Chicago in the 1920s was "hog butcher to the world," smokestack capital, the country's railroad center, the "metropolis of America's heartland." A rough, tough, dynamic city—exciting not just to work in but as a place to live. The city fascinated me, perhaps because it was so unlike my native New York. Parochial, yes: politically benighted—newsbound by the flag-waving *Chicago Tribune* and bossed by the grotesque Mayor William Hale Thompson (then running for reelection on the slogan "Keep King George out of Chicago!"). He was kept in power by a Republican machine more solidly entrenched than Daley's Democratic one, decades later. Battleground of Al Capone, Dion O'Banion, and the five Genna brothers and scene of the St. Valentine's Day Massacre,[2] Chicago was still a strong "union town," with bold and "advanced" leadership. The Chicago Federation of Labor had adopted a resolution favoring U.S. recognition of Soviet Russia. Mettlesome John Fitzpatrick, the federation's president, admired Senator Robert M. LaFollette ("fighting Bob") and acclaimed the Conference for Progressive Political Action sponsored by the Brotherhood of Locomotive Engineers and the International Association of Machinists. The

2. The Genna brothers owned a grubby-looking but wonderful Greek restaurant on Blue Island Avenue which served the best food in town at moderate prices. Elizabeth Gurley Flynn, who drew close to the Party during this period, loved it. So did I. We used to go there whenever she came to town. In 1912 and 1913 "Gurley Flynn" had been "the glamor girl of the IWW." Neither she nor the IWW had any glamor now but Elizabeth was still earnest and charming, a delightful companion.

144

Chicago Federation of Labor assembly included Jack Johnstone, Charlie Krumbein, Arne Swabeck, and Nels Kjar—all known Communists—delegated by union locals in which they had been especially helpful on picket lines. Fitzpatrick welcomed them, not as Communists but as good union men. So, though we were unable to build up the Party, we did have some sense of real accomplishment in Chicago.

As agitprop director I had charge of arranging meetings, lining up speakers, and preparing handbills and other printed materials for local distribution. In addition I conducted a class called Rudiments of Marxism-Leninism. By now I had done quite a bit of collateral reading, and was one of the probably not more than half a dozen American party members who had read all three volumes of Marx's *Capital*. Besides, like teachers everywhere, I learned a lot while preparing the lessons. In short, "working for the Party" proved a hell of a lot more like full-time employment than the job at Sears Roebuck had ever been!

Though my salary was set at ten dollars a week, I rarely got that much—sometimes I got five dollars, often only two. It depended on what was available. The Party's sources of income were scanty: collections at meetings, entertainments, bazaars, and so on, plus the occasional donation from some prosperous sympathizer. Throughout its history, the Party received a regular subsidy from Russia. The amount was a secret to all but a two-man committee; I knew only that it came earmarked for specific elementary purposes. We understood, of course, that it was trifling in comparison with the largesse afforded our large and embattled brother parties in Europe. In my seven years as a "paid Party functionary," I could never count on full salary for several weeks running, and it was the same with everybody else on the payroll. We managed, nevertheless: "took in each other's washing," borrowed, and once in a great while there came a windfall of back pay. There was time, and money, for recreation, too: Oak Street Beach, the movies, picnics at Chernauskas Grove, Sunday morning confabs at the Radical Book Shop, Ben Hecht evenings at Dill Pickles, and a certain amount of carousing with Prohibition gin or *mustikha* in other comrades' homes.

In the Party setup Chicago was both Chicago and Chicago Plus; for the city organization was administrative center for District 8, which

Oak Street Beach, Chicago, 1922. Foreground, left to right: "Manuel Gómez," Rose Carmon, "Natalie Gómez," and Dorothy Day.

included Illinois, Wisconsin, Minnesota, and parts of Michigan and Indiana. Late in 1922 my City Central Committee experience got me elected to the District 8 Executive Committee, and I became district agitprop director. For a while I delegated most of the "agit" stuff to others and concentrated on quiet "prop." I set up an educational lecture circuit for the district and took to the road as lecturer. I delivered two short lecture series, Revolutionary Marxism and History of the American Labor Movement. The public was invited, admission was free, and I did this five nights a week, each in a different town.

The most challenging stop on my circuit was Milwaukee. A city famous for three things: (1) beer, which flowed freely even during Prohibition, (2) Germanism—the heaviest concentration of German people in America, and (3) Socialist Party politics. The vitality of the last was exemplified by the city's perennial mayor, Dan Hoan; its perennial representative in Congress, Victor Berger; and its top-circulation daily newspaper, *The Milwaukee Leader*. Berger was the first Socialist ever elected to the U.S. Congress.

Milwaukee had been a center of opposition to President Wilson's war policy (chiefly, it was said, out of sympathy with Germany), but in general the Milwaukee brand of socialism was conservative and

146

provincial. The Socialist Party there maintained only an arms-length (practically nominal) affiliation with the national SP, and modeled itself on the extreme right wing of the German SPD.

Not every socially minded Milwaukeean liked the local SP. Some of the more progressive young people were impatient with the stodgy Hoan-Berger line. Thus, even though we Communists had no real footing in town, my lectures attracted a comparatively large audience. The first one seems to have thrilled (their word) a young couple who introduced themselves as Girolamo ("Nemo") Piccoli and his wife, Juanita. I sensed, from the beginning, a rare personal sympathy between these two youngsters and me, and they evidently sensed it, too. They attended all the rest of my lectures in Milwaukee, and each time I stayed overnight at their place. In Milwaukee they belonged less to the world of politics than to that of art. Nemo, a promising American sculptor, had been born in Palermo, Sicily, and brought to this country as an infant. Juanita, a native Milwaukeean, was one of his pupils (her mother was a Milwaukee-German hausfrau, her father a Cuban cigarmaker of French parentage). At the time of our first meeting, the couple were just flirting with social leftism. In time, I converted them into unconditional Communist Party loyalists (the conversion was in fact too thorough), but they never participated in the day-to-day movement. That such a personal sympathy existed between the Piccolis and me was a bit of a mystery then, and isn't wholly explicable even now, though it lasted a lifetime and survived even a long and acrimonious break.

While Milwaukee was probably the "least Communist" stop on my circuit, we did have one prodigious Party member there. This was Thurber Lewis, a wiry, hard-fisted, cocky young hell-raiser with personality, imagination, and brains. A self-educated man of Welsh descent, he had, as a boy, traveled the country with his widowed father, a popular itinerant old-time Socialist wheelhorse. While the old man spoke, the boy handed out leaflets. In his early twenties, when I first me him, he was a militant sophisticate of the working class movement. He could laugh at the Party, live it, work like hell for it. In Chicago, to which the Party soon shifted him from Milwaukee, Thurber and I developed a relationship as close as the one I had with the Piccolis—and in some ways more confidential.

Lewis would have become a national leader of the Party if it hadn't been for his wild streak. On one of his bouts of irresponsibility, he disappeared for weeks, sailing as a deckhand on a freighter between New York and Hamburg. When he returned, he could describe every whorehouse on the Rieperbahn. (In Chicago, the only woman he looked at was his wife; he was crazy about her, though she seemed to have an eye for every man but Thurber.)

During my years in Chicago, I had more friends than at any other time in my life: George Maurer, Harrison George, Kitty Harris, Tom O'Flaherty, Max Shachtman, Al and Viola Tiala, Charlie Krumbein, Bill Dunne . . . and of course the Carmons. We were joined by a heady feeling of comradeship born of the conviction that our lives were in tune with history. My preferred companions were Bill Dunne and Thurber Lewis—we three were real cronies—and, Tom O'Flaherty, the free-swinging revolutionary columnist. I had a give-and-take with Bill, Thurber, and Tom which I didn't have with the others. Tom, with his barbed humor and brogue-slurred speech, was, when sober, a complex of talents. Unfortunately, the succeeding years would find him less and less apt to be sober.

When I first heard of William F. Dunne he was already a famous character. Born in Kansas City around 1890 of an Irish immigrant father and a French-Canadian mother, he'd been raised in Minnesota. At twenty he was an electrician and active in the electrical workers union in British Columbia. He went to Butte, Montana, during the first phase of the war, in 1916 or '17, to work at his trade in the Anaconda Copper Mining Co. In 1917 an explosion in one of the Anaconda mines took a terrible human toll and provoked a strike that eventually involved 28,000 miners. The electrician Bill Dunne became chairman of the joint strike committee and editor of the strike-spawned *Butte Daily Bulletin*. The strike was a bitter one. Anaconda called in the Pinkertons; Frank Little, labor organizer from the IWW and a cripple, was lynched; and on occasion Bill and his young wife, Marguerite stood guard, guns in hand, all night at the *Bulletin*'s printing plant. Under Bill's continuing editorship the *Butte Daily Bulletin*, adopted as the official organ of the Montana State Federation of Labor, became the largest labor daily west of the Mississippi. Elected to the 1918–20 Montana State Legislature as a write-in Democrat (though an announced Socialist), Bill was the first legislator in the country to introduce a resolution calling for withdrawal of U.S. troops from Siberia, and the first to introduce one for the recognition of the Soviet government.

One day while I was talking to Jack Carney, Dunne came into the *Voice of Labor* office. He was a short, stocky, powerful-looking man with a heavy Irish face, black close-cropped hair, and mild blue eyes. He asked what I, as a Mexican, thought of the rendering into English of certain terms in some new book on Mexico (I hadn't read it). We talked animatedly of this and that, political and literary. The range of his interests surprised me. I walked him home and met Marguerite, a sunny petite woman with a loose friendly mouth and round brown eyes. I also met Little Bill, the Dunnes' only child. Both parents adored the spindly six-year-old, who used to call me Comrade Manny. Marguerite lived for her husband, and over the years had her full portion of thrills and heartbreaks. We were fond of each other, and she confided in me. Never had an affair, though we came close to it once or twice.

Bill had ugly moods. Like Thurber and Tom, he drank heavily. People told me I ought to try curbing them, but I was not my friends' guardian and drank along with them when I wanted a refresher. At the end of an evening's political rally, Bill and I generally sat up late, exchanging stray thoughts and observations, ideas, witticisms, and long silences. I was always the first to call it a night. Afraid of no person, Bill would be afraid to go to bed with his reveries.

Our Workers Party interjected itself into the country's electoral process hesitantly and weakly. In 1922 it presented only four state tickets and half a dozen isolated candidates elsewhere. In the meantime, Fitzpatrick and Ed Nockels of the Chicago Federation of Labor had organized a skeleton Labor Party—symptomatic of a growing Farmer-Labor Party movement—with centers in Minnesota and the Dakotas. Here was an opportunity to forge a United Front.[3] A 1922 Comintern thesis had asserted that "the problem of the United

---

3. During the Third Congress of the Comintern it had become clear that the times were not ripe for revolutionary action. The small, often isolated Communist parties were therefore directed to build bridges to the social democrats and other working class parties and associates in the hope of winning members. This so-called United Front tactic was viewed by many left Communists as pure casuistry.

Political Front of Labor in the United States is the problem of the Labor Party." The favorable status of the Communists in the Chicago trade unions and Fitzpatrick's high regard for William Z. Foster gave the Workers Party an opening wedge. He and Foster had collaborated during the great steel strike, and also in organizing Chicago's packinghouse employees. In 1923, then, when the Fitzpatrick-Nockels outfit sponsored a convention to set up a national Farmer-Labor Party, the Workers Party was invited to attend.

This, however, was not enough for our Party's bosses in New York. Thus, a plethora of "fraternal delegates" from shadowy organizations with such names as the Council for the Protection of the Foreign Born, International Workers Order, and International Labor Defense descended upon the Chicago convention. Fitzpatrick, no yesterday's child, thereupon proposed that the convention consider itself preliminary and adjourn until a wider and more representative gathering could be convened. Foster thought our people should play along with Fitz, and all of us Chicago Communists agreed, for he was one of our few links with the progressive leadership in the American labor movement. But the Central Executive Committee in New York said no, and the packed convention, much of it operating under strict Communist discipline, declared itself the constituent assembly of a National Federated Farmer-Labor Party. Amid cheers, Fitzpatrick and the bulk of the bona fide trade union delegates walked out. The Minnesota Farmer-Laborites never affiliated with the new party. In name at least there was now a Federated Farmer-Labor Party, one that was secure from petit bourgeois compromises. The Central Executive Committee claimed that the new organization represented a great victory in the class struggle; others laughed, while some found the whole affair just too painful. This simulacrum of a federation cost real money to maintain, and such influence as it had was negative. Before long it dropped from notice, quietly abandoned.

The Federated Farmer-Labor fiasco naturally precipitated bitter recrimination within Communist ranks. We Chicagoans, and our entire District 8 membership, blasted the Central Executive Committee for ruining one of the Party's few contacts with progressive trade union leadership. The CEC in turn assailed us for having been party to a Foster-Dunne-Cannon policy of "United Front from

Above" (that is, an alliance worked out with the heads of the unions) instead of "United Front from Below." We replied that ours had been a policy of United Front from Above *and Below*, and that the CEC's line was no more than infantile leftism.

At that time the CEC in effect meant Ruthenberg and his twenty-three-year-old chief strategist, Jay Lovestone, a contemptuously glib whiz kid out of the City College of New York. With their conferees, Will Weinstone, Max Bedacht, Bob Minor, Israel Amter, et al., they ran the Party.[4] The Party's third national convention was only weeks away, however, and convened early in January 1924. I (Manuel Gómez) was a delegate, a member of the Foster circle in daily confab with Foster, Bill Dunne, Jim Cannon, Earl Browder, and Jack Johnstone. The only one in that group never to have belonged to a trade union, I was also bourgeois in upbringing, a fact that grieved me. In the Party of the Proletariat even the intellectuals, the Bert Wolfes, the Mike Golds, the Joe Freemans were, or pretended to be, proletarian by origin. I admit, with amusement, that in my first days in Chicago I said I'd been a coal miner.[5]

The convention wrought a complete change. We Fosterites, in alliance with Ludwig Lore's Volkszeitung group and supported by the big Finnish Federation, wound up with a majority of the delegates, chose the new CEC, and took over the Party. The Foster group leadership (now reinforced by Alex Bittleman from New York) moved the Workers Party headquarters to Chicago, where it should have been before. To this point, the Party had no daily English-language newspaper. The new CEC established one, the *Daily Worker*, with Bill Dunne as editor. (Moscow, recognizing the obvious need, provided funds.) A merger of three existing magazines, the *Liberator*,

---

4. "They ran it" under the guiding hand of one Joseph Pogány, alias John Pepper, a temerarious Hungarian who had arrived in New York mid-1922 with the aura of having been, for a time, war commissar in the Bela Kun (March 21–August 1, 1919) Soviet Republic of Hungary. As "John Pepper" he became a voice in Ruthenberg-Lovestone policy.

5. At that time, I accepted on faith the oft-repeated precept that the working class was humanity unblemished. Time and observation have undeceived me. "Bourgeois intellectual" and "petit bourgeois intellectual" were corrosive epithets. It was of course possible for intellectuals to appear from the ranks of the working proletariat, but the only one I ever met was Bill Dunne. He was a true working class intellectual.

Greetings!

Illustration from the *Workers Monthly*, August 1925. This issue's lead article was "La Folletism without La Follette," by Manuel Gómez.

Soviet Russia Today, and the *Labor Herald* (organ of Foster's old Trade Union Educational League [TUEL]) created a new forty-eight-page magazine called the *Workers Monthly*, which combined the features of its three predecessors. The titular editorship went to Earl Browder, Foster's TUEL aide, but I was editor de facto. I still have copies of the *Workers Monthly*, the lead articles signed "Manuel Gómez." The magazine carried analyses of international political developments, American labor reportage, stories, poems, book reviews, and cartoons (with cover decorations by Juanita Piccoli, and a couple of drawings by Nemo).

The magazine was an official organ of the Workers Party, so designated on the colophon. How interesting, in the light of subsequent events, for it to have featured in 1924 and 1925 monthly installments of the *History of the Russian Communist Party* by Grigori Zinoviev! (I was reminded of this only when looking over my old copies.) Zinoviev was a name to reckon with in those days. The downfall of the MacDonald Labour government in the general election of October 29, 1924, was universally attributed to the so-called Zinoviev Letter, which the Tories had released only four days before. The letter, later proved a forgery, supposedly contained Comintern instructions for a revolution in Britain. The "History of the Russian Party" has of course been rewritten many times since Zinoviev's version was published, and is now being rewritten again.

21 The Anti-Imperialist Department

In addition to editing the *Workers Monthly*, I headed what was known as the Anti-Imperialist Department of the Party. All Comintern parties in important capitalist countries had such departments, which sought to implement "the Leninist program of uniting all revolutionary working class movements in the home countries of imperialism with the National Liberation struggles in the oppressed colonial and semicolonial countries." The issues? In our case independence for Puerto Rico, liquidation of the Guantánamo naval base in Cuba, withdrawal of U.S. forces from Haiti and the Dominican Republic, and an end to all U.S. exploitation in Latin America and the Philippine Islands. We also called for a free China. We cultivated good relations with militant nationalists among the Latin Americans and Filipinos living in the United States, and I haunted Chicago's Chinatown (the Wentworth Avenue–Twenty-second Street area). Everybody I encountered there was pro-Kuomintang, but I made no secret of my Communist connections. In China at that time the Kuomintang admitted Communists to membership and was battling the Japanese with Russian advisers—notably Michael Borodin, my old mentor.[1] I acquired friends in Chicago's Chinatown and developed an affection for this people which has never left me. In Chicago we had a good group of sympathizers, including laundrymen, restaurant workers, and a few University of Chicago students. I shipped a number back to China to fight—some, I must admit, to die.

For a time we thought the Anti-Imperialist Department's responsibilities would include the struggle against the oppression of Negroes within the United States itself. But eventually it was decided that the issue must be addressed by the entire Party organization, not just the Anti-Imperialist Department. (By the late 1920s the Party would be combatting the Marcus Garvey and other "Back-to-Africa" movements by calling for the self-determination of the Black Belt, that large contiguous region stretching across several southern states where the majority of the population was Negro. This demand for self-determination acknowledged that the Negroes should have the right to carve out an independent black nation.)

In April 1925, I spent ten days in Mexico where I was assigned to represent the Workers Party at a convention of the Mexican Communist Party, and to help establish a front organization called the

---

1. In 1927, following a right-wing coup by Chiang Kai-shek, the Communists were thrown out of the Kuomintang and the Russian advisers sent home. Borodin got only mediocre Soviet assignments after that. The Comintern had dispatched my old friend Roy to China soon after sending Borodin. There he had attacked Borodin's policy inside the Kuomintang as too conciliatory, but Roy's "more independent line" proved ruinous and led to his downfall (see note 5).

All-America Anti-Imperialist League. It was hoped that the latter would eventually have sections throughout Latin America which could cooperate with the section in the United States.

The Mexican Communist Party I found in 1925 was not the one I had left behind a few years before. José Valadés and José Allen had disappeared, and the only old activist I recognized was Manuel Ramírez. Though the party was clearly in disarray—the Central Committee report contained no membership figures—some not unpromising rebuilding was under way, thanks to a lanky, dyspeptic American in his twenties named Bertram C. Wolfe. The party had a vigorous new general secretary (Rafael Carrillo) and was publishing an astonishingly good weekly or monthly paper called *El Machete*. The Central Committee included two of Mexico's world-famous painters—David Alfaro Siqueiros and Xavier Guerrero. They, like the others, tended to follow Wolfe's lead.[2] Siqueiros's temperament was that of an anarchic gangster, while Guerrero was a brooding sphinx never able to find words. Bert and his sweet-faced wife, Ella, put me up in their house. I was to know Bert Wolfe for many years, first (there in Mexico) as a friend, later as a factional opponent in the Workers Party, then again as a friend. (As friend and as opponent I respected him greatly.) He and Ella were temporary in Mexico; I forget just what brought them there. Bert had been with Jay Lovestone at CCNY, with him in the American Socialist Party left wing, and with him in the breakaway to communism. Bert was a second whiz kid—without Lovestone's underlying hint of cynicism.

Although the weak Mexican Communist Party did not provide much of a nucleus for a broad front organization, the general population's hatred of sticky-fingered *Yanquilandia* provided a strong base for our All-America Anti-Imperialist League. Nominally at

2. I have a letter from Bert Wolfe in which he says that when he arrived in Mexico the Communist Party "was primarily a party of painters." And so he characterized it in his *Fabulous Life of Diego Rivera*. Rivera was in and out of the party during much of his life—back in near the end, worshiping the Stalin he once reviled as a Trotskyite. I met Diego once, in 1920; had dinner at his house in fact—in company with Felipe Carillo, Mayan-speaking spellbinder of Yucatan's peasants, and "Roberto" Haberman, Carillo's mastermind. Though not yet a Communist, Diego was clearly a socialist. It was a wonderful and gargantuan dinner. "The philosopher of the brush" impressed me as gargantuan in every sense, and sociopolitically as an unstable sentimentalist.

Mexico City, April 1925. Third National Congress of the Communist Party of Mexico. Manuel Gómez, emissary (fraternal delegate) from the U.S. Party, in center of 2d row. Bertram Wolfe in rear, center. Two famous Mexican painters, Xavier Guerrero and Alfaro Siqueiros, at left and right ends of front row respectively.

least, the organization there (*Liga Antiimperialista de las Americas*) served as the center of truly international endeavor. We already had certain extraordinary individual contacts elsewhere: Julio Antonio Mella in Cuba, Victor Raúl Haya de la Torre in Peru (both these men proved themselves giants). Though we later acquired connections in Panama, Guatemala, and Nicaragua, they never (except in the notable case of Nicaragua) amounted to more than occasional correspondence.

Though I'd been named secretary at the United States section of the All-American Anti-Imperialist League, that section in fact still had to be created. The organized labor movement was not interested; indeed, the speakers we sent to meetings of trade union locals usually failed even to be admitted. However, many progressive unions subscribed to a news service (the Federated Press) whose Chicago Bureau—Carl Haessler, Leland Olds, and Art Shields— were all more or less radical, and the All-America Anti-Imperialist League idea appealed to them. They gave us publicity, and a wealthy Chicago liberal named William H. Holly gave us money. Liberals like William Pickens (of the NAACP), Roger Baldwin, Robert Morss Lovett, Paxton Hibben, Lewis Gannett, Freda Kirchwey, and Arthur Garfield Hays allowed us to print their names on our letterhead—in company with Scott Nearing, William Z. Foster, William F. Dunne, and Manuel Gómez. Until the Nicaragua crisis a couple of years later, the league was largely a matter of propaganda—bulletins, petitions, lecture materials, etc.—most of it emanating from my office.

Art Shields and Esther Lowell, his cherished consort, became personal friends of mine. On the surface, they seemed an unlikely combination: he an ex-Wobbly roustabout, she a Boston Lowell. They were equally gentle people, both of them warm-hearted, kindly, generous, idealistic. And they were thieves. When the mood seized them, or when they thought they needed something—as perhaps they often actually did (their living scale was lower working class)—they simply took it. Art stole books from the public library. Esther told of stealing coats. She explained her method: "When you go into the store you have a coat hanging over your arm. You lay that coat down, look around until you find one you want, put it on and stroll out. If they stop you at the door you can always say, 'Oh, I thought it was mine.' " (I knew nothing of Art's and Esther's thievery during my Chicago days. I learned about it years later from my dear Sylvia, who met them as friends of mine. While it was all news to me, I was hardly surprised. For me, Art and Esther remained the quintessence of honor. After all, the public library was a "bourgeois" library and the stores were "bourgeois" stores. Wobbly, and Leninist, philosophy scorns bourgeois morality as a capitalist prop. The shame, I have long since realized, is that we defied "bourgeois morality" while possessing only the merest scraps of a viable substitute.)

In the Party, this was a particularly intense phase in the factional fight that lasted, with shifting alliances and reversals of position, throughout the life of the Party as I knew it. Like the similar struggles in other Comintern parties, it was fatefully linked to changes in Soviet Russia. In the spring of 1922 Lenin had undergone surgery for removal of the bullet Dora Kaplan fired at him in 1918. A stroke followed, leaving his right side partially paralyzed. He had a quick recovery but suffered two additional strokes in December. In 1923 he was able to work only now and then, dictating from his sickbed. In the meantime, dismissals and promotions were occurring in the party-state's pervasive organizational personnel. Lenin died on January 21, 1924. No one else commanded his authority.

Trotsky was the most illustrious and most popular, but he found key positions in the party-state aligned against him. A triumvirate of Zinoviev, Kamenev, and Stalin emerged and, invoking the pre-1917 Bolshevik Old Guard, excoriated Trotsky for his one-time Menshevism and his prerevolutionary conflicts with Lenin. Suddenly Trotsky was under violent attack. A systematic campaign exhumed his little-known (and even less understood) theory of Permanent Revolution, and accused him of seeking to replace Leninism with "Trotskyism." The party (and state) press was practically closed to his replies. The Zinoviev-Kamenev-Stalin triumvirate ruled (Stalin was regarded as the junior partner) with the support of Bukharin and the Old Bolsheviks generally, and few dared to speak out in Trotsky's favor. Those who did (Radek, Sokolnikov, and a few others) were quickly shifted to minor posts.

These developments were rapidly reflected in the American party—the Workers Party. In the CEC, a Ruthenberg-Lovestone resolution proposed "unqualified support of the Bolshevik Old Guard." The Fosterite majority demurred, maintaining that we ought to wait for more information. The resolution was held up, but at a subsequent meeting, after repeated hints from Moscow, it passed—without opposition.

The fourth national convention of the Workers Party—its name changed to Workers (Communist) Party—was now set for late August 1925. The battle for delegates was furious—and not without abuses. Rationalizing that we acted for the Party's ultimate good, we of the Foster group used Party funds to finance group caucus travel. The Ruthenberg group did the same. Indeed, I think they did more of it than we, but it didn't help them. When the delegates convened, we Fosterites had a big majority: 40 to 21.

At this point a cable arrived from the CI (Communist International) and was read aloud by the CI representative. (We were rarely without a "CI Rep." This one was Sergei Ivanovich Gusev, under the extraordinary pseudonym "P. Green".) I have a copy of the cable, which stated:

(1) The Communist International has decided the majority group must not be allowed to suppress the Ruthenberg group because the Ruthenberg group is more loyal to the CI and stands closer to its views.

(2) Ruthenberg must be renamed party secretary and the new CEC must include Lovestone.

(3) This new CEC must be fixed by a Parity Commission with an equal number of members from each group and Comrade Green acting as parity chairman.

The convention heard this in stunned disbelief, and then burst into outraged protest. But Comintern discipline was inviolable. Injured and angry, I subscribed to the resolutions myself, and the final vote accepted the decision unanimously.

We had not yet heard the worst, however. "Parity" proved to be a fiction. At the first meeting of the Parity Commission, Comrade "P. Green" announced that he, as chairman, would cast the deciding vote—and would cast it for the Ruthenberg group, "because of that group's greater loyalty to the Comintern." We accepted this, too, but without grace, resolved to be ready for anything next time.

The new CEC, and its trick majority, included Bert Wolfe. Bert had returned from Mexico before the convention and was a prominent Ruthenberg group spokesman throughout the proceedings. (He and I fought a verbal duel over anti-imperialist policy—mostly by flinging conflicting quotations from Lenin at each other. According to comments I heard—*from our side*—I had much the best of it.)

The Ruthenberg group now controlled everything, and one of their insiders (Weinstone, I think) had the nerve to call the group "the U.S. Communist Old Guard." They took over quickly, putting Israel Amter in place of Charlie Krumbein, whom we had installed as district organizer in New York. At the same time they made Bert Wolfe the national agitprop director, appointed Max Bedacht editor of the *Workers Monthly,* and reduced Bill Dunne's *Daily Worker* status to coeditor with J. Louis Engdahl. Etc., etc.

In all communications from Moscow, "Bolshevization" was now the predominant line. Every Comintern party had to be "Bolshevized," structurally and otherwise. Our American party was to be restructured on the basis of where the members worked instead of where they lived or what language they spoke. Now, this was a plausible idea, but few of our city members worked together in the same establishment. We compromised, transforming the local territorial branches into "street nuclei." For all its absurdities of nomenclature, then, this structural Bolshevization accomplished something good, eliminating the anomaly of separate language federations.

Apart from this restructuring, our "Bolshevization" consisted chiefly of "hush-hush" work for Soviet Russia. Comrades would simply vanish. "What happened to them?" "Hush hush." You stopped asking. You knew they had been absorbed into the secret apparatus of the Commissariat for Foreign Affairs or the OGPU or the Intelligence Section of the Red Army or the Technical Service Bureau or some other, acting under Party discipline.[3] As good Communists they had no choice. Friends of mine in the Party—Harrison George, Kitty Harris, and many others—disappeared in this way. (Earl Browder, whom I knew to have once been Kitty Harris's sweetheart, confided to me years later that she had been commandeered in 1925.) At one stage of my own career I might well have been deemed suitable for some "drop-out" job. If so I would have obeyed the summons unhesitatingly. I hate to think of what such an action would have done to my life. By 1925, however, my too open role in the Party ruled out anything of the kind.

Natalie had adjusted her life to mine as best she could, running a Communist-oriented household on little or nothing, with serenity

---

3. The OGPU (Unified State Political Directorate) had in 1923 succeeded the GPU (founded in February 1922 to replace the Cheka) as the primary extrajudicial organ of repression. It would in time develop into a vast apparatus of systematized terror.

and discretion, whatever the hours and whoever might drop in unexpectedly. She went with me to Communist-run picnics, festivities at comrades' homes, and so on, but never to political meetings, public or private. In effect a constituent of the Chicago Communist-Foster group, she probably never believed in communism for a moment, either in Russia or Mexico, or in the United States. In fact she was becoming more and more American, and less dependent on me. Midway through 1926 we broke up. It should have happened sooner. She bored me and was getting less and less companionship from me. In the final months—and years—I treated her abominably, hurting her with derogatory remarks on her Hollywood tastes, her idle daydreaming, and her intellectual vacuity. My behavior was destructive and cruel. I was ashamed of myself afterward, and resolved never again to act that way toward another human being.

I left our basement apartment on Belmont Avenue near Clark to Natalie and went to live with Thurber and Marguerite Lewis over on the West Side not far from the *Daily Worker* office. Natalie soon found consolation. A teller employed by a bank where the ILD (International Labor Defense) had an account moved in with her.

I enjoyed being with Thurber and Marguerite—except for the physical inconveniences. Whenever I wanted a bath I had to go somewhere else because the bathtub was full of coal for the pot-bellied stove around which we huddled in winter. The kitchen sink had to do for washing hands and face; for Marguerite's batiks occupied the bathroom washbasin—sometimes with an admixture of her hair dye. Since Marguerite slept late, Thurber and I regularly breakfasted without her. (An incidental note: Thurber was the only person I ever knew who ate six eggs for breakfast—when he could afford them.)

For some undisclosed reason Ruthenberg, Lovestone, and Company, when using the axe on us Fosterites, left me undisturbed at the head of the Anti-Imperialist Department. Perhaps they hoped to win me over to their group, and, indeed, Lovestone's enigmatic pleasantries at the time struck me as a come-on. Or perhaps what my department was then doing made a change inopportune. After all, the U.S. Marines were about to intervene in Nicaragua for the third time, and the Anti-Imperialist Department thus had an emergency on its hands. In 1926 the marines had invaded to bolster a native reactionary dictatorship. This time they could not just land and take over the country. A liberal guerrilla army led by General Augusto C. Sandino offered stubborn resistance for seven years, with widespread peasant support. We of course supported the guerrillas, and in direct opposition to the marines' recruitment campaign we issued the slogan "Enlist with Sandino!" I found the general's brother, Socrates Sandino, living in Brooklyn, and his name helped bolster our cause. Through the United States section of the All-America Anti-Imperialist League we raised funds for Sandino to buy munitions, medical supplies, and bandages. Our league slogan was "Stop the flow of Nicaraguan blood!"[4] Haiti had been under continuous U.S. occupation since 1916, and the Dominican Republic since 1915. We conducted campaigns on their behalf. But the fighting in Nicaragua made that our focal point.

In February 1927 I was delegated to the Congress against Colonial Oppression and Imperialism in Brussels, organized by communism's entrepreneurial genius, Willy Münzenberg. I can't say the congress accomplished anything, but it was surely a star-studded affair. The delegates included Jawaharlal Nehru, Chou En-lai, Mohammed Hatta, Julio A. Mella, and Victor Raúl Haya de la Torre (all destined for vital roles in the future of their respective countries), along with Henri Barbusse, Ernst Toller, George Lansbury, and others of similar note. The 180-plus delegates naturally included Sen Katayama and Roy (just before his eclipse).[5] With me from the United States came Roger Baldwin, Scott Nearing, Richard B. Moore, and Chi Ch'ao-ting. Both Moore and Chi were Commies, though their credentials suggested otherwise. Chi was a discovery of mine, a University of Chicago student whom I originally re-

4. In 1934 General Sandino was seized treacherously and executed. Unlike the Sandinista regime, he and his movement had no communist ideology or predilection.
5. In 1927 Roy was sent to China to help patch up the alliance between the Kuomintang and the Chinese Communists. As this policy failed, the Executive Committee of the Communist International denounced him as "adventurist." When Stalin refused to see him, he knew he was doomed. He was expelled from the Indian Communist Party and the Comintern in 1929 and returned to the Subcontinent, where he was arrested on a prior charge and imprisoned for six years. Roy died in 1954.

Brussels, 1927. Congress against Colonial Oppression and Imperialism. Prominent were (seated) Sen Katayama, Japan; Willy Münzenberg, Germany; Mohammed Hatta, Indonesia; George Lansbury, England; and Jawaharlal Nehru, India. Also (standing) Roger Baldwin and Manuel Gómez, U.S.A., and Julio Antonio Mella, Cuba.

cruited for Chinese nationalist work and then initiated into the Party. Chi was a scholar, a man of action, and a brilliant public speaker (in both English and Mandarin).[6]

On cabled instructions from Chicago, I detoured from Brussels to Essen in order to attend the Eleventh Congress of the German Communist Party. One of many foreign fraternal delegates at the

6. I learned the subsequent history of Chi Ch'ao-ting sometime in the mid-1980s from a comparatively recent friend of mine, Phil Jaffe. Chi had married a cousin of Jaffe's and had been associated with him in the Institute of Pacific Relations and in the editorship of the widely publicized and controversial magazine *Amerasia*. Chi returned to China sometime in the early 1940s, and was in secret communication with Chou En-lai until the establishment of the Communist regime in China in 1949. He occupied various posts under Mao Tse-tung, and died in Peking in 1964 at the age of sixty-five.

Essen, Germany, 1927. Eleventh Congress of the German Communist Party addressed by Manuel Gómez, fraternal delegate from the Workers (Communist) Party of the United States.

Parteitag, I made a ritual speech (in English) of greeting from the Workers (Communist) Party of the United States. Whatever little it may have meant to that immense gathering, to me it was thrilling.

In March 1927, Ruthenberg died. Though I had sat in with him for years in Party proceedings, I never really knew him—nor Gitlow, nor Bedacht, nor Amter, nor Stachel, nor Ballam—all the leading figures of Ruthenberg's group. After his death, it became "the Lovestone group," but except for Jay Lovestone and Bert Wolfe— and Weinstone when he came over to us—I had little more than a formal acquaintance with any of "their" leaders, even their secondary leaders. So deep was this factional split in the Party that it extended to the district committees and even the Young Workers (Communist) League.

Lenin had been in his mausoleum less than two years when the Zinoviev-Kamenev-Stalin triumvirate fell apart. Zinoviev and Kamenev had begun to fear they would have to oppose Stalin's enveloping organizational network or become its hostage. Therefore,

Kamenev made a rather bold speech to the Party, protesting "Stalin's use of the Secretariat as a political instrument." Zinoviev supported him, but with Bukharin siding against them their politico-organizational power soon crumbled. Zinoviev lost his Leningrad stronghold, and Kamenev suffered the humiliation of being demoted from Politburo member to mere *kandidat* (alternate). Repenting their previous vituperation of Trotsky, Zinoviev and Kamenev now made overtures to him. In 1926 the three joined forces, forming the United Opposition. A belated conglomerate of two crippled groupings, it met its foredoomed end in 1927 when Trotsky, Zinoviev, and Kamenev were expelled from the Party, in the company of numerous supporters. On what grounds? Factionalism. Defiance of the Central Committee. "Political deviations from Leninism: underestimation of the peasantry." Zinoviev and Kamenev recanted and were readmitted—but in a humbled capacity.

Bukharin, the "best-loved" Bolshevik, was also acknowledged the Party's most gifted theoretician. His name gave the Bukharin-Stalin concordance an indispensable prestige. The chief editor of *Pravda*, he would soon succeed Zinoviev as president of the Communist International.

Jay Lovestone had an inside track to Bukharin. In the course of his watchdog commutes to Russia, Jay had reached what amounted to an understanding with the Soviet leader regarding the groupings in their respective countries. Small wonder then that the Fifth National Convention of the Workers (Communist) Party received a strong Lovestone group endorsement—reinforced by the new CI Rep. The result was a complete Lovestone triumph. Weinstone, who had entered into a bloc with us before the convention, crept back. Bill Dunne was reduced to assistant editor of the *Daily Worker*, under Bob Minor. The Party's national headquarters were moved from Chicago to New York (on the grounds that New York was the center of world finance capital!).

When the national headquarters moved to New York, all the departments moved with it—including me. The *Daily Worker* moved too, as did such outfits as the ILD (International Labor Defense), CPFB (Council for Protection of the Foreign Born), ANLC (American Negro Labor Congress—later the League of Struggle for Negro Rights), and so on. I set up the Anti-Imperialist League office in a dusty room at 32 Union Square—adjoining the dusty suite occupied by the *New Masses*. The *New Masses* was a Communist pseudo-revival of the impudent Max Eastman–Floyd Dell political-literary-art magazine that had been hospitable to radicals of whatever description before the war. The Anti-Imperialist League paid rent to the *New Masses*, when we could, and the *New Masses* paid rent to the landlord when it could.

The ILD was conducting tumultuous demonstrations in Union Square to protest the scheduled execution of Nicola Sacco, a shoe-maker, and Bartolomeo Vanzetti, a fish peddler, who had been con-victed of murder in an atmosphere of unparalleled prejudice six years before and had been confined in a Massachusetts jail ever since. The Sacco-Vanzetti case had aroused the sympathy of the combined liberal, radical, and working class world, but not of the trial judge, not of Massachusetts Governor Alvan T. Fuller, and not of tight-lipped President Coolidge. Appeal after appeal had been de-nied. Some of the Union Square protests tended toward riot. I at-tended one with Bill Dunne which was broken up by club-swinging police. An Irish cop moving in our direction through the crowd seemed to size up my companion, stopped abruptly, and muttered to Bill, "What are you doing among these foreigners?"

Pleas and petitions, one a mile long, succeeded in staying the ex-ecution for another year, but Sacco and Vanzetti died in the Charles-town prison electric chair on August 22, 1927.

No other "Communist-front" organization did more effective work than the ILD. Most notably in the Scottsboro case, where its early and persistent intervention was no small factor in saving the lives of eight Negro boys convicted by an all-white jury in racist Scottsboro, Alabama, of raping two white girls in 1931. (One of the girls recanted her previous testimony.) Some of the boys' other de-fenders (the NAACP and the Independent Scottsboro Defense Com-mittee) opposed the ILD's role and methods, but many blacks approved. The ILD undoubtedly won friends in the Negro commu-nity as a result of the Scottsboro case.

My first home in New York (as Manuel Gómez) was a "hall bed-room" in the apartment of Liston M. Oak and Margaret Larkin on Thirteenth Street east of Second Avenue. Neither Liston nor Marg-aret was a Party member but both sympathized with it. Liston had worked for Amtorg, the Soviet purchasing agency in this country. Margaret wrote publicity for the textile and other labor unions (which, I believe, paid her fairly well). I was one of two or three (or more) subtenants accommodated down a "bowling alley" hall from the quiet sizable Oak-Larkin combination living room and sleeping quarters. For long stretches my rent remained unpaid. Neither Liston nor Margaret ever reminded me of how much I owed them. And their icebox was open to me—for breakfast or snacks. I lived as one of the family.

Liston—gaunt, gray-eyed, with an organ-deep voice—had the easy familiarity of his native California plus a genuine love of people and a compulsion to do things for them—individually and collectively. He was my age (a month younger), which in 1927 meant thirty-two. Margaret, still in her late twenties, was a statuesque, olive-skinned, doe-eyed charmer from New Mexico and the University of Kansas (where she had won poetry prizes). She entertained with gusto, self-accompanied by guitar. Their hospitality, attractiveness, and verve made their place a sort of East Thirteenth Street salon for friends and friends of friends. Arriving home late from a night of one harried meeting after another—at least two or three—I might find Jessica Smith, Genevieve Taggert, Jimmy Harris, Alex Gomberg, Adelaide Schulkind, or other guests in the living room. I usually joined the gathering, knowing there'd be no one coming to my office before ten or eleven in the morning.

I was busy most of the day and a lot busier at night, generally with Anti-Imperialist League work, though I also taught labor history several nights a week at the Party-run Workers School headed by Alexander Trachtenberg (later by V. J. Jerome). The fighting in Nicaragua was at a critical stage and Sandino needed all the help we could get him. To complicate matters I had to defend our pro-Sandino activities against factional sniping within the Party. In spite of our "Enlist with Sandino" slogan, we were being accused of pacifism. Referring to one of our other slogans ("Stop the flow of Nicaraguan blood!"), Lovestone, with characteristic Lovestonian wit, branded our activities "Gómez's Kotex campaign." A foul blow, but it hurt.

In theory, factionalism had no "right" to exist in the Workers (Communist) Party. After a statutorily provided brief period for

Brooklyn, New York, September 30, 1928. Superscription: "Haitian Patriotic Union Banquet to Mr. Manuel Gómez, Secretary of the All-American Anti-Imperialist League." (Gómez in center of front row.)

thrashing out differences, the Party was supposed to be—as in Soviet Russia, and throughout the Comintern—a monolith. In the Russian case, as we have seen, factionalism was ended through the suppression of all opposition. There had been a difference in Lenin's time. Both before and after the revolution, Lenin had open disagreements with every member of the Central Committee at one time or another. Very serious disagreements. But almost invariably these disagreements were settled by persuasion or vote, and the confreres proceeded to work together as before. Lenin usually—though not automatically—prevailed. Without Lenin this collegial approach lapsed. Trotsky, Zinoviev, Kamenev, Radek, Rakovsky, et al. had been read out of the Central Committee, out of the Party—even written out of the Party's official history—with the barest pretense of a chance to defend what they stood for. In early 1928 some thirty of the opposition leaders, headed by Trotsky, were exiled to remote parts of the country. Others submitted contrite public statements and applied for readmission to the Party. As a political force the Left Opposition was crushed. All the expelled leaders, including Trotsky, had the right of appeal to the Communist International. But the Comintern's Executive Committee was dominated by the Russians, and Bukharin was its president. We in the American party accepted the decisions from Russia unanimously. On the basis of the information available to us, no one doubted that Trotsky and his followers had been wrong. At the same time, some of us in the Foster group—and I include myself—deplored the machine-like procedures employed in the affair.

22   Moscow after Eight Years

The Sixth World Congress of the Comintern met in Moscow in the summer of 1928. Our "monolithic" American party sent two rival delegations, one from the Lovestone group, one from the Foster group. The Fosterite delegation consisted of Bill Foster, Alex Bittleman, Bill Dunne, Jim Cannon, Jack Johnstone, and Manuel Gómez. (My presence at the Second Congress as Jesús Ramírez in 1920 had admittedly been rather fortuitous; now in 1928 as Manuel Gómez I was a delegate in my own right, with a legitimate constituency.) The Sixth World Congress would be the first in four years—an unprecedented interval.[1] On the way over we speculated how things would look when we got there. The intervening years had, after all,

1. The first four congresses had met annually, 1919–22. The Fifth met in 1924. After the four-year wait for the Sixth came a seven-year wait for the Seventh. And the Seventh proved to be the last. The Comintern as such was dissolved in 1943, under the circumstances of wartime cooperation between Allied governments. Contact between Moscow and the various Communist parties continued, however.

seen tremendous changes in Soviet Russia and throughout the world. Among the most important was the election of Field Marshal Paul von Hindenburg as president of the German Republic, a fateful event that would have been avoided had Communist votes gone to the Social Democratic candidate. Instead, the Communists had persisted in calling the Socialists "the main enemy"—"social fascists," and so on.

We soon found that the New Economic Policy (NEP) had unmistakably improved the Soviet economy. Lenin had forced through the NEP in 1921 as a substitute for the desperate conditions precipitated by the policy of War Communism. At the outset Trotsky had opposed the new policy as a dangerous step backward, and proposed the creation of a "militarized labor force" instead.[2] But Trotsky, like all the other leaders, soon accepted the NEP as the only realistic alternative. Through temporary, manageable infusions of small-scale private enterprise in both the rural and industrial economies, the country would take a more gradual route to socialism. Bukharin, who soon became the primary ideologist of the NEP, argued that the peasants should and could be made to grow gradually and peacefully into socialism. In a Leningrad speech he added that "the class struggle in our country will diminish little by little until it dies out in communist society without any Third Revolution."

The Sixth World Congress opened on July 17 and lasted until September 1. At a couple of sessions Stalin sat impassively on the platform without speaking once. Bukharin, as head of the Communist International, presided throughout, delivering the traditional Main Report, leading the discussions, and presenting the final summation. After some last-minute amendments from the Russian delegation, the report and the summation were of course approved unanimously.

Two major themes dominated the proceedings. First, it was acknowledged that world capitalism had entered its "Third Period," during which "its partial and temporary stabilization is beginning to show evidences of breaking down." Second, great emphasis was

2. Reassignment of workers serving in the Red Army to new duties in armies of labor, and use of the War Commissariat for industrial administrative purposes. Trotsky had also proposed that the trade unions be incorporated directly into the state apparatus.

placed on the achievements and future security of Soviet Russia, which had embarked upon the historic task of building "socialism in one country." As the high court of the International, the congress also had to deal with Trotsky's final appeal against his expulsion from the Russian party.

From his exile in Alma Ata Trotsky had sent a lengthy document defending himself and denouncing Bukharin and Stalin for Thermidorism and for stifling Party democracy. The congress as a whole never heard Trotsky's opus, which was instead referred to a special committee whose members received numbered copies to peruse and return (sections were leaked surreptitiously). The committee's report recommended that Trotsky's appeal be rejected. Like every other delegate present, I voted to approve that report. I believed the decision to be necessary and proper, though I hardly subscribed to the method used in attaining it. Whether or not Trotsky's expulsion had been justified in the first place, his reinstatement was inadmissable. He had set himself up as an independent party center in exile and promulgated a destructively ambiguous position on the interrelation of world revolution and the building of socialism in Russia. He was correct to condemn the stifling of Party democracy, but the situation would have been just as bad (or worse) under Trotsky.

In the corridors of the congress one began to hear of differences between Bukharin and Stalin. "Socialism in one country," it now turned out, had more than one meaning. Bukharin envisaged it as an evolutionary outgrowth of NEP. Placing an overwhelming emphasis on the peasantry, he predicted that the private peasant economy would develop cooperatives for marketing, supply, credit, and eventually production, and that these would provide the framework for socialism. At first Stalin had encouraged this view, though he never placed the same emphasis on the role of the peasantry. He needed Bukharin's political support against the Trotsky-Zinoviev coalition, and Bukharin's "face to the countryside" coincided with his own outcry against Trotsky's "underestimation of the peasant." But Stalin always stressed industrialization, and heavy industry in particular. Unless Soviet Russia were rescued from abroad, the construction of a socialist society according to the Bukharinist agenda would take, as Bukharin himself admitted, a long, long time. Too long for Stalin. He was thinking not of evolution but of acceleration.

He had elaborated his ideas into a coherent doctrine—invoking the international Communist revolution even while he insisted that one country could achieve socialism through its own efforts. And it had long been part of Stalin's doctrine to insist that Soviet industry be made independent of "kulak caprice" by setting up more and more collective and state farms.

Now Stalin's political position was strong enough to force the issue, and a critical shortfall in grain procurements provided the necessary spark. Bukharin proposed to deal with the situation by raising grain prices and thereby inducing the peasants to part with their surpluses voluntarily. Stalin said "caressing the peasants" had gone too far. Bukharin, as always, enjoyed the support of Rykov (Lenin's successor as chairman of the Council of People's Commissars) and Tomsky (head of the All-Russian Trade Union Organization). Bukharin, Rykov, and Tomsky were all Politburo members.

In my own view, the overall Bukharinist program was hopeless, whereas Stalin's plan was ingenious, revolutionary, and made good sense. Though I had no love for Stalin's personality even then, I strongly hoped that he would prevail—as did Foster, Dunne, and others in our delegation. Foster obtained an interview with Stalin, while Bittleman and I got one with V. M. Molotov, who was then virtually Stalin's alter ego. Molotov understood no English, but the Russian-born Bittleman did the talking and made a strong case for our group's position in the American party conflict—not forgetting to mention Lovestone's closeness to Bukharin. Molotov listened without comment, but shook our hands with special warmth and somehow managed to convey that he was not displeased with our visit.

No reference to a conflict between Bukharin and Stalin disturbed the serenity of the congress auditorium. Except for the Russian delegation's ambiguous last-minute amendments to his report and summation, Bukharin seemed to exert more authority than ever. In fact, the struggle had already reached its climax. In the corridor-congress Heinz Neumann, the rising star of the German party, and V. V. Lominadze, a knowledgeable source within the Russian party, both hinted to us that Bukharin was on his way out.

Foster, Bittleman, Dunne, Johnstone, and I gathered at the hotel to consider things. We all understood that the congress would adjourn in apparent harmony, but we agreed that the real political denouement would follow fairly quickly. Moreover, we agreed that the outcome would probably be what we considered favorable—defeat for Bukharin. Jim Cannon was the only one of our group's delegates not present at this gathering. Jim had missed several sessions of the congress (no doubt from considerations that were to emerge later), and we had not seen much of him lately.

As we prepared to leave for home, I reflected that I had never been hungry in the Moscow of 1928, as I had been part of the time eight years before. The hotel plumbing worked better, too. In spite of the current difficulty in procuring grain, life had eased for everybody under NEP. The people in the street looked better fed—and much better dressed. Shops were no longer boarded up everywhere. New buildings were going up. Still, I missed the exhilaration of 1920—the bold challenge of War Communism.

As we returned home after the Sixth World Congress, our party changed its name one last time: from Workers (Communist) Party to Communist Party, U.S.A. For the time being at least the Lovestone group remained in control, and I was now fired from the directorship of the Anti-Imperialist Department. It did not trouble me. The Party had a national convention scheduled in a couple of months— November 1928—and I welcomed having some extra time to do advance factional work.

What did trouble me was the appearance of an American Trotskyism. Evidently Jim Cannon had committed himself to this line while in Moscow, and now he converted those closest to him: Max Shachtman and Marty Abern. The three built up a small—very small—secret following, but one that included Bill Dunne's brothers in Minneapolis. Then they made a careful approach to Bill and me, and we blew the thing wide open. I appreciated Trotsky's prodigious gifts and revolutionary achievements. But now, with a makeshift "party" of his own, he was attacking the Party from the outside—and planning for a Fourth International to supplant the Comintern. I never doubted Trotsky's courage or his integrity, but then I could say the same thing of Emma Goldman and Alexander Berkman. His followers represented a splintering from the only party organization capable of leading the world communist revolution, and they had to be denounced. I felt compromised by the fact of Cannon's association with our group, which had at one time even been known as the Foster-Cannon group. Bill and I reported what was going on—first to the group and then to the CEC. Arraigned before the committee, Cannon, Shachtman, Abern, and the others made a demonstrative profession of their Trotskyism. That was the end of them in the Party, and they were expelled on March 26, 1929.

A month or so later, Cannon, Shachtman, et al. organized a pro-Trotsky mass meeting at Irving Plaza, and I tried to break it up. I went there, grabbed a front seat, tried to confuse the first speaker with persistent heckling, then jumped up and clamored for everybody to walk out. Classic Communist-gangster procedure. They'd expected it, and a "security squad" gave me rough treatment. I was hustled from the hall with a black eye.

For an hour or so I felt like a paladin. Gradually, though, my feeling changed to shame. What had I hoped to accomplish? Shut the opposition up? Prevent free discussion of what should have been discussed openly long before, inside the Party and out? Cannon and the others were expelled with no intra-Party hearing beyond the CEC, and rank-and-file members learned of the action only through the official announcement printed in the *Daily Worker*. Here was the same privation of healthy intra-Party discussion that had distressed me under the Zinoviev-Kamenev-Stalin triumvirate. There had been, as I have stressed, abuses—serious abuses—of Bolshevik "democratic centralism" even in Lenin's time. But Lenin never hid his disputes with Trotsky, Zinoviev, Kamenev, Bukharin, Piatakov, or Stalin. He met them and defeated them (or was defeated by them) in argument. And he did not shrink from public debate of the differences when they were important enough. With the expulsion of Cannon the U.S. party had lapsed into an insidious confusion of ends and means—a confusion I detected in my own attitude, too.

How far this tendency had taken us became clear on the first day of the national convention (which, by the way, had been postponed to March 1, 1929, so that we could see how the power struggle in Russia would end). As the meeting opened Jack Johnstone (undoubtedly prompted by Foster) rose to amend the traditional motion "Fraternal greetings to the Communist Party of the 'Soviet Union.'" He shouted, "The greeting is not good enough. It won't do these days to mention only the CPSU. It must be the CPSU under the leadership of Comrade Stalin." I never recovered from the shock. I sat silent throughout the convention. Johnstone's amendment was approved by "unanimous vote" (my unraised hand escaping notice). The delegates, a majority of them elected as followers of the Lovestone group, were already responding to the Soviet Politburo's February resolution condemning Bukharin, Tomsky, and Rykov as "Right deviationists." Lovestone himself (along with Ben Gitlow) introduced a resolution that his friend Bukharin be removed as head of the Comintern. The resolution did not help him; for the brand-new CI Rep produced an open letter from the Communist International to the Communist Party, U.S.A., proposing that Foster be named general secretary of the Party and that Lovestone be "withdrawn from work in America and put at the disposal of the CI." Read aloud to the convention, the "proposals" (designed, said the text, to eliminate factionalism in the American party) were accepted without question or debate.

Did the proposals go into effect? Not entirely. Lovestone went to Moscow, as required, but engaged in a stubborn confrontation with Stalin. After several months, his friends in the OGPU hurried him out of the country without Stalin's knowledge. That of course finished him in the Party. Bob Minor, Max Bedacht, and other leading members of his group repudiated him. The few who stood by him (Bert Wolfe among them) were expelled along with him in June 1929. They carried on for several years as a Communist splinter group, at the opposite end of the spectrum from the Trotskyites.

23 Temporary Refuge in Wall Street

It gnawed at me that the traditional greeting to our brother party in Russia was no longer "good enough," and that we must now append praise for *the leadership of Comrade Stalin.* I wondered how much Stalin's personality had to do with the stultification of Communist

Party life. Lenin, in his so-called Testament—notes written by the dying man and presented to the Thirteenth Party Congress (May 1924) by his widow—had proposed Stalin's removal as the Party's general secretary. The "Testament" charged Stalin with being personally "rude" (harsh, insolent), and accused him of having "concentrated boundless power into his hands" while general secretary. The proposal to remove him had been made, it was stated, in hopes of avoiding a split in the party.

I first became acquainted with this document in a 1925 book entitled *Since Lenin Died*, by Max Eastman, then a Trotsky supporter. Though Eastman claimed Trotsky as his source, Trotsky disavowed the book and called the Testament a fabrication.[1] (Later, he—and others—circulated clandestine copies widely.) Without considering its authenticity or fradulence, I now recalled this Testament and perceived how Stalin had used the secretaryship, previously a purely technical office, as the organizational base for a political power drive that, in successive ruthless maneuvers, had made him the master of the Soviet party-state.

Stalin, I now believed, was the nemesis of Communist freedom. To work in support of him was degrading, but to work against him impossible—if you raised your voice you were out. Unable to breathe the Stalinist atmosphere, I stopped going to Party meetings, including my own unit's. I still considered it my party, the party destined to head the revolution that would forge a new society. I was not a Trotskyite, and never became one. I placed no hope in splinter groups. Stalin's paralyzing power could not endure forever, and the Party would right itself in time. I would be watching. I continued to see my personal friends in and around the Party, and for the time being avoided any intimation of politically dissident notions.

In the meantime, since I was no longer on the Party payroll, I had to think about making a living. This was 1929, the stock market was booming, and every business related to it was short-handed. A daily paper called the *Wall Street News* advertised for an experienced

1. Its authenticity was established beyond doubt after Stalin's death, by Nikita Khrushchev in his sensational "secret" report on Stalinism and "the cult of personality" at the Twentieth Party Congress (1956).

man to edit a column of advice to investors. Able to cite my impressive former connections with the *Chicago Economist* and *Investment News*, I bluffed my way into the job. I had hesitated about applying—not because I was unqualified (which, God knows, I was) but because of my doubts that it would be right for a professional revolutionary, hating the capitalist system, to take on such a job. I discussed my doubts with Bill Foster in his Union Square office before deciding.

Bill scratched his bald head and said, "Manny, one capitalist job is like another. Down there in Wall Street you'll be talking to capitalists against capitalists, not against workers. So what the hell. . . ." He pondered a bit and added, "But you can't go down there as Manuel Gómez. If they find out who you are you'll be finished." I turned to Ethel, his secretary, who had been taking dictation.

"Ethel," I inquired, "what's your last name?"

"Shipman."

"Thanks, I think I'll adopt it."

So for business I became Charles Shipman. I picked "Charles" for a first name without realizing, for the moment, it was the one I'd been born with!

The *Wall Street News* occupied an old two-story building on New Street near Wall. Although I had never heard of the paper before, it employed thirty or thirty-five financial reporters and had a fairly sizable circulation. Every day brought a batch of readers' inquiries. Was General Motors as good a buy as General Electric? How about Consolidated Edison? What did we think of the market in general? With a boy assistant just out of high school, I answered them, most by mail, a selected few in my column. As during my brief stint with *Investment News*, I lifted my responses from other financial publications—the *Wall Street Journal* and such. I was often unsure of the lingo, and realized that my attempt to advise investors was laughable—outrageous from a moral standpoint. But to me, still a devout Leninist, "bourgeois morality" was humbug.

For the stocks "analyzed" in my column I stuck to widely known ones, those written about everywhere. I emphasized "bearish" recommendations when I could find them, and gave a negative twist to some "positive" recommendations. I liked to say don't buy it, sell it; this is a false boom, a reckoning is near—a collapse—a world crisis. In this I held true to my own inner convictions: I was giving them the Party line.

The Party, after all, had been talking crisis year after year—mistakenly. But I happened to be talking it to Wall Street in August, September, and October 1929, and when the October crash occurred people marveled at my "astuteness"! My negative comments persisted—while John D. Rockefeller announced, "I and my son are buying stocks," while J. P. Morgan assured us that "this is a temporary thing." When stock prices improved in the first three months of 1930, the pundits said the worst was over. But Charles Shipman remained bearish, and in April the upswing lost its steam. It seemed I couldn't go wrong. So in May, when the prestigious *Wall Street Journal* absorbed the *Wall Street News*, I was one of the few staff members to be absorbed with it. I was now the investment expert of the *Wall Street Journal,* with a secretary, three assistant analysts, and my own daily column, "The Inquiring Investor."

Most people who knew me as Manny Gómez had no inkling of my *Wall Street Journal* manifestation. I led a double life. Although I no longer attended Party meetings, I wrote for the *New Masses* and taught classes on Leninism at the Workers School. The *Wall Street Journal* work challenged me to educate myself in the world of finance. Though I really wanted to do a good job, I was not able to give myself over to it fully. Ideologically, emotionally, even socially, my life was tied to "the movement." I never socialized with Wall Streeters; I was on the opposite side.

While still with the *Wall Street News* I'd been earning enough to move (in January 1930) from Liston's place to an "apartment" (one room and kitchenette) at 1 Sheridan Square. Once rescued from the bedbugs—which required an exterminator—I was quite comfortable there. I liked being in the Village. And near the subway. Liston and Margaret helped me fix the place up, and I did a bit of entertaining, most of it with the old Chicago gang: Bill and Marguerite Dunne, Wally and Rose Carmon, Fred Ellis, and Thurber, when he was in town. Wally was acting editor of the *New Masses.* Liston now edited *Soviet Russia Today.* Under Comintern pressure the Party's leadership had again been "rearranged." Foster had been shifted from general secretary to the new (figurehead) post of chairman.

Earl Browder, fresh from a long stay in the USSR, was now secretary. With Bob Minor and Max Bedacht at his bidding and no "factionalism" tolerated, Browder ran the Party. Bill Dunne remained a prominent CEC member, but he was no longer one of its inmost circle. He and I used to get together over drinks and anathematize the Browder regime. Now and then I tried to hint that the evil was linked to Moscow, but Bill refused to listen. To him, as it once would have been to me, denigration of Comintern authority was unthinkable.

24 Definitely Sylvia

During this period, I was chummy with Catherine Larkin, Margaret's good-looking sister. One evening in mid-February 1930, Catherine and I arranged to have a late dinner together, and then meet up with a girlfriend of hers, a Sally Feningston, and crash a party over on Thirty-eighth Street at Lexington. I don't recall if Catherine introduced me to Sally, but my arm was around her waist when we rode up in the elevator and her arm was around me, and it seemed the most natural thing in the world. I never knew what became of Catherine at that party. I said hello to our hosts, waved at people here and there, picked up a couple of drinks, and backed Sally into a corner. She said she was twenty-nine years old (versus my thirty-five), an actress, divorced (or getting divorced) from a renowned composer of modern music (Roy Harris), and in the midst of an affair with a writer of some distinction (Harvey Fergusson). Her name, it turned out, was Sylvia, not Sally. She was Jewish, the youngest of five sisters whose parents had run a mom-and-pop hardware store in the Bronx.

She mocked my cocksure bolshevism. I belittled her as a condescending political dilettante. She called me overbearing. I called her affected. It was a flirtation by combat, and it went on and on. I had no thought of stopping. But Sally (Sylvia) sent me for a cigarette and when I was there again she wasn't. Deserted and hurt, I left the party abruptly and walked home—all the way from Thirty-eighth and Lexington to Sheridan Square.

But of course it couldn't be the end. I waited more than a week and then, on February 22, 1930, Washington's Birthday, I phoned her. It was nine o'clock in the morning, and I asked for the entire day with her. Sleepy-voiced, she accepted without hesitation.

We took the ferry to Hoboken—a favorite haunt of holidaying New Yorkers because it defied Prohibition by being "a wide open town." On the way over Sally (Sylvia) told me more about herself. Her parents had come to this country from Russian Poland, where her father had peddled "second-hand" (used and dried) tea leaves. After the Bronx hardware experience, he became a wholesale grocery salesman and bought a house in Mt. Vernon, New York. Sylvia went to school in Mt. Vernon, as did her four sisters. The parents were Fenigsteins, the girls Feningstons. Madeleine, the eldest, a nonconformist by nature, imbued the others with radical—broadly socialistic—sympathies early in their lives. Barbara, the second youngest, eventually married Ben Legere, an itinerate IWW-type labor leader, prominent for a time in One Big Union agitation in Canada. Sylvia spent a year at Cornell, and over a year writing copy for a New York advertising agency before deciding, at twenty-two, that she wanted to be an actress.

Dusty old Hoboken was almost brilliant with sunshine that day. We roamed the hilly streets all morning, then stopped at a waterfront "oyster bar" for two hours or more of drinks and lunch and exploration of each other's minds and tastes and sympathies. We argued—but without the same animus as at the party. We were friends now, frankly taking pleasure in each other's company. We made a night of it at 1 Sheridan Square, and to this day we consider February 22, 1930, our anniversary.

At this time, Sylvia's chief interest was the ambitious theater group she had recently joined. She'd been chosen, like the group's other aspiring actors, by three intense people with a prescription for revitalizing the American theater: Lee Strasberg, Harold Clurman, and Cheryl Crawford. Lee and Harold developed their ideas from Stanislavsky's program, and in time their theory of acting came to be known as The Method. Over a long, not uninterrupted period, they indoctrinated their actors through preparatory weekend lectures, "effective memory" exercises, and improvisations. In the meantime the young actors supported themselves in various ways—some rather strange. After a stint with an industrial spy agency over on East Twenty-third Street, Sylvia began to do publicity for the ILD (International Labor Defense), an important Communist front organization. It seems that my relentless proselytizing had converted her to the cause. She never did join the Party, however—and, after all, I was only half in it myself.

About the time that Sylvia went with the ILD (May 1930) I learned that my father, whom I had not seen for many years, was critically ill. I had contrived to see my mother and Anna now and then, but too seldom to claim that I was really in touch. Harry I saw a bit more often, and it was he who informed me. Though we lived different lives and spoke different languages, there was always some sort of tie—and corresponding affection—that linked me with Harry, Anna, and Mother. For my father I had only resentment and hostility.

All the same I went to see him. I found him lying in bed, ashen and shriveled, his lips compressed in pain. He had cancer of the liver and this was his deathbed. He recognized me with a faint, apologetic smile. I bent and kissed his cheek. I can't say I felt a surge of love for him. I didn't. But I did feel commiseration. He had been a well-intentioned man but weak, and overjealous of his station in America. My mother leaned down and told him Charlie had an important job with the *Wall Street Journal*. That seemed to please him, as if I had redeemed myself. He died on June 1, 1930. I had visited him three or four times in the interim.

At the *Wall Street Journal* (as previously at the *Wall Street News*), I had pretty good rapport with my fellow newspapermen, but we were not intimates. I knew little of their lives and they knew nothing of mine. I had a cozy position. My department, which at this time included two willing assistants, was virtually autonomous. I was getting a financial education and being paid for it.

That I was contributing to so quintessentially capitalist a publication gave me no qualms, and I actually enjoyed it most of the time. But not always. On entering the office one summer morning (August 3, 1930) I had a sudden feeling of revulsion. Without a word to anyone I got up from my desk, grabbed my hat, and walked out.

Front page of the new CPUSA membership book issued to Manuel Gómez on the occasion of his payment, in 1930, of back dues—his last payment ever.

I took the subway and went to see Sylvia at the ILD. I said there was something urgent, she must step outside with me. I didn't really know what I had in mind, but when we got into the street I found myself telling her the first thing I wanted to do was to pay up my back dues in the Party. We walked together to the Amalgamated Bank in Union Square—a "labor bank" owned by the Amalgamated Clothing Workers. I withdrew all there was in my account, and walked from there to the Party's district office on Twelfth Street. I paid my back dues. About sixty dollars. Little as it seems today, it represented quite an accumulation. The moment we walked in I heard "Manny Gómez! Manny Gómez!" I got a prodigious reception from everybody. With the dues stamps pasted in my book—plus some special relief-assessment stamp—I felt euphoric.

Leaving Sylvia the next morning I wondered what I had accomplished by paying my dues. I still knew I could never function in the Party under Stalin. Nothing was changed since the previous morning except that I had put myself in good standing. An empty gesture, as I now saw it, undertaken to deal with some inner emptiness—to give myself an illusion of accomplishment—rather than for any objective purpose. I was right back where I had been before, but with a stronger sense of helplessness. It was the last time I paid dues to the Party. It was still my party, and there could be no other. I remained a Leninist—waiting.

Sylvia went to California in the fall of 1930 to visit her sisters, but in March 1931 we were back together in New York, this time for good. That summer the Lee Strasberg–Harold Clurman–Cheryl Crawford theater group, having raised some venture capital, moved up to Brookfield Center, Connecticut, to prepare for the fall opening of their first season. Some thirty actors and actresses, Sylvia among them, were to live in close association for two months or more of exhaustive workouts under Harold and Lee. The acting company included Franchot Tone, Elia ("Gadget") Kazan, Stella and Luther Adler, Clifford Odets (not yet thought of as a playwright), Sandy Meisner, Bobby Lewis, Morris Carnovsky, and others whose names would become well known to Broadway and Hollywood. I was there weekends, visiting Sylvia. I argued with Harold and Lee against the "classless ideology" of what would soon become the Group Theatre, while they openly resented my indoctrination of

Sylvia. (Paradoxically, both Harold and Lee no doubt harbored anti-capitalist sympathies at the time. As the Depression deepened they became almost, if not quite, Fellow Travelers.)

Their season opened at a Broadway theater on September 23, 1931, with *The House of Connolly*, a play by Paul Green. Sylvia had a very small acting part but also understudied the leading lady. The newspaper critics, though unenthusiastic about the play (one of those things about a decadent Southern family), eulogized the acting. There was even flattering talk of "an echo of the Moscow Art Theatre."

A few days later Sylvia and I transferred our household goods from the one room and kitchenette at Tenth and Fourth to a four-room spread farther uptown—at 434 West Twenty-ninth Street, way over near Ninth Avenue. It was a terrible neighborhood, gangster-ridden, not far from Hell's Kitchen. Dead bodies had been found on our street, and there were shrieks in the night. The street was a row of dingy rooming houses, but 434 West was not bad. We had the top floor, four flights up, a skylight, ample windows, and cross ventilation. The rent, I think was seventy dollars a month.

When Sylvia got home from the theater, she had to have a lox and cream cheese on rye, or whatever I had ready. Then rather than go to bed we sat and read aloud to each other, mostly Dickens and Dostoyevsky (Dostoyevsky's *House of the Dead* was a great discovery for us). Those were among our best times. We delighted in each other as well as in what we read.

25 My "*Demarche* into Cultural Work"

It was in March 1932 that I read a startling headline in the *Daily Worker*: MANUEL GOMEZ EXPELLED FROM THE PARTY; FOR PETTY BOURGEOIS TENDENCIES. A bolt from out of the blue! What bourgeois tendencies? My connection with a Wall Street newspaper? I doubted that the connection had leaked out. In any case, I had cleared it in advance with Bill Foster, the Party's candidate for president of the United States in 1932. My life-style? It had not changed appreciably. Except, of course, that I was no longer attending Party meetings. And not paying dues. And dodging Party discipline. Except. Except. Except. The expulsion was more shock than surprise. I knew I had been courting it. Even so, the headline shook me. I had a sinking feeling at the sight of it. The body of the story relieved me considerably. It said Gómez would be reinstated "if and when he satisfies the Party he is prepared to abandon his petty-bourgeois tendencies." So I was not banished to outer darkness, was not to be regarded as an enemy. I had been given what amounted to a comradely slap on the wrist. My friends treated me as before. To them I was merely on sabbatical. All of them knew the Party was my religion.

In fact, these were months that confronted me with a serious personal dilemma. It was like this. I had been none too happy with my prolonged disengagement from the day-to-day work of the Communist Party. I had kept in touch with it through my Communist friends, in touch but out of the action. I could easily have gotten back into the party—by agreeing to accept party discipline and so on. But no, I couldn't do so while Stalinism endured. But though work inside the Party was an impossibility for me, should I not be able to work *along with* the Party? For its general objectives? I had felt I should from the first without knowing a modus operandi. Now the modus had suggested itself. As the Depression deepened, more and more people, including prominent professional people and intellectuals, were beginning to challenge the economic and political foundations of American society. I would take this path, too—assign myself to influence the left-moving intellectuals to move still farther leftward. I would work among them systematically, not as an individual but through an appropriate United Front company. Accordingly, I joined the John Reed Club, created under the Leninist dictum that "art is a weapon." So began, with some enthusiasm, what I designate my *demarche* into the cultural field.

The John Reed Club was, in some respects, a huge success. Among those who cooperated with it (for short periods or long) were such luminaries as Theodore Dreiser, Edmund Wilson,

It Had to Be Revolution

Sherwood Anderson, John Dos Passos, Waldo Frank, Franz Boaz, Sidney Hook, Heywood Broun, Eva Le Gallienne, Richard Wright, William Phillips, Phillip Rahv, Harriet Monroe, Alfred Kreymborg, and Adolf Dehn. They were the front. The organization, as such, was the work of Communist Party designates: Mike Gold, Joe Freeman, V. J. Jerome, and others, the old reliables of the Party's agitprop establishment. They operated the club, kept it going. The club ridiculed liberalism, denounced social democracy ("the main danger"), and endorsed the Communist Party's ticket of William Z. Foster and James Ford. It might have accomplished more with a less sectarian line. Still, it spawned the epochal *Partisan Review* (which in due course broke with the Party—as did most of its writers). The *Partisan Review* would become a forum for the early writings of Mary McCarthy, Saul Bellow, Lionel Trilling, Clement Greenberg, Dwight Macdonald, and others worthy of such company.

The club brought me, for a time, into close relations with Mike Gold, who qualified as the party's number one cultural liaison man. He was a politico-literary paradox: a nonintellectual middlebrow personality with a talent for colorful and forceful expression—a Party hack sustained by the lasting promise of his book *Jews without Money*. Mike and I had roomed together in a Christopher Street basement, taught English together in Guadalajara, collaborated on the book and lyrics of *The Last Revolution*, teamed up on General Alvarado's newspaper in Mexico City—all without becoming close. Back in the U.S. we had rarely seen each other, in the Party or socially. I never liked Mike, and I think he suspected as much. His flashing smile and boyish charm concealed a churlish nature. And besides, he was lazy—though great at meeting new people.

Earlier in the year, Sylvia had resigned from the Group Theatre, primarily because of her disappointment with the trifling roles she'd been assigned. Though this separation ended her professional acting career, she almost immediately established a new theater connection, and this time I was involved, too. We joined up in a new venture "to produce worthwhile Class Struggle plays" in competition with the bourgeois commercial theater. We got in during the planning phase, in response to an invitation to join the self-constituted producing board: Charles and Adelaide Walker, Liston

My *Demarche* into Cultural Work

new masses

Fight Against Fascism!

An Article by Joseph Freeman

Statements by Newton Arvin, Roger Baldwin, Heywood Broun, Lewis Corey, Waldo Frank, Michael Gold, Horace Gregory, Granville Hicks, Sidney Hook, Horace Kallen, Scott Nearing, James Rorty, Isidor Schneider, Edwin Seaver, Revolutionary Writers' Fed.

The Bank Crisis

Manuel Gomez

15 c

Andre Gide Goes Left

Edward Sagarin

APRIL, 1933

Poems - Drawings - Stories - Reviews

Oak, Margaret Larkin, Paul Peters, Albert Maltz, George Sklar, and Michael Blankfort—all of them Communist Party sympathizers.

We had met the Walkers through Margaret and Liston. Charlie, about forty in 1932, had participated in various Communist-inspired doings, yet retained some special relationship of a corporate kind with Yale University (his alma mater). Paul Peters I knew from the John Reed Club, and from his writings in the *New Masses*. I had not previously met Maltz, Sklar, and Blankfort, three young and earnest offspring of Professor Carlos Baker's famous Yale University drama course.

I'm not sure how these assorted individuals got together, though I think the project originated with Charlie, who had collected some modest preliminary working funds. As I said, although all had Communist Party sympathies, none was a Party member—except Liston, who had joined in 1929 (just about when I quit going to Party meetings). Though independent of Party control they were anxious not to violate "the correct line" in their productions. And that is why they invited Manuel Gómez, not as "a theater person" but as a recognized Leninist in close touch with the ins and outs of Party practice. The board was subsequently "broadened" to include two well-known Socialist Party personalities, Mary Fox and Samuel H. Friedman, after which it could operate as a nonpartisan entity within the general orbit of the fragmented "class-conscious" labor movement. We called ourselves the Theater Union and, with a reputation for theatrical experiment, soon attracted some of the most interesting people in New York theatrical circles. Thus, John Hammond and Joseph Losey sometimes sat in our board meetings, as did H. William Fitelson, New York's preeminent theatrical lawyer and a major player in the American Civil Liberties Union. Bill donated valuable legal services—and a bit of cash as well—and soon became a regular (and active) board member. We thought him an advanced liberal, but, as he told me years later, he was a secret Trotskyist at the time. Charlie Walker became the Theater Union president and was, in fact, its animating spirit, organizational resource, and administrative bulwark.

For our first Theater Union production we chose *Peace on Earth,* an antiwar play by George Sklar and Albert Maltz. A thirty-eight-year-old university professor, wholly devoted to his wife, daughter, and university teaching, is unwittingly drawn into contact with longshoremen who refuse to load munitions for a looming European war. They win his sympathy, and while he is speaking on their behalf somebody fires a shot. The professor is framed for murder. War is on in Europe. Blackout. A female blues singer, spotlighted with hips swaying to music, belts out: "I want a man with a uniform on. . . . " As the professor goes to his execution, offstage noises indicate that the U.S. has now joined in the war.

The script was much stronger than this trite outline suggests, but I, with my political commissar approach, insisted on revisions to make it a "Theater Union" play. I thought the present version encouraged opposition to all war, not just the capitalist variety, and the ending struck me as too defeatist. At a hastily called caucus I proposed correcting these "defects" with two simple changes. First, we'd insert the following: "When we go out to fight it ain't gonna be for the bosses. It's gonna be for a world where there won't be any bosses. Or wars." Second, the sounds indicating that the U.S. had entered the war would be countered by workers chanting that their fight goes on. George and Albert made the changes, and the socialist members of the board offered no objection.

To house the production—and indeed to serve as a permanent home for the Theater Union—Charlie and Bill arranged for us to take over Eva Le Gallienne's lease of the grand old Civic Repertory Theatre, located, appropriately enough, in the proletarian atmosphere of Fourteenth Street and Sixth Avenue. Charlie's magic had unearthed not only rent money, but also the preliminary financing for *Peace on Earth*. With this cash in hand we were able to hire our large cast, plus the director, scene designer, stage manager, and backstage crew. We even managed to pay for some advance advertising.

With *Peace on Earth* scheduled for the fall (1933) Sylvia took a two-month spring vacation in Europe, the guest of Aline Barnsall, the oil heiress and former patron of Roy Harris. In Sylvia's absence Nemo and Juanita Piccoli, our good comrades from Milwaukee, moved in with me at Twenty-ninth Street. New York, in the Depression, was rugged for the Piccolis; there was only a minimal demand for paintings, and none at all for sculpture. So many people I knew were out of work in those days that my secure job seemed more than ever an anomaly. As a matter of fact, I had by then acquired considerable respect for the *Wall Street Journal*, both as a newspaper and as a power in the financial community. I'd arrived in Wall Street assuming that the paper was merely a tool of big-business insiders and of its advertisers. Instead, I found it boldly independent. To my amazement it demonstrated quite as much integrity as the *Daily Worker*, perhaps more. Experience of the Dow-Jones organization from top to bottom taught me something I ought to have known since graduating from adolescence: there are honest and dishonest, intelligent and unintelligent, courageous and cowardly people on every side of every question.

In June 1933, I took a first fling in the stock market, selling "short" one-hundred shares of International Paper. Timing was with me. The stock dropped in a day, and I took my quick profit of a few hundred dollars and bought my first automobile. When Sylvia returned from abroad the brand new Model-A Ford was on the pier beside me, with Nemo at the wheel. I did not know how to drive.

That August we learned Sylvia was pregnant. Obviously this was an accident, for children had no place in our life plan. We reviewed our predicament, then agreed—as I would not have believed possible—to let things take their course. At this point we were giving all our spare time to the Theater Union. In order to supplement newspaper publicity for *Peace on Earth*, Sylvia and I, like several other board members, extolled the play to trade union locals, workers' recreation clubs, and so on. Though we hoped to attract "uptown" theatergoers of one kind and another, we realized that our audience backbone had to be working class. Without that—our raison d'être—we'd be nothing. We kept our admission prices low: thirty-cents to $1.50—and anyone claiming to be unemployed got in free.

26　A Father out of a Job

*P*eace on Earth opened December 29, 1933. Often enough (though not always) for sixteen successive weeks it filled the large Civic Repertory Theatre, more than justifying our expectations. The production got respectful—in general surprisingly appreciative—notices from the regular drama critics, and raves from the labor press—Communist, Socialist, and otherwise.

Our second play proved a smash hit. It was a sensitive yet explosive piece by Paul Peters, in which black workers are roused to fury. A lynch mob is hounding an innocent one of their number who has been accused of raping a white whore. When Paul first presented his script to the board its title was "Wharf Nigger"—just right for the play, but of course we couldn't allow it. "Nigger" was taboo even where it belonged, and we changed the title to *Stevedore*. When it opened on April 18, 1934, *Stevedore* made the Theater Union famous. It played the Civic Rep for twenty-three weeks (138 performances) to large and wildly applauding audiences. These audiences included numerous blacks, and the cast was composed primarily of blacks, some of whom were (or became) famous: Georgette Harvey, Leigh Whipper, Rex Ingraham, Canada Lee. The run at the Civic Rep provided something we had never expected to see, substantial profit. Emboldened by our own success, we sent the show on the road, bungled the matter, and promptly lost our windfall!

While Manuel Gómez devoted nights to the Theater Union, Charles Shipman was performing daily at the *Wall Street Journal*, where the compensation was by no means exclusively monetary—I was picking up all kinds of fascinating knowledge. And I met some remarkable people in the financial world. In November 1933, just after the presidential election, I became acquainted with a very serious young man, twentyish, with independent opinions on everything. Undersized, puffy, dimpled, blinking through thick glasses, he offered his views in a peculiar nasal whisper. Deferential yet positive, he had a headful of facts, supplemented by memoranda on bits of paper stuffed into his pockets. Everybody called him Izzy, and for many years to come he enjoyed a unique career among Washington newshounds, writing, editing, and publishing his own four-page newsletter, *I. F. Stone's Monthly*. Few knew of it and fewer read it, except in newspaper and U.S. government offices. There it became a must, recognized for the combination of industry, honesty, fearlessness, and uncanny nose for fact which were characteristic of its undersized reporter-editor-publisher.

It Had to Be Revolution

When I met Izzy, he was writing editorials for the *New York Evening Post*, a metropolitan daily that had existed over half a century. It was a revered conservative paper, and its financial section was the largest and best in the city. The paper had just been bought by J. David Stern, who renamed it the *New York Post* and brought in staff members (including Izzy) from the Stern-owned *Philadelphia Inquirer*. An ardent FDR supporter, Stern aimed to capture a popular rather than an "elite" readership. In time he converted the *Post* into a Hearst-style yellow journal with an ultra-liberal slant, and finally into a tabloid. At first, however, he left the paper's physical appearance and standard feature divisions substantially intact, and hired an esteemed liberal intellectual, Ernest Gruening, as managing editor.

In February 1934 Izzy Stone came to my *Wall Street Journal* office with his managing editor, whom I had heard of but never met, and Gruening promptly offered me the *Post's* financial editorship. Here was an extraordinary challenge and opportunity. How could I not be tempted? Still, I had a good and secure situation at the *Wall Street Journal*, a paper so remote from the capital-labor battlefront that I did not have to feel uncomfortable about anything it printed. So I said no. But Gruening kept after me, and eventually I succumbed. My contract granted me exclusive jurisdiction over what was to be said and not said in the financial section, plus a salary of $150 a week (a lot of money then, at least in the newspaper business).

When I checked in at the *New York Post*, Ernest Gruening was no longer managing editor. What ended his brief engagement with J. David Stern I know not, but I now reported directly to Stern, who ran the paper himself. The financial section I took over retained the format and character inherited from the *New York Evening Post*, and I intended to keep it that way. But Stern, I later discovered, had a very different notion. Instead of a conventional financial section covering stocks and bonds, he wanted pieces about everyday money matters and economic problems, written from the FDR point of view. For weeks he left me on my own. Then, without warning, he presented me with a bold new masthead for my section: "The New Deal in Business." I was horrified. I'd been hesitant to surrender the ideological insulation of my *Wall Street Journal* position, and I certainly wasn't going to lend myself to New Deal propaganda. FDR was anathema to me—"a fascist" in our Communist idiom. I told Stern to forget it, and before I knew what was happening I was out. Fired. It was May 21, 1934, the day my daughter was born.

In the hush of dawn I had driven Sylvia to Lenox Hill Hospital (I had barely learned to start and stop the car). Carlota had been born around nine. With Sylvia resting, I had decided to put in a few hours at the paper and then return. A hell of a time to say I was out of a job! I was not, thank God, devoid of resources. My contract had a cancellation clause, and getting rid of me cost the *Post* a full year's pay.

Carlota emerged from the womb a wrinkled red blob. Sylvia said, fancifully, that she resembled a Chinese fish. We had considered naming her "Manuela," accenting the Hispanic Manuel Gómez affinity. But Sylvia disliked that name, so we settled on the no less Hispanic "Carlota." Down through the years—until her marriage in fact—she signed herself Carlota G. Shipman (the "G" for Gómez). The infant, like a billion others, giggled and bawled, her signals of contentment and discomfort not to be ignored. Withal she was a merry imp. And she transformed us into a family. Such chores as changing diapers and getting up in the middle of the night to prepare and administer the formula seemed (most times) not chores but secret privileges.

Out of a job, I refused to worry. I could quit being Charles Shipman altogether, give up this double-life business and be myself, Manny Gómez. Indeed I did not look for another "capitalist job" until December of 1935, devoting most of my time to the John Reed Club, the Theater Union, and my family. The old Chicago bunch were, as ever, my best pipeline to the inner workings of the Party. And Bill Dunne was the most important of all.

I think again of the place Bill—and Marguerite—had in my life for so many years. There was complete confidentiality among us. One night Marguerite brought me two ornamental daggers—one from Tashkent, the other from Outer Mongolia—which Bill had acquired during a trip to Russia some time before. "Manny," she said simply, "Bill is drunk and I'm afraid of him with these daggers in the house. Please take care of them." They decorate a wall in my home as I write this.

27 Bertolt Brecht and the Theater Union

On July 1, 1934, with Carlota barely five weeks old, the Gómez family plus Nemo, Juanita, and assorted luggage squeezed into the Model-A and drove to the far end of Cape Cod. We'd hired a long, rambling house at Wellfleet through September. The house sat high on a hill, and we got it cheap because it was lying vacant. The charm of the Truro region's lonely dunes lured a sizable scattering of artists, writers, academics, and others. Our friends Charlie and Adelaide Walker, who knew everybody, were summering in Truro and introduced us to Edmund Wilson, John Dos Passos, Carlo Tresca (the most famous of anarchist-IWW strike leaders), and Margaret de Silver, Carlo's plump girlfriend. (Dos Passos obviously did not remember our 1920 *entrevista* in the reading room of the Ateneo in Madrid, and I did not remind him.)

That summer Carlota's crib was a wicker laundry basket. Asleep in it out back of the house on a sunny day she looked cherubic. Nemo had fashioned a miniature awning to keep the sun off her face. We took Carlota along with us in her basket on our daily before-breakfast dip in Long Pond. Or whenever and wherever. Otherwise leaving her with Nemo and Juanita or down the hill in care of Mrs. Lee, a benevolent and sturdy Finnish woman who raised corn, gave wise counsel, and took in washing. We went regularly for the mail (including the *Daily Worker*) and a how-do with Mr. Dalmas, the postmaster, our landlord. Bought fresh seafood from Mr. Lombard on the bay side—at a hole in planks on shaky stilts over the water. After lunch I shut myself up in the spare room—not to be disturbed before four unless the house caught fire. Working on a play, a satire of Wall Street. (Never got beyond the first act.) At four we swam, Sylvia and I at least, in the overwhelming icy rollers and horrendous undertow of South Shore ocean. Emerged buffeted, goose-pimply, and euphoric.

We returned to New York at the end of September to find that our lease would not be renewed. Through December we camped out in a grubby flat on Nineteenth Street, then rented the upper part of a two-family house in the semi-suburban Sunnyside part of Queens. It would be our home for nearly six years.

The second Theater Union season opened with *Sailors of Cattaro*, a dramatization of a World War I mutiny in the Austrian Navy. Mike Blankfort had adapted the play from one by Friedrich Wolf, a noted contemporary German playwright. One of the actors, Harold C. Johnsrud, was married to Mary McCarthy and she came to some of the rehearsals. Mary admired the play immensely, but the Broadway critics were lukewarm. Clearly we did not have another *Stevedore* on our hands. Still, with the help of theater parties booked in advance through labor organizations of one kind and another, we got comparatively good houses, but did not make money. We were pressed for time in choosing a play to follow *Sailors*, and none of those submitted captured our enthusiasm. Since we could not afford to keep the rented Civic Rep empty, we went ahead with the one we liked best, and it held the stage for the rest of the season.

By that time we had something to start the next season, a jewel of a play with occasional music. Paul Peters had come upon an ingenious German drama based on Maxim Gorky's novel *Mother*. The uniquely bare and direct drama was set in prerevolutionary Russia. Its main character was a poor, ignorant old widow, Pelagea Vlassova. As the play opens, she is cooking watery soup for her metalworker son, Pavel, and lamenting what will become of him. His wages have been cut again and, what is worse, he is mixed up with the malcontents at the factory—people who could get him into trouble. That night Pavel brings home some fellow workers with a hectograph and a batch of paper. They drape a heavy cloth over the window and start to duplicate a leaflet protesting the wage cut. A rap on the door. They hide everything. The police come, look around, leave. They begin work again.

Pelagea overhears that tomorrow it is Pavel's turn to hand out the leaflets. Assured that there's no danger, she bursts out bitterly: "No way out of it, but no danger. No danger but no way out of it. We're already suspected but there's no way out of it. That's why there's no danger. . . . Just slip your head into the noose, no danger. Give me those leaflets. Pavel won't hand them out. I will."

Thus begins a process that draws her, step by step, into revolutionizing experiences. She sees those caught with the leaflets being arrested, and on May Day watches as the tsar's police shoot down unarmed workers. Mother and son now have a new bond in the solidarity and peril of their common embroilment in the workers' struggle. When Pavel is killed, the mother carries on. The play ends in February 1917, on the eve of the tsar's overthrow, as Pelagea Vlassova carries the red flag at the head of a demonstration. She refuses to relinquish her heavy load, and as the curtain falls, a worker speaks directly to the audience: "She marched with us, never tiring, all morning and into the late afternoon."

The German playwright whose work Paul had adapted was Bertolt Brecht. Brecht's *Mother* (in some respects a forerunner of his *Mother Courage*) is representative of his *Lehrstücke* period. It was among the last of these direct propaganda plays, and the only full-length specimen. Together with the adaptation, Paul showed us a literal translation of the play. His adaptation humanized Brecht's text, making several characters less stereotyped and supplying a bit of added motivation. We voted unanimously to accept *Mother*, in Paul's version, for presentation in the fall of the year (1935). Although we'd never heard of Brecht, we found Hans Eisler, the composer who scored Brecht's lyrics, living in New York (an exile, like the playwright, from Hitler's Germany). Eisler gave us Brecht's address on the outskirts of Copenhagen, and we mailed him a copy of Paul's script—along with a standard agreement for assignment of rights. In the meantime we picked a director, set designer, and so on, and proceeded with preparations for a November opening.

Summer 1935 found both me and Sylvia free, so we again headed off to Wellfleet. It was a good summer, until early in August, that is, when Victor Wolfson, Paul Peters, and "the boys" (George Sklar and Albert Maltz) arrived from New York bearing calamitous news. Brecht had cabled, calling Paul's script a distortion and mockery, and denying us production rights for the play. With the Walkers and the Gómezes and Mike Blankfort handy, an emergency Theater Union meeting ensued right there on the Cape.

Since Eisler had said Brecht spoke no English, we wondered how much of Paul's version he could have understood. And what did he know of the Theater Union? We reasoned that by talking to him directly we might change his mind. Since *Mother* was scheduled for November production, someone had to go to Denmark. It would be a mistake to send Paul, and I was the only other board member who knew any German at all. I agreed to go, and Charlie cleared it by phone with the other members of the board.

I sailed for Europe with a passport issued to Charles Shipman, "occupation Theatrical Producer." Even before the *Isle de France* cleared New York harbor, I studied German furiously. I also read—and reread—the English versions of Brecht's play, and soon found myself preferring the literal rendering. Paul had smoothed edges, doctored unnatural transitions, rounded out characters—and in so doing given the boldly original work a tinge of the commonplace. My mission, however, was to get Brecht's signature to the agreement sent him by the Theater Union, authorizing our production of Paul's version. What an assignment!

Brecht and his wife had rented a cottage near a seaside resort outside Copenhagen. I remember my first glimpse of this emaciated, stunted man darting up and down in front of the house, chewing an unlit black cigar. He wore a torn leather jacket, and the leather cap of a European workingman perched on his close-cropped black hair. The jacket and cap, I later learned, were habitual, as were the soiled white shirt, dirty fingernails, and a five-day growth of beard.

A Theater Union cable had told him to expect me. He greeted me as *Genosse Gometz* (Comrade Gómez), but the abruptly withdrawn handshake was about as hospitable as a prickly pear. Brecht once described himself to me as *ein unbequemer Mensch* (an uncomfortable person). He meant that he made people uncomfortable, which, God knows, was true, but I also think that people made him uncomfortable. Actually he was glad to see me, having assumed that I'd come to work out a modification of the production agreement we had first proposed. He wanted a Theater Union production very much, but for *his play*. He seemed informed about us and satisfied with both our "Marxism" and the professionalism of our actors and staging.

In my tortured German I explained that only one version of *Mother* interested the Theater Union, and that was Paul's. I told him I had no authority to change things, but did let on that personally I now preferred his version (that is, the literal translation) to Paul's.

He seemed bewildered by this admission, but when I announced that the board hoped he would accompany me to America, he pondered for a minute and then agreed.

He went into the house, came back with the production agreement, signed it, and handed it over to me. Tomorrow he would go to Copenhagen for an American visa. He told me frankly that once on the spot in New York, he, Bertolt Brecht, "formidable" Marxist and peerless artist, would take over everything: the working script, the direction, the use of screens, the lighting, and so on.

During the several days before his visa came through, he accommodated me in the cottage. Each morning we walked on the beach until his wife had breakfast ready. Except for "*Morgen, Genosse Gometz!*" and an aside to Brecht, the mistress of the house rarely spoke at table, as though it wasn't her place. (I later learned she was a gifted actress and had helped Brecht in his work. Her name, Helene Weigel, was illustrious in German theater.) Brecht spent much of the day in his room alone, presumably writing. After doing the supper dishes, the wife retired, leaving the husband and me to talk. *He* talked. I had crammed an astonishing amount of German into myself during the trip over, but I could understand it better than I could speak it. And Brecht was, by disposition, a better talker than listener. He prided himself on his "formidable" Marxism and claimed that the first volume of *Capital* had enabled him to understand his own early plays. Though he declared himself a Communist during the abortive 1929 rising in Berlin, he never joined the Party.

We shared a second-class cabin on the boat home. Brecht rarely washed, never changed his shirt, and left chewed black cigars everywhere. We never got on a first-name basis, remaining *Genosse Gometz* and *Genosse Brecht*. Much of the time we just sat on deck together and read.

At intervals he reiterated that *we* (he and I) must force the Theater Union board to save *Mother* from Paul's "kitsch bastardization." I warned him not to expect too much. Our ship would reach New York on October 11 or 12. The opening was announced for late November. Victor Wolfson would be rehearsing his cast in a matter of days, and though Brecht's presence would make a difference—maybe a big difference—there were obvious limits. I would support him as much as possible, but I was not the director, and only one voice on the board.

Welcomed at the dock by Theater Union board members, Brecht bowed stiffly and muttered, "*Sehr angenehm*" ("Pleased, I'm sure"). Escorted to the Hotel Albert in Greenwich Village, he declined our invitation to dinner. When I called for him next morning Hans Eisler was with him, and I took them to the Civic Rep. The auditorium, stage, and equipment all impressed him, and he declared himself gratified at the "proletarian" Fourteenth Street neighborhood. Both men then participated in a Theater Union board meeting. Brecht recited a marathon speech which I translated as best I could. Now that he was on hand he would, of course, supervise the presentation of his play. He would see that the lines were spoken correctly. He did not propose to disturb existing arrangements regarding the director. Comrade Wolfson doubtless had merits, but what could he know about Epic Theater, Brecht's basic concept of dramaturgy? Eisler kept nodding approval to everything Brecht said.

Though Brecht's shocking discourtesy and truculence disinclined me to say a word in his favor, I had to make my position clear. After giving them Brecht, therefore, I announced I had some comments of my own. I told of studying the two scripts en route to Copenhagen and explained why I had come to prefer the original. I said I had told Brecht of my preference, yet had warned him that his signature would authorize production of Paul's version.

The next day we met again with Brecht and Eisler. The board as a whole remained unconverted, but not inflexible. Brecht's persistently offensive manner did not prevent his being treated with respect, and it was resolved that we would go ahead as before on the basis of Paul's script—subject to adjustments made during production. Brecht would sit in and advise.

Seated in the darkened auditorium at rehearsals, Brecht and Eisler objected to every aspect of the staging: entrances and exits, blocking, gestures, delivery of lines, singing of this and that phrase of a song. They always had a reason, but delivered it so insultingly that they antagonized our actors. Every rehearsal was constantly being interrupted by Brecht's peremptory "*Genosse Gometz! Genosse Gometz!*", and everything stopped while Comrade Gómez

199

hurried over to be told what to tell the director. The director (Victor) wasn't much bothered by all this, but script changes were another matter. Paul, who had been attracted to the play in the first place and obviously sensed much of its rare quality, wanted to meet Brecht halfway. He rewrote and rewrote, but his revisions never yielded the precise meaning Brecht sought. In addition to his constant verbal expostulations (with Eisler's invariable *Ja! Ja!*), Brecht showered me with handwritten complaints penned (in the dark) in almost indecipherable German. When the objection seemed picayune, I often told him, "I agree, but we can't persuade the director. The point is insignificant, so why press?" Sometimes he answered by jumping up and yelling, "*Sitzung! Sitzung!*" (demanding a meeting of the Theater Union board).

In Brecht's original script, the old widow enters the Bolshevik Party, but Paul's adaptation did not call the Party by name. Brecht fumed at this "truckling to petit-bourgeois prejudices." Here was a point on which I disagreed with Brecht, reminding him that our board included two Socialist Party members and that we aimed for relatively wide audiences. At this he hit the ceiling, demanding that we go to *Genosse* Browder for "a ruling." And thus Brecht, Eisler, and I marched to Communist Party headquarters to meet with Browder. Once there, Brecht and Eisler even asked that he "order" us to remove Victor as director! Browder, being not quite an idiot, said what was to have been expected: we would have to settle matters among ourselves. This rebuff shook Brecht, but he continued to interrupt rehearsals and yell for *Sitzungs*. It got so bad that no one wanted to meet with him. Only one thing kept us from telling Brecht to go to hell and take his play with him: we loved what we had.

Few others shared our love, however. Opening night (November 19, 1935) was a disaster. The press pronounced the play a dud— even most of the left-wing labor press. Once the advance-sale tickets were gone, attendance plummeted. After the opening Brecht disappeared. Where he went, what he did, we never knew. His personal life in New York, if he had any, was a mystery. I have read that he left New York for Scandinavia early in 1936.[1]

1. He was back in the U.S. (Hollywood) in 1941, remaining for several years. A

Mother was still playing when I realized that the Gómez family needed money. Sylvia had snagged a Christmas Seal job but it was short-term. The time had come for Manuel Gómez to resume the Charles Shipman role. I couldn't afford to be choosy and realized there was plenty of room at the bottom for a Charles Shipman— even in a depression. Standard & Poor's Corporation, 345 Hudson Street, the last resort of the needy security analyst.[2] I just walked in and was hired. December 2, 1935.

The Standard & Poor's layout resembled a factory. The place employed printers, typists, secretaries, copyreaders, "statisticians," librarians, account executives, salesmen, and rows and rows of "analysts," junior and senior. Because of my *Wall Street Journal* credentials they took me on as a senior. Apart from salesmen (greatly esteemed), account executives, and a few top people, everyone was underpaid. I got fifty-five dollars a week. As at Sears, employee turnover was terrific, but I stayed on for fourteen years.

The Theater Union survived the "Brecht-Peters" *Mother* to present five additional plays. While all these got larger audiences than *Mother*, none was a howling box office success, and on August 8, 1937, the *New York Times* reported: "The Theater Union, after eight plays in four years, has dissolved, unable to finance chronic deficit operations." Production costs for our eight plays had averaged $3,000, practically all raised by Charlie Walker. The four-year attendance totaled 523,000, including 23,000 without charge. In spite of its difficulties, the Theater Union must be classed with the WPA Theatre Project and Orson Welles's Mercury Theatre as one of the most noteworthy American theater experiments of the 1930s.

Our financial problems might have been solved, but there was something else. When Margaret Larkin switched from Liston Oak to Albert Maltz it poisoned relations between Liston and Albert. These personal disaffections, however, simply aggravated the basic

---

magazine write-up says "he worked on some fifty film projects but sold only one, for which he received no credit." In 1947 he was "an unfriendly witness" before the House Un-American Activities Committee. Asked if he had ever applied for Communist Party membership, he replied "No, no, no, no, never," and "within hours fled the country." He became an Austrian citizen but settled finally in East Berlin, where he founded the Berliner Ensemble. There his real fame began.
2. At the time its name was Standard Statistics Co. It became Standard & Poor's Corp. shortly thereafter, having taken over Poor's Manuals.

discord in the Theater Union board, which was political. Charlie and Adelaide Walker had gone to Mexico to see Trotsky and had come back Trotskyites. Ditto Mike Blankfort. That broke up the pro-CP caucus. Albert, George, Margaret, Liston, and I plotted in secret caucus against the Trotskyite influence, and the secret caucus itself harbored secret divisions. Albert had become unconditionally Stalinist, with Margaret his ardent disciple. Liston, though a Party member since 1929, appeared shaky on Stalin, while Sylvia and I were irreconcilably opposed. We had formed the Theater Union to produce "class struggle" plays, but most of the struggle now seemed to be among ourselves.

28   Painful Disillusionment

In the latter part of 1936 the New York newspapers featured Edward VIII's insistence on marrying the divorced "Wallie" Simpson at the cost of his throne, and pushed the Spanish Civil War to one side. Coinciding with this first stage of the fighting in Spain was a new Stalinist horror in "the Socialist homeland" at the other end of Europe. Imprisoned after a secret trial for "complicity" in the 1934 murder of Kirov,[1] Zinoviev, Kamenev, and I. N. Smirnov now had to be prosecuted in public—for "treason"—and, of course, executed. The charges included plotting (with Trotsky, and Nazi agents, and agents of the Western powers) to murder the entire Bolshevik leadership, bring down the Soviet regime, and restore Russia to capitalism. The shock of this first of the Moscow "show trials" was indescribable. All the past Stalinist indignities had not pre-

---

1. Sergei Kirov was a key Stalin protégé, closer to him than any other collaborator, with the possible exception of Molotov. His assassination on December 1, 1934, became the excuse for the succession of wholesale arrests, persecutions, and Party "purges" that followed. It is now widely believed that Stalin himself arranged Kirov's assassination as a pretext for his assault against the Old Bolshevik cadres.

pared observers for the transparent absurdity of these allegations, the hypnotic atmosphere of the courtroom, the dazed Old Bolsheviks stumbling through their extorted confessions, the prospect of Kamenev (about to be executed) begging his sons to devote their lives to "our great Stalin."

I felt that I could no longer piddle around with the John Reed Club, the Theater Union, and such. There was bound to be latent opposition to Stalinism inside the Communist Party, U.S.A., and someone had to organize it. I had been indulging myself at the Theater Union up to then, showing more interest in theater as theater than as weapon.

For the formidable task of "boring from within" I had one exceptional resource. Bill Dunne was a front-rank Party leader, wise in its ways, uncowable, and my best friend. I had never ceased criticizing the Party to Bill—as well as to Thurber Lewis and a few others. All of them disliked the Browder regime. But what about Stalin? The fantastic trial of Zinoviev, Kamenev, and fellow Old Bolshevik leaders shocked Bill and the others as much as me. Their initial responses encouraged me, but the only one who would hear a word against Stalin was Liston Oak, and he would not commit himself. I tried and tried, but the shell refused to crack. The second show trial of illustrious Old Bolsheviks (Karl Radek, Iu. L. Piatakov, et al.), the "confessions," the swift executions—none of this made any difference. In the meantime, invited by Intourist (the official Soviet tourist agency), Liston led a group of American sightseers on a tour of Russia. The visit completed his disillusion with Stalin, and he went to Spain to serve the Loyalists in the foreign press division. I tried to reach him in Barcelona, but he never received my letter. Ubiquitous Stalinist censors must have waylaid it, because it fell into the hands of the New York *Daily Worker*. With it they "unmasked" Manuel Gómez as a vicious renegade, a paid counter-revolutionary long known to be in the service of Wall Street. The ineffable Mike Gold ran a column denouncing "four Trotskyites of the defunct Theater Union: Charles Walker, Adelaide Walker, Liston Oak, and Manuel Gómez."

This was October 9, 1937. A day or two later I received a missive signed William F. Dunne, severing all relations with me. Lofty, verbose, oratorical, it wound up: "In that sector of the barricades where

I command you will be shot on sight." Bill's communication must have been eight pages long. Soon thereafter I received a short one from Albert Maltz, dismissing me with a condemnatory quotation from Lenin which I had taught him. A bit later, Liston, who had stopped off in London on his way home, attacked the Party and the Comintern publicly, much to my surprise—and disapproval. At this Nemo and Juanita, who were practically family, came to Sunnyside with an ultimatum: they rejected the *Daily Worker's* characterization of me, but they would stop seeing Sylvia and me unless we broke with Liston. We told them "too bad"; we loved them dearly but . . . Other comrades cut us off without bothering to inform us. The Party was now definitively closed to me.

Without access to the party of Lenin, how could a conscientious Leninist carry on? I considered turning to the Trotskyites, but only for a moment. They were a futile sect, going nowhere. So I waited, without knowing what I was waiting for. I was still waiting in 1938 when the third—and most bizarre—of the Moscow show trials struck. On the prisoner's bench sat the last of Lenin's old comrades in arms—Bukharin, Rykov, N. N. Krestinsky—plus a conglomeration of alleged Trotskyites, physicians, and G. G. Yagoda (who as head of the NKVD had set up the first show trial).[2] Charges included the medical murder of Maxim Gorky and a 1918 plot to assassinate Lenin. All but Krestinsky "confessed." Most were shot.

This ultimate phantasmagoria—and the acquiescence of the Communist parties throughout the world—forced me to reexamine the structure of my beliefs. Things that had disturbed me since my first contact with Bolshevik reality came to mind one after the other:

The contrast between Borodin the plenipotentiary of proletarian revolution and Borodin the high-living epicure.

The Bolsheviks' prompt dumping of the Left–Socialist Revolutionary allies who had collaborated with them in the seizure of power.

Dispersal, by armed force, of the Bolshevik-summoned Russian Constituent Assembly as soon as it proved to have a Menshevik–Socialist Revolutionary (rather than Bolshevik) majority.

2. The NKVD (People's Commissariat of Internal Affairs) was established in 1934 as a successor organ to the OGPU. It united all police functions under its control.

Finding Marx's Dictatorship of the Proletariat interpreted to mean dictatorship of its "vanguard," that is, the Communist Party.

Watching the Russians operate as a unit vis-à-vis the other delegates at the Second Congress of the International—and maneuvering themselves into control of every phase of the proceedings.

The bloody suppression in 1921 of the revolutionary Kronstadt sailors who had mutinied in support of striking Petrograd workers.

"Democratic centralism" converted into a euphemism for rule from the top down, within the Party. And internationally, from Moscow.

Emergence of Stalin as boss of the Russian party and rule by "organizational methods." Elimination of Trotsky from power before most of the membership knew what was happening.

The rubber-stamp nature of the 1928 Sixth Comintern Congress; Trotsky's appeal rejected summarily—without discussion; Bukharin simultaneously lauded and on the skids.

Disgust with my own part in the expulsion of American Trotskyites (Cannon, Shachtman, et al.)—and my outrageous conduct at a Trotskyite mass meeting.

The series of arbitrary persecutions and "purges" before and after Kirov's assassination—culminating in the Moscow show trials.

Against lingering emotional resistance and with great pain, I recognized that the seeds of Stalinism lay in Leninism, that the Leninist ideology and methods that had made the October Revolution possible were also responsible for its corruption. My disillusion was stupefying. It left me incapable of believing in anything.

That year, 1938, was the first one in which neither May Day nor November 7 gave me a lift.

29   More Shipman than Gómez

May 21, 1939: Carlota is five. I wrote her a little "booklet" in advance: *The Three Shipmans: The Story of Two People and How They Came to Be Three.* When I wrote *The Three Shipmans* we were already more Shipman than Gómez. I still responded more readily to "Manny" than to "Charlie" (which nobody called me except at Standard & Poor's), but the sobriquet belonged to a life beyond resuscitation. Every call for "liberation of the masses" was suspect to me now. Some disillusioned Communists turned to the Socialists; some to extreme capitalist reaction, but I couldn't do either. We continued to get the radical magazines, out of habit, but when they came I hardly glanced at them. I knew what they would say without turning a page. Instead I reread *Nicholas Nickleby*, discovered Proust, and started on the memoirs of Ulysses S. Grant.

Both Sylvia and I had jobs to distract us, she with the U.S.O. in Newark, I at S&P. In Sunnyside we visited with neighbors like Irwin and Rose Rosen (essentially apolitical), and of course saw Liston and occasionally Charlie and Adelaide Walker (not Trotskyites anymore). Liston was now assistant to the managing editor of the *New Leader*, the weekly organ of (extreme) right-wing socialism. He had become more political than ever, an (independent) Norman Thomas Socialist, indiscriminately active in his anticommunism.

When the war in Europe began that August, I reacted according to the old Communist logic that viewed ordinary capitalist countries and the Rome-Berlin Axis as tweedledee and tweedledum. At the same time, I knew in my bones that a Nazi victory would be a disaster for civilization. When the Nazis overran France I shuddered. I thrilled at the doughty endurance of the British under the Blitz. I couldn't accept France's defeat, nor could I accept the fact of French collaboration. My compassion for the victims had nothing to do with the fact that I was a Jew myself, though it would later on. I was—and am—an atheist, without any distinctive Jewish culture. I regarded myself as an American citizen kin to all humanity. Now I regard and proclaim myself also a Jew. Birth did not make me Jewish. Hitler did.

By the fall of 1940 Sylvia and I had had enough of Sunnyside. We longed for something farther out, more rural, and rented an unpretentious but sound cottage in what seemed an idyllic setting, RFD, Holmdel, New Jersey, the scene of the bizarre incident narrated in the Preface to these memoirs. We were more or less happy there, but the regional public school disappointed us badly, and would probably have cut short our stay had the FBI not come knocking first.

I've already described our flight to Kansas City, and what we did as Mr. and Mrs. Gordon and daughter. In response to Liston's coded message, I returned to New York alone and went directly to the American Civil Liberties Union, where Roger Baldwin was expecting me. He knew my early history—including Camp Upton—and I had complete confidence in him. Of course no one could match Baldwin's experience in the field of civil liberties. No, he had nothing definite on the FBI visit to Holmdel, but Roger could assure me that such visits were not, in themselves, alarming. When I emphasized how knowingly the young fox with the southern accent had questioned me—the sequence and word-for-word detail of the questions—Roger replied, "I can show you a dozen identical cases that amounted to nothing. If I were you I would come back and go about my business." He explained that in many small towns the postmaster reports it if the *Nation*, the *New Republic*, or the *New Masses* comes addressed to you.

Next I went to see Morris Ernst, a top-notch liberal attorney, whose views echoed Roger's. I still wanted confirmation, so I determined to put in an appearance at Standard & Poor's and try to find out whether or not the FBI had been there. The president received me icily—I had after all deserted my job—but his questions persuaded me that no FBI follow-up had occurred. It soon became clear, moreover, that I wasn't even going to lose my job. S&P always had trouble keeping good security analysts, and by their measurement I was one of the best. This realization gave me the chutzpah to request two months in California at half-pay, in return for which I promised to mail in a certain number of field reports weekly.

A few days later I astounded Sylvia by driving up to our Kansas City abode in the old Ford. In the morning we settled for our efficiency and headed west for San Francisco and Sylvia's sister Billie. She and her husband, Zev, took us into their lives without reserve. Every weekday morning I did my stint for Standard & Poor's, inspecting industrial plants in and about San Francisco. By mid-afternoon I was free for sightseeing or whatever, with Sylvia and

Carlota. San Francisco proved an enchantment, in the morning fog, when the fog suddenly lifted, and not least with the setting of the enormous western sun into the Golden Gate. We hated to leave for the trip back east.

By early fall 1941, though, I was back once more at Standard & Poor's, where I found a stir of trade unionism among my fellow employees. A chapter of the New York Newspaper Guild was starting up, and I became a charter member. Almost simultaneously I joined the New York Society of Security Analysts. For the first time I recognized myself as a professional security analyst. I had no training for anything else, except as a professional revolutionist.

30   A Different Man and a Different War

When Hitler unleashed his *Wehrmacht* against Stalin's Russia in June 1941, he and the world expected the Nazis to be in Leningrad and Moscow before winter. They came close, but by October they had stalled. I asked myself what it was that gave the Russians their miraculous counterpunch: Stalin's Socialism in One Country? The great Mother Russia that had destroyed Napoleon? Whatever the reason, the *muzhik* millions were fighting back, aided by tanks, guns, ammunition, and food from the West. Many Americans, probably a majority, agreed with those who characterized the hostilities as "that European mess." Okay, Mr. President, people said, aid the Allies in every way possible, short of entering the war. The isolationist "America First" agitation was not confined to defeatists, pacifists, and pro-Germans; it had a very broad following until "the date that will live in infamy."

I was a different man from the one I had been in World War I, and this was a different war. For once my brother, Harry, and I saw things the same way. He had come out of World War I a captain. During the Depression a textile business owned by him and two partners had failed, and Harry lost everything he possessed. He began by selling life insurance for an agency headed by one of his many friends, and was a phenomenal success at it. Now, unhesitatingly, he interrupted his prosperous insurance career to reenter "the service" as a major in the Air Force. Of course he was too old to fight, and so drew an administrative assignment at a gunnery school in Las Vegas. With my record I couldn't have gone into the service even if I'd wanted to. Any kind of government service, military or civilian, was closed to me. They had my fingerprints.

In 1939 Standard & Poor's had made me its railroad editor. I headed a department that furnished the railroad data for *Standard Corporation Records* and *Standard Stock and Bond Guides*. We issued a specialized weekly advisory service entitled *Railroad Securities*, handled all inquiries concerning railroads and railroad securities, and cooperated with the bond ratings department in its ratings of rail bonds. I undertook week-long inspection trips over railroad lines, peering at track and roadbed, sauntering through yards and roundhouses, quizzing the man on the job. At first unable to distinguish between neglected and well-maintained mileage, an old locomotive and a new one, I learned from the men I was quizzing. I acquired and retain to this day a special fondness for railroaders and railroading. Officers of the railroads, eager to satisfy Standard & Poor's, often accompanied me on inspection trips over their lines.

In 1942, we moved uptown to the top floor of one of those old Seventy-second Street brownstones between Park and Lexington, within easy reach of Carlota's new school. On answering the phone one Sunday afternoon, we got a surprise. "It's Juanita. Nemo and I are in the neighborhood. Can we come over?" The Piccolis! The last word from them had been to break off relations, eleven years back. I took a breath and told Juanita we'd be happy to see them. As I hung up I thought of our three flights of stairs and the fact that Nemo had had a "heart condition." Then remembered, with relief, that it had been declared psychosomatic. The visit went off fairly well, though awkwardly. We had guessed Juanita would never have called unless they had abandoned communism. The wrong guess. The personal

Charles Shipman (standing) as head of Standard & Poor's railroad department, 1947.

had bested the political. With "certain subjects" out of bounds, we were friends again.

Meanwhile I was at odds with the New York Newspaper Guild. I had had to give up my (charter) membership on becoming head of the railroad department. I received the union's "honorable withdrawal" card and continued to regard myself as a union man. But personnel dilemmas began to intervene. A starting analyst whom I called unfit just before the end of the contractual thirty-day period begged for a little more time: "One week, to prove myself." Out of common human sympathy I acceded. But when the week was over I couldn't get rid of him. He appealed to the union and of course the union upheld him. There was another analyst, still worse, who had been with the department so long that both he and I knew that I was stuck with him. He was an old crab, unable to read a balance sheet and unable to write English; and a hedgehog to touch. He took more of my time than the seven other analysts combined: before publishing anything of his I had to recast every paragraph for both content and grammar. At this time he claimed a grievance, asserting that his work was rated too low, and the union defended the claim before our company grievance committee. The company's president appeased the union by proposing a permanent arbitration board for my department.

I announced my resignation. The president refused to accept it. Things could be worked out, he said; he didn't believe that I actually meant to quit. The truth is I had surprised myself. But the more he tried to reassure me, the more strongly I felt my position had become untenable. I cleaned out my desk and left. Only then did I remember that our bags were all but packed for Mexico. We were going on a summer-long vacation; Standard & Poor's had granted me a much-needed leave.

31 Railroading and High Finance with Robert R. Young

So I was jobless again, having surrendered thirteen years of pension credits. I was living in a comparatively high-rent apartment, my wife was not working, my daughter was at an expensive school. I had no prospects and was nearly fifty-three years old. Sylvia was appalled. I wasn't: I was exhilarated, like a worker going out on strike. Our vacation trip was only a week away and I proposed that we go ahead as planned. I would use the intervening week to explore job possibilities.

The week proved an eventful one. I had not imagined it, but I had only to announce my availability and people wanted to hire me as a senior analyst. Meantime, on a hunch, I journeyed to the forty-fifth floor of the Chrysler Building and had myself announced to Robert R. Young, the five-foot, 130-pound colossus and enfant terrible of the railroad industry. Eleven years earlier Young, then an obscure stockbroker, had had the gall to challenge J. Pierpont Morgan—and the wit, tenacity, and assembled resources to lick him. In partnership with Woolworth heir Allen Kirby and backed by Cleveland financier Cyrus Eaton, he had "robbed" the J. P. Morgan Group of a railroad empire. He had taken control of the vast Chesapeake & Ohio system and other property through the magical device of a railroad holding company, the Allegheny Corporation (Kirby furnished three-fourths of the cash).

The Robert R. Young I went to see at the Chrysler Building that day in 1948 was chairman of Allegheny's board of directors. I knew Mr. Young to be the recognized boss of everything from Allegheny down, that is, including the Chesapeake & Ohio and the other roads in which Allegheny had a stake: the sprawling Missouri Pacific and the Texas & Pacific. Among Wall Streeters, he had the reputation of an egomaniac, freebooter, and cutthroat—a man who respected nobody and nothing. But in my occasional interviews with him for Standard & Poor's, he had seemed benign. He had sandy, thinning hair, mild blue eyes, and an inviting smile. To the toughest questioning he had responded affably, with apparent frankness and never a dodge.

Mr. Young was out of town that day. But Robert Purcell, vice chairman of both Allegheny and the C&O, asked me in. I had come with the vague notion that perhaps somewhere in the vast Allegheny organization there might be an opening for me. I informed him immediately that I had quit Standard & Poor's, and why. I was thinking how to continue when Purcell said encouragingly, "Would you care to work with me, Charlie? Sort of assistant?" Would I! "I certainly would, Bob. Assuming a good enough salary." Next a bold afterthought: "And a title." He scratched his prematurely bald head and considered. Then in his North Country twang: "On salary I know we can get together, Charlie. The title thing I'll have to clear with Mr. Young."

Mr. Young was in town the next day and wanted to see me. Bob Purcell was with him when I got in. Without preliminaries they offered me double the salary I had been getting at Standard & Poor's, and two separate titles: Assistant to the Vice Chairman of Allegheny Corporation and Assistant to the Vice Chairman of the Chesapeake & Ohio Railway Company. I would have a private office on the forty-fifth floor of the Chrysler Building and such help as I might need. This was too much. In fact, it was scary.

Whatever they expected of me would top anything my journalist—security analyst experience had equipped me for. I'd be safer with Keystone Custodian Funds, the big Boston investment outfit that had made me an offer earlier in the week, but the Allegheny offer was tempting. "Could I let you know tomorrow, Mr. Young?" "Yes of course, Charles. Or the day after, if it's all right with Bob." Bob said, "Fine." With my hand on the doorknob I heard myself venture, almost involuntarily, "I was expecting to take my wife and daughter to Mexico for the summer . . . until Labor Day. . . . I don't know whether . . ." He replied immediately, "Have a pleasant vacation, Charles. Report the day after Labor Day. We'll need time to line up your assignment."

Neither the rigors of Mexican travel, nor anything we ate or drank, was new to me. During those three and a half months I seemed to thrive as never before. But somewhere along the way I must have picked up a bug, because I arrived home, the Saturday before Labor Day, a sick man. Doctor Wechsler diagnosed viral pneumonia and prescribed weeks in bed to be followed by a month of rest and quiet in the country. "Doctor," I exclaimed, the sweat pouring out of me, "I have to report for work on Tuesday." "Well, you can't," he told me. "Do you realize how sick you are?" "This job is my future, doctor. I can't afford not to show up on time the first day." He looked incredulous. "Do you want to die, Mr. Shipman?" In return I asked, "Will you guarantee I'll die if I go to work on Tuesday?" When he replied that he would not guarantee it, I told him that I would go to work as planned.

On Tuesday I had a temperature of 105 and felt awful. Sylvia refused to help me dress; she called me an idiot, and almost cried when I left the house. I reached the forty-fifth floor of the Chrysler Building in a daze. I felt that I couldn't face Mr. Young, and gave the receptionist Mr. Purcell's name. After all, I was assistant to the vice chairman and he was the vice chairman. It turned out that Mr. Young was away anyway. Bob didn't notice I was sick and I didn't tell him. Escorting me to the office I'd been assigned, he said that I should spend the next few weeks just looking around. "Talk to people, go over our files, read reports. Get the general picture." I asked him what I would be doing after that and he told me that, frankly, he didn't know. "Hire yourself an assistant and a secretary," he said. "The thing will work itself out." And he left me.

I sat alone in my large office, picking up and laying down papers, hardly reading a line. My hand shook. After a decent interval I went down for lunch: a cup of tea. I walked half a block and went back up feeling worse. A little after two o'clock I went home, straight to bed. The next day I was home by noon. I found that as long as I showed up in the morning I could fake it. I saw Mr. Young only a few minutes that week and my immediate boss, Bob Purcell, not much more. Before either of them called me in for a conference Doctor Wechsler had pronounced me recovered. Sylvia credited "Gómez luck."

"The thing" did work itself out. My first assignment was a confidential review for Mr. Young of Allegheny's investment position. My responsibilities included seeing people who came to the forty-fifth floor of the Chrysler Building with propositions they wanted Allegheny (or Mr. Young personally) to put money into. I was expected to sift them through—to listen, ask questions, examine supporting documents, check credit ratings, sometimes visit a plant or a building site, talk to one of our lawyers. If I was satisfied that something was worth Mr. Young's attention, I talked it over with him or simply wrote him a memo. He relied on me more than I myself believed prudent. It seems that he and Bob Purcell had been impressed by my doggedness as an analyst for Standard & Poor's. Their confidence put me on my mettle. Sizing up unfamiliar properties is often a guessing game, but I did, I think, develop a sort of knack for it. Somehow I have always had an intuitive aptitude for interpreting—but not computing—figures.

The first Allegheny coup in which I had a part, and the biggest ever, originated in December 1948, three months after my employment started. Bob Purcell learned—hush-hush—that control of a billion-dollar business could be had for $3 million. The business was Investors Diversified Services (IDS), a complex of savings, insurance, investment trust, and mortgage institutions based in Minneapolis. IDS revenues had been disappointing for years and the firm was going under. Its controlling stockholder was tired of the situation and wanted out, but neither the general financial community, nor the IDS president, nor its employees knew. Bob Purcell asked me to go up and take a look. Pretending an interest in buying a $100,000 savings certificate, I was shown all around. I saw that there was vitality in the unique organization, and spent the next couple of weeks investigating. I got hold of documents, examined the SEC records in Washington, found a lot of data in newspaper morgues and in the files at Standard & Poor's.

It was true that IDS was in bad shape, with its common stock far short of asset value; but there were pluses. They included Investors Mutual, which was the biggest "balanced fund" in the country and one of three investment trust affiliates. Fees for managing its conservative portfolio were fairly secure, and were bound to rise with the general recovery of bond prices. Another of the trusts, smaller and speculative, had a good growth potential. The IDS insurance and mortgage divisions were comparatively new and already growing. But what most impressed me was the advantage of governing a billion dollars of assets. My final report was affirmative, and Bob Purcell endorsed it. Mr. Young decided IDS was for Allegheny, in spite of adverse outside legal advice.

IDS proved a Golconda, a veritable diamond mine, for Allegheny. Within a few years its cost was returned in quintuplicate. Besides the direct profit there were the influence and power inherent in controlling great and growing assets—soon exceeding $2 billion, and growing eventually to $8 billion. My part in the acquisition made me solid at the Chrysler Building.

You got good pay working for Robert R. Young, if you performed well. Nor was payment limited to salary. Mr. Young himself owned the controlling interest in a moderate-sized film company, Pathé Industries. In May 1951 he gave me an advantageous option to buy 2,000 of his personal shares of Pathé's stock. In the next month I found myself elected to Pathé's board of directors; and similar arrangements continued to come my way. Mr. Young had a mild side and a hard side. Kindly with strangers, generous to those who kept faith with him, he could cut the heart out of an adversary. I have never known a more implacable hater.

Palm Beach, Florida, 1950. Group at Robert R. Young's winter home—photographed by Charles Shipman during a business visit. Young and David Baird in center.

Away from Wall Street his two main power allies were Cyrus Eaton and the senior Clint Murchison. Murchison, a rawhide Texan whose schooling never got beyond the third grade, had made zillions in oil and was spreading himself. Mr. Young and he would agree on some proposition in general terms, long distance, and I'd take the first flight to Dallas to follow through. Old Clint would greet me at the door of his alabaster mansion with a Bloody Mary for me in one hand and a bottle of Coca-Cola for himself in the other. We'd work in his air-conditioned conference room all afternoon or evening, making and comparing notes. We sat side by side on a long, padded, steel locker crammed with refrigerated Coca-Cola. Every so

Longview, Texas, October 1950. Charles Shipman of Allegheny Corp. addressing a gala dinner party. With him at the speakers' table (left to right): Gene Tunney, John Wrather, and Texas Governor Allan Shivers.

often old Clint would reach down for a Coke and drink from the bottle. I say old Clint because everyone called him that. He wasn't so old, probably not sixty. In contrast to the typical Texas drawl, his twang was the fastest I ever heard. He thought fast too, mathematically. He could reach the bottom line as quickly as a present-day computer. When we had things worked out he'd ring for a man to take dictation. He maintained a sizable all-male retinue, which reminded me of gangster movies.

Cyrus S. Eaton, Cleveland's great independent capitalist, was of a different order. He was complex, cultivated, silver-haired, and benevolent-looking. You might have mistaken him for a sophisticated Anglican bishop. He and his much younger, crippled wife explored philosophical and social questions together. He sponsored important annual science conferences at his Nova Scotia birthplace. He was an acknowledged intimate of the Soviet leaders and was perhaps the foremost capitalist apologist for Soviet Russia. Yet his chief occupation was the practice of financial wizardry: he made, lost, and remade several huge fortunes. When I was a *Wall Street Journal*

columnist, the gossips accounted him a sharper. But Cyrus Eaton
was the pride of Cleveland and a power in steel, coal, and other industries at the time I met him. He was well into his seventies and
erect as a church steeple.

Closer to Mr. Young than either Murchison or Eaton was a million-
aire New York stockbroker named David G. Baird. He too was an
original. Like the rest, he spent overlong working hours in concentrated pursuit of the dollar. He pursued it with intense fervor, with
vision, sureness, virtuosity, and self-effacement. He loved the game
of it. But when Dave Baird made a killing most of the proceeds went
to one of his three personal charitable foundations, through which
he gave away money every single day. He gave money to hospitals,
religious institutions of all creeds, schools, orphan asylums, and
homes for the aged, needy, or crippled. His offices were, by any
comparison, spare. He had just a cheap metal desk in one big room
with fifteen or twenty employees placing and accepting phone calls
from all over the world. Yet Baird & Co. was the country's tenth largest security broker in volume of business.

32 I'd Rather Be in Wilton

I was so close to the inside of this world of high finance that I could
hear the wheels whir. It was enthralling, but it never engaged me
fully, perhaps because I had the recurrent sensation that I was an
interloper. My off-the-job associations, affinities, and behavior remained as if I had never entered Wall Street, the Chrysler Building,
or the Terminal Tower. Though no longer a political leftist I was, in
a sense, still leading a double life.

During a weekend's recess from the forty-fifth floor, I had a long-
ing to see old friends from the Chicago days. Bill Dunne, of course,
but also, and unaccountably, Walt and Rose Carmon. I say unaccountably because, while I had known them longer than anyone
else in Chicago (Wally since my days of exile in Mazatlán), I never

had the "correspondence of personality" with them that I enjoyed with my closest friends. Neither Bill nor the Carmons might want to talk to me, but the worst they could do was throw me out. I located Wally and Rose in a rat-trap of an apartment on the Lower East Side. Rose hastened to make me a cup of tea, as in the old days back when. Wally was in bed, coughing and wheezing, emaciated with disease. He shook my hand and perked up a bit. They gave me news, mainly of the Chicago people I had known. "Natalie Gómez" ran a Mexican handcrafts shop on Eighth Street; she had been living with Sterling Bowen, but no more. Thurber Lewis was dead. Tom O'Flaherty was in Ireland, Harry Freeman still worked for TASS. They did not mention politics directly. Nor did I. They did, however, tell me where to reach Bill and Marguerite Dunne, in part of a second-floor loft on Union Square East.

Marguerite opened the door, squinted into the dim hallway, and shrilled, "It's Manny!" She threw her arms around me. Bill came in from behind a curtained-off space, naked to the waist, wondering. Then, affectedly casual, "Get yourself a chair, Manny." But before I could move he was squeezing my hand and giving me a bear hug. The three of us sat side by side on a lumpy sofa. I was so happy I almost cried. We talked. "Disgusted with how this Browder pipsqueak was hog-tying the Party," Bill had gone up to British Columbia and worked as a cook in a lumber camp. Returned, he had "taken the Browder apparatchiks apart" in an open meeting and was now damned as a factionalist. Sure he was still a Communist. What the hell did I think? Nevertheless, he appeared to have forgotten his "that-section-of-the-barricades-where-I-command" letter of 1937.[1]

He asked what Manny Gómez was doing these days; I said earning a living with Allegheny Corporation and the C&O railroad. He seemed relieved to hear me say C&O. "So you finally decided to be a proletarian. I congratulate you, Manny." (A proletarian? He actually believed it, or wanted to.) I told Bill I was in fact an assistant executive. He insisted it didn't matter, that a paid employee in an essential industry was "engaged in socially useful labor." Bill's

---

1. Actually, Dunne had been expelled from the Party in 1946, though he continued to be associated with various splinter groups. He died in 1953.

rationalizations didn't comfort me. They were the same old double-talk, the same pseudo-Marxist clichés. Coming from Bill, and after all we'd both gone through, they caused me dismay. We could hardly communicate. When we got on to personal recollections we did better, and for a time we were almost the old Bill and Manny. But not for long. We were trying to be ourselves with each other and it was awkward as hell. I never tried to see Bill again.

At the forty-fifth floor one afternoon, two men whose names I did not recognize asked to see me on personal business. As soon as they were alone with me, they flashed FBI badges and announced they wanted to talk to me "not as Charles Shipman but as Manuel Gómez." They evidently had no wish to expose me. They were, they assured me, convinced that I was now "a good American." They wanted me to identify others, and handed me fifteen or twenty photographs to study. The faces were new to me, every one of them. What I would have said if I had recognized anyone I don't know. I reminded my callers that I'd been out of things for a long time. They were understanding and promised their visit would remain an FBI secret. Several weeks later they were back with more photos, with the same lack of result. That was the last I saw of them.

Naturally their visits upset me. Not through fear of exposure as Manuel Gómez: I accepted their assurances on that. The FBI people could have no purpose in disclosing that Shipman was Gómez. Gómez was not wanted for anything, at least not then. But if they knew Shipman had been Gómez, did they also know who Gómez had been? On reflection I realized that they did not necessarily know anything. Although a number of ex-comrades might have revealed the Shipman-Gómez connection, few knew of an earlier name. But one thing was sure, I must avoid incriminating the Shipman persona in anything that might provoke an investigation of the past. I must never again sign an official document swearing to false information about my date and place of birth, the names of my parents, and so on, as I had done on my passport application for the Denmark trip. In practice, this meant that I must resign myself to never having another passport.

After twenty-one years of cohabitation, Sylvia and I became a married couple on May 5, 1951. Not through some sudden belief in the sanctity of wedlock; with or without was all the same to us. We did it out of legal and practical considerations. My niece, Edith, knowing my complicated history, wondered if the marriage was legal. It was. The 1920 marriage of Manuel Gómez and Natalia Mikhailova had been bigamous and therefore did not count. My legal wife at the time was Eleanor, but Eleanor had divorced me on May 5, 1937. (She did it without my cooperation or knowledge. After the fact she mailed me the decree, with a request to be reimbursed for the cost! I was mean enough to refuse.) The ceremony occurred at the city hall in Hoboken. Sylvia went over on the ferry with two witnesses, Edith and Liston's daughter Joanne Lancaster. I arrived late and hung over, having flown from Minneapolis after an IDS office party the night before. An air of the surreptitious hung around Hoboken's city hall. A little red-nosed man demanded and got ten dollars to serve as the required resident witness, and an acting magistrate hurried through the perfunctory ritual, in a vestibule.

At this time we decided to make a radical change in our lives: we moved to a house and eighteen-plus acres in Wilton, Connecticut. It was my idea, and I persuaded Sylvia to try it. Before the end of June 1951 we were property owners. By fall we said it was the smartest thing we'd ever done. I discovered that I loved outdoor work. I hacked away at heavy underbrush, cleared out ubiquitous poison ivy, planted buckwheat and rye, later even some corn and a few tomato plants. But I wasn't a gardener, for the most part I did strictly unskilled labor. I did, however, become expert at rough work with stone. Every weekend, and many weekday evenings, I was out among the rocks, rebuilding the broken-down dry wall along our several hundred feet of road frontage. Everyone admired the result. There was a swampy hollow on our land which we thought might be converted into a swimming pool. Having heard the U.S. Department of Agriculture was offering free help for such purposes, we contacted our agricultural agent and in due course had a nice, if somewhat muddy, swimming pool. "Don't call it a swimming pool," the agent warned. "It's a pond, an upgrading of rural land. That's what the department pays for."

Developments in my personal life did not hinder my uninterrupted concern with politics, though I was now merely an onlooker. Stalin had loosed the Cold War by fastening totalitarian regimes on most of Eastern Europe and East Germany, in defiance of the

1945 Yalta and Potsdam agreements. The United States responded with the Truman Doctrine and the Marshall Plan, which saved Europe from economic collapse. As time went on, the Cold War— and the hot one in Korea—became disturbing influences in American domestic affairs. President Truman ordered "loyalty checks" for federal employees in 1947. There was an atmosphere of fear and accusation, in which innocent people were undoubtedly sent to prison.[2]

33 A Proposal That Could Not Be Refused

In January 1952 Mr. Young said to me, "Charles, you are going to the Orient." The trip concerned the American Mail Line, a steamship company in which Allegheny and the Murchisons had a controlling investment. Charged with watching over that investment, I had become convinced that it would never have much of a future unless it developed a better "freight mix." Its main cargo was copra. It carried a lot of copra, which was nice business. But the copra was all outbound from the Philippines; this meant a costly reverse movement of empty bottoms. Clint Murchison had come up with the idea of establishing a trading company with offices in Manila, Singapore, and either Tokyo or Yokohama, which would work with the steamship company. Well, Mr. Young said, I was to go out there, spend some time in each place, and consult with public officials and others, to whom Clint evidently had access.

2. American liberals, herdlike as their opposites, tended to assume that everyone accused was innocent. Take the famous case of Alger Hiss. The evidence, plus a jury, plus repeated findings against him on appeal, plus the manifest integrity of his accuser, Whittaker Chambers, satisfy me of his guilt. No doubt he acted from high motives, as I would have been doing if, when a Communist, I had been similarly situated. I knew Whittaker Chambers when he was writing for the New Masses. He was an oddball but as principled, decent, compassionate, and fair-minded a man as one could dream of.

He no doubt expected me to purr; it was a real plum. But unlike trips I had made to Mexico for the C&O, overseas travel required a passport. I recognized the danger at once. "Mr. Young," I said lamely, "are you sure I'm the best one to go?" He was unbelieving: "For Christ's sake, Charles, this has been your baby from start to finish." I tried to make objections, but he had answers for each of them; there was plenty of time, my wife could come along, I would be able to finish the project I was working on, and so forth.

When I got home Sylvia said, "You'll have to get out of it. Because you can't go and you know it." I had a confidential talk with Bill Fitelson, whom we still kept up with. Bill said he would have some people in Washington ferret out what kind of dossier they might have. A few days later he called me up and said my record down there was so bad that if I ever thought of applying for a passport I should just forget it. I decided to do everything possible to get out of the trip, but if there was no out I'd have to take my chances. I had used the name Charles Shipman on the passport for Denmark without a hitch. I no longer remembered certain things I'd said in that application—including my mother's name!—but the chances were good that a new application would be handled mechanically and I'd escape notice.

A month passed. Sylvia fretted. Mr. Young began asking when I was going down to see Clint about the trip. Finally I told Mr. Young that the trip would have to be postponed because my wife wasn't well, and that a man named Jim Clark should go in my place. After some discussion he gave me a sharp look and said, "You don't want to make this trip, do you?" I had to answer. "Well, if you put it that way . . . Mr. Young, if you want me to go I'll go. But if you're asking if I'd rather have you send me than Jim Clark, I'd say no." "Okay. It will be Jim Clark."

I was troubled. Yes, I could tell Sylvia that I had escaped going. But Mr. Young was plainly disgruntled. He wasn't forcing me, nor did he show anger. But I felt a chill. Time passed and I dismissed the incident from my mind. On the surface things were as before. (It happened that neither Jim Clark nor anybody else made the accursed trip, because Allegheny-Murchison's interest in American Mail Line evaporated. An opportunity to sell out at a good profit came up and was accepted.)

Mr. Young's stockbroker-philanthropist friend David G. Baird now entered the picture. A frequent visitor to Mr. Young's office, he and I had had frequent dealings together and had become "Dave" and "Charlie" to each other. One morning in June 1952, Baird made me an interesting proposal. He and I would set up a business together for financial counseling, management of investment portfolios, getting out corporations' annual reports, and so on. I would be president and run things, with an annual salary of $27,500 guaranteed by Baird personally. He would have a 75 percent stock interest in the company, and I'd have 25 percent. He would lend the firm $25,000 to start with. Of course it would entail my leaving Allegheny and C&O.

To say I was startled is and was an understatement. But what followed was even more surprising. "Now I want you to understand, Charlie," said Dave slowly, "that if when you were younger . . . you happened to do something foolish, shall we say not too patriotic . . . I mean for a long time mixed up with . . . subversives? . . . Charlie, I want you to understand that as far as I am concerned it is all over and done with, and does not make the slightest difference to me. I want you to understand I have every confidence in you, Charlie." Dave's remarks were generous indeed. But they told their own story. It was clear now that Mr. Young had had me investigated, and that he no longer wanted me identified with Allegheny and C&O. The solution he and David Baird came up with was very kind, and indeed not unflattering.

I ignored Dave's reference to my past and went directly into questions about the operation and prospects of the proposed new company. I knew I was going to accept, because David as a partner was a bargain on any terms. But I told him I'd have to talk with Mr. Young.

My conversation with Mr. Young was almost as strange as the one with Dave. He said, "Charles, David's proposition is one in a billion. Grab it." Then he went on, "If you do it you will be close to me, Charles. Goddamn close. You and David can count on enough business from C&O and Allegheny, and from my own personal affairs, to cover your overhead. You have my word on it. Whatever outside business you get will be gravy. Go ahead and draw up a budget." I had a rough budget and showed it to him. It called for gross annual receipts of a million dollars. "It looks pretty good," he said. "Okay, I'll guarantee you that much business." He also proposed that I resign as of the end of the year, to enable me to realize a profit on my Allegheny stock. Mr. Young was not kidding me about future relations. I had the benefit of his collaboration and trust until his death five and a half years later.

Our new company began business August 12, 1952, in a three-room suite at 250 Park Avenue, subleased from the New York sales division of IDS. We had a catchall name: Coordinated Financial Services, Inc. David Baird and I were the only officers and the only stockholders.

In 1954 Allegheny Corporation, through a series of complicated maneuvers—including a Cyrus Eaton deal, Murchison cooperation, and a fierce proxy battle—swapped control of the Chesapeake & Ohio Railway for control of the famed but needy New York Central. Mr. Young had itched to get his hands on the New York Central and restore its profitability, as he had done with other properties. He would begin by getting the Central a new president. I recommended Alfred E. Perlman, then chief operating officer of the small but flourishing Denver and Rio Grande Western.

Al Perlman was a transportation genius, recognized as such by railroad men everywhere. I had traveled with him for two days back when I was at Standard & Poor's, had listened to his wide-ranging comments and watched him in action with trainmen, shopmen, and district supervisors. He'd have been president instead of chief operating officer but for one thing: he was Jewish. Jews were rare in railroading and a Jewish president was unheard of. Authorized by Mr. Young, I flew to Denver and asked Perlman if he'd be interested in the presidency of the great New York Central. Al Perlman became the first Jewish railroad president in America. He did a fine job with the Central, and the market price of its stock rose from 12 to near 90.

In the meantime, our own company became involved in developing two shopping centers in Western Canada. We got people to put money up as an investment in the project and were able in both instances to sell out at a profit to the investors. We never intended to manage the shopping centers, and sold as soon as they were built and most of the leases signed. We went on to a housing development in Florida and a land deal in Puerto Rico. Once, the public-spirited International Basic Economy Corporation commissioned us to test out an ingenious brick-making tool for peasant use in Colombia. I went to Colombia myself in this connection; no passport was required!

Though my salary as president of Coordinated increased from time to time, as resources permitted, it remained relatively modest. It must be said that Coordinated never set the world on fire, although it might have if I'd been a better promoter. I lacked talent for that, and dislike it still.

34 Rich and Poor in New Canaan

After awhile we changed the name of the company to Coordinated Services, to give us more room for maneuver. Around the time of the name change I said to Baird, "Dave, when you approached me with the proposition of our going into business together, you made a peculiar remark. I ignored it then but now I'd like to have it cleared up." I didn't need to say which remark I meant. Dave replied, "I shouldn't have said it, Charlie. I thought you must guess that I knew. I just wanted to assure you of my confidence in spite of it." I asked him exactly what he knew and how he had learned it. "Mr. Young had a routine checkup done on you. They discovered you had been a longtime Communist under a different name. It made no more difference to Mr. Young than to me, but Mr. Young has enemies. He has to be like Caesar's wife. He felt he couldn't afford to keep you in his organization. I was glad to cooperate, as much for my own sake as yours." This recital left no doubt that, as I had always suspected, the American Mail Line episode was responsible. Neither Dave nor I ever referred to the matter again.

But there was to be one more evocation of my shady past, a final visit from a U.S. government agent to my Coordinated office. Not FBI, not Department of Justice, but an immigration officer! He said,

"Mr. Shipman, we understand you are a Mexican and your real name is Manuel Gómez. Can you produce papers to show you are not in this country illegally?" I admitted I had used the name Gómez, and explained I was not Mexican but American Jewish. I was a native American, born in Kenosha, Wisconsin, and I could prove it. A comparatively few words with me convinced him that I was not a Mexican or any other kind of foreigner.

On January 25, 1958, Mr. Young blew off his head with a shotgun in the billiard room of his Palm Beach home. I was in Bogotá, Colombia, and got the news by cable. I stumbled up and down my hotel room, too distraught to pack. This fabulous man had, yes, befriended me—consistently, and under circumstances that would have prompted others in his place to drop me like a hot poker. No one knows for sure why he killed himself.

The next year Coordinated Services, Inc., went out of business. Mr. Young's death had deprived us of our most valuable client and source of venture capital, but that would not necessarily have made us fold. By this time, however, more and more of my time had been preempted by other activities. In fact, I had already stopped collecting a salary from Coordinated. In January 1957, eleven associates and I had bought two sizable steel warehouse companies, one in Buffalo, one in Rochester, New York. The organizer of the buying syndicate, I was in personally for $200,000 (one-half of it borrowed from David Baird). I headed both companies, with a nice salary plus a percentage of the profits.

The Shipmans now occupied an estate, a manicured property in New Canaan, Connecticut, protected by a seven-foot stone wall with iron gates. (It had been used originally by Bernard Baruch for off-the-record conferences during World War II.) For three years my take from the warehouse companies exceeded expectations: one year they approximated 100,000 in pre-inflation dollars. Then with the opening of the St. Lawrence Seaway, Buffalo became an economic disaster area. Profits turned to losses at both Buffalo and Rochester, my salary stopped, and I resigned as responsible head of the companies. Our syndicate agreement prohibited any of the twelve from selling out singly, so my investment was locked in. I knew I'd be able to get my money out in the long run; but the long run turned out to be just that!

Charles and Sylvia Shipman at home in New Canaan, Connecticut, 1956.

I told myself how much better it would have been with Mr. Young alive and Coordinated still active. Yet I was half-glad with things as they were. I was through as a businessman: I was never meant for such a life in the first place. Sure, it had beguiled me for inordinate years, but through infatuation rather than love. Now in 1960, at sixty-five, I was free. I did not "retire." Instead, as I like to say, I changed my vocation. I worked as a playwright with Spanish-language plays, adapting them, recreating them in English, trying to make them my own. I went to my desk faithfully and eagerly, every morning.

My new vocation titillated and invigorated me but paid no bills. The New Canaan house had to be sacrificed, a realization that came to us with a sense of deliverance. We sold to the first bidder at a sacrifice price. Rid of the damned property, and the mortgage, we gloated. A third of the sale money bought our Redding house, a pleasant, sunny, wood-shingled little place on six-plus acres of lovely Connecticut countryside.

35 Italy, Israel, and Rumania

Sylvia and I now began to travel extensively abroad. Yes, I took the chance of soliciting a Shipman passport, and had no trouble. I even got it renewed.

One of our trips began with a bizarre reunion in Italy. The Piccolis (Nemo and Juanita), both of them artists in retirement, had built themselves a studio in a tiny mountain village called Anticoli Corrado, fifty-odd miles from Rome. A cable invited us for Christmas in 1968. We arrived on Christmas Day around noon, just in time for the big meal—to find, similarly invited, an old friend named Clarina, whom we had known as Clarina Michaelson. She was with her incongruous new husband, whom I had known in the early 1920s in Chicago as a dull-witted CP local Myrmidon. We soon learned that Nemo, Juanita, Clarina, and Andy remained devoutly pro-Soviet. Hard core. They eulogized the recent smashing by the USSR and assorted satellites of the liberal (Dubček) movement in Czechoslovak communism. Sylvia and I had resolved to be on our good behavior, but this was too much. A confrontation erupted; and for a moment an all-around fist fight seemed likely. From midday to almost evening (when Clarina and Andy would have to leave), we berated our hosts and fellow guests, while they reviled us. But suddenly Nemo blurted out, "Well, we love each other anyway!" And, like magic, there were *abbracci*. Sylvia and I stayed on with the Piccolis for several weeks.

Israel proved a disenchantment. Those of our Jewish friends who had journeyed to the Jewish sanctuary said it had thrilled them with a proud sense of belonging. Not Sylvia and not me. We admired the plain heroism of the Israelis—casually going about their business in a wisp of a nation enveloped by enemy, less than half a year after the Six-Day War of June 1967. And their constructive achievement: "making the desert bloom" (with the not inconsiderable help of American money). But we were appalled to find Israel a xenophobic theocratic state—without, I believe, the excuse of true

Redding, Connecticut, 1972. Charles Shipman and librarian aide at the Mark Twain Library.

spiritual or cultural commitment. When we got back to Italy, we felt we had come home.

Our second peregrination, in 1975, was even more "historic." Juanita (Nemo had died of cancer a few years back) got us included in a three-week trip to Rumania, chartered by a leftist Italian labor group. It was my first visit to an Iron Curtain country since my missions—as an "insider"—to Soviet Russia. We touched down at the Bucharest airport, where I noted a red star and a large photoprint of Nicholae Ceauşescu, president of both the Socialist Republic of Rumania and its Communist Party. Formalities seem to have been waived for our group, but we were required to provide ourselves with Rumanian currency, at the official rate of four and a half lei to the dollar. Bucharest, an indestructibly beautiful city in part, looked badly run-down and dreary at its core. Our hotel was okay, but it was a hotel for foreigners, who stayed there in total isolation. We soon moved on to our final destination, Neptun, a health resort not far from the Black Sea.

When we enplaned at Rome I had no notion that the objective of Juanita, and the group, was nothing less than the Fountain of Youth. An apparently renowned *elixir vital* could be obtained only in Rumania, during weeks of daily "health treatments." Juanita had been there the year before, though we saw no signs of rejuvenation in her. She herself doubted the cure had had any effect, but was so plagued by infirmities that she was disposed to try anything. Besides accompanying her in her "free time," Sylvia and I wanted only to glimpse Rumania. We had no intention of taking either the elixir or the treatments, and in fact did neither.

During our first breakfast in Neptun one of the Italians confidentially inquired whether Sylvia and I would like to exchange some money. Eight lei per dollar, versus the official rate of four and a half. Virtuously, we declined. Later, when we told the story to a chum of Juanita's, he laughed and assured us that "everybody deals black market." So . . . , when a man in the street offered twelve to the dollar, we promptly did business.

Our hotel, indeed the whole town, was restricted. Rumanian nationals drove the minibuses, served in bars and restaurants, clerked in stores. Otherwise, one encountered only (transient) foreigners, most of them West Germans. Either from an inadequate stock of foreign phrases or out of reluctance to say a lot, the people who dealt with tourists avoided unnecessary conversation. The language of our transactions was usually German or French. But in one store a clerk bawled out in cognoscente English, "Gimme a cigarette," and the cashier of another echoed with "Gimme your fountain pen."

The young commissionaire of our hotel was an exception. He could and did talk readily, in whatever language, for this was his job—answering our questions, taking care of our reservations, international phone hookups, and so on. He was super-accommodating, too, as I discovered when a tooth broke off from my partial dental plate, leaving a conspicuous hole. There was no dentist in Neptun, so the young man conveyed me to a dental clinic in an unrestricted town, where three or four men in frayed white coats stood leaning against old-fashioned dentist's chairs. The only one who spoke English at first pretended not to understand me. But at a reassuring nod from my chaperone he led me into a hallway, took my denture, and mumbled that he would fix it. If I told anyone, however, he would call me a liar. Moreover, I'd have to pay him, not the cashier, in advance: ten thousand leis. When I said that was impossible, it turned out that he could accept American money. Ten dollars, to be exact! I handed them over, relieved and astonished. All bets on the value (sic) of the leu were off.

Our helpful commissionaire had a buddy of about his own age, bronzed and broad-shouldered, who sometimes dropped in on him at the hotel. Once when Sylvia and I were in the lobby, chatting with my savior from dental gap, he introduced us to this friend as "hotel guests but special." The broad-shouldered man was multilingual, a sailor who had been able to travel outside the country. How, we asked, could the authorities be sure he'd come back? Because he had a wife and family in Rumania. He was so confiding that we inquired if the average Rumanian was satisfied under communism. The two men looked uneasy. Nervously surveying the lobby, our commissionaire suggested we transfer the conversation to a bar across the street.

In the deserted bar our two companions outdid each other in execration of Rumanian Communist rule: the most totalitarian in all of Eastern Europe, cynical, brutish, corrupt, duplicitous. Ceauşescu had made the country his exclusive preserve. Ordinary Rumanians were tyrannized, spied upon, riddled with fear, while Ceauşescu's jackals enjoyed good pay, plus the spoils of their graft and thieving. Few Rumanians were allowed to travel abroad, those who did were kept on a short leash.

Segregated in Neptun with the other transient aliens, Sylvia and I had no way of checking out these confidences. But nothing we experienced between entering and leaving Rumania contradicted them.

232

36 After All

August 10, 1980. Eighty-five years old. Birthday party on the terrace back of our house. Essentially a ritual. Sylvia, Carlota, and the grandchildren, supplemented by offshoots of the family I was born into: Phillipses and Phillips kin. I seem to like the members of this ramified body, and wish I knew them better. Those I know best I regard with some affection, but our relationship (unavoidable pun) is hardly one of uninhibited intimacy.

Of course I am long quit of the blind alley of politics. Quit of participation. But the curse is on me. Political intelligences—local, national, and international—are what I read first in my morning newspaper. Skeptically, yes. Although even after my very thorough 1938 disillusionment I was, once, almost hopeful of a progressive break in the totalitarian stranglehold on Russia. The Khrushchev phenomenon, and especially his speech at the closed session of the Twentieth CPSU Congress (February 25, 1956), denouncing the 1937-38 purges and "the grave perversion of party principles, party democracy, and party legality" under Stalin. Alas, on November 4, 1956, less than nine months after the Twentieth CPSU Congress, the USSR, led by this same Khrushchev, put an end to Imre Nagy's moderate Communist regime in Hungary with 200,000 troops and 2,500 armored cars and tanks.

There is no point in carrying these memoirs further. My eighty-fifth year provides an appropriate if not overdue stopping place. That I have survived to eighty-five is a miracle. I ought, logically, to have died when I touched the Long Island Railroad's electrified third rail at the age of five.

Epilogue

On November 27, 1989, Charles Shipman died in his sleep at his home in Austin, Texas, after an illness of several months. He was ninety-three years old. Sylvia and he had moved to Austin in the early 1980s to be near their daughter. They left their beloved Redding, Connecticut, only when doctors told them that they could no longer live in the relative isolation of their home there. Sylvia died of a stroke on September 15, 1985. Charles Shipman was a volunteer at the public library, went regularly to classes at the University of Texas, and read at least two newspapers a day. He led an active life until the very end.

INDEX OF NAMES

Index of Names

Index of Names

Index of Names

Index of Names

Library of Congress Cataloging-in-Publication Data

Shipman, Charles.
  It had to be revolution: memoirs of an American radical / Charles Shipman.
     p.   cm. — (Studies in Soviet history and society)
  ISBN 0-8014-2180-2
  1. Shipman, Charles.   2. Communists—United States—Biography.
3.   Businessmen—United States—Biography.   4. Journalists—United
States—Biography.   I. Title.   II. Series.
HX84.S55A3 1992
324.273'75'092—dc20
[B]   91-57896